MIGRANTS OF THE MOUNTAINS

Meto settlement in late 1964 showing villages A and D

Migrants of the Mountains

THE CULTURAL ECOLOGY OF THE BLUE MIAO (HMONG NJUA) OF THAILAND

BY

WILLIAM ROBERT GEDDES

CLARENDON PRESS · OXFORD

1976

Oxford University Press, Ely House, London W.1

GLASGOW NEW YORK TORONTO MELBOURNE WELLINGTON
CAPE TOWN IBADAN NAIROBI DAR ES SALAAM LUSAKA ADDIS ABABA
DELHI BOMBAY CALCUTTA MADRAS KARACHI LAHORE DACCA
KUALA LUMPUR SINGAPORE HONG KONG TOKYO

ISBN 0 19 823187 3

© OXFORD UNIVERSITY PRESS 1976

PRINTED IN GREAT BRITAIN
BY WILLIAM CLOWES & SONS, LIMITED
LONDON, BECCLES AND COLCHESTER

PREFACE

MY interest in the Miao was aroused by meeting a number of them at the Chinese National Institute of Minorities in Peking which I visited in May 1956. It was enlivened by talking with Dr. Fei Hsiao Tung, the Vice-Director of the Institute, whom I had known previously in London, about the studies of Miao culture which he was supervising. At the time I was considering studying a mainland group practising shifting cultivation as a comparison with the study of the Dayaks I had made earlier in insular South-East Asia. The Miao promised to be a colourful, exciting, and ethnographically important group for this purpose.

I hoped to obtain Chinese permission to visit them in their heartland either in Yunnan or Kweichow but when in later correspondence I sought Dr. Fei's help in this he replied that as he was studying them in China it would be more useful if I were to study them outside China, and then we could exchange notes—an intention unfortunately never fulfilled because of Dr. Fei's fall from official grace.

Awarded a Rockefeller Travelling Fellowship in 1957 I decided to devote part of it to a study of the Miao in Laos or Thailand and finally chose Thailand as the easier of the two countries in which to work. By November I was resident in Pasamliem, a village situated at a height of 5,000 feet on a ridge near Chiengdao mountain in Chiengmai Province. Apart from a courtesy call on the Provincial Governor, who gave me an introduction to a Thai tea planter who in turn gave me a guide to Pasamliem, I had no official connection during this period, and no official visited the village during my stay there. I lived in Pasamliem until May 1958, when I left for Europe, and again from October 1958 until January 1959.

It took no time at all to discover that the Miao were a proud and independent people. After I had enjoyed brief notoriety as a not too attractive oddity, they treated me with indifference, assuming that I had come either to buy or to beg opium. I could purchase no food from them and had to transport it all on my own pack-horse. They would not help me to build a house even when offered quite a high price, so I had to employ opium addicts from a Thai village lower down the slopes. As the first months passed I gained a low status as a provider of second-hand entertainment, through having a tape-recorder, as a photographer, and finally but most valuably as a medicine man. Gradually relationships warmed and when I returned for the second period the Miao came down to the road with their horses to bring in all my supplies.

In 1962 I returned to Pasamliem to find it abandoned but I spent a short time with a group of the old residents who had formed a new small village a few miles away.

My field-work amongst the Miao might have ended there had not other unexpected events intervened. In 1961 the Department of Public Welfare of the Government of Thailand initiated a socio-economic survey of the Hill Tribes and sought the help of U.N.E.S.C.O., which provided the services of the Austrian anthropologist, Dr. Hans Manndorf, as an advisor. One of his recommendations was the establishment of a Tribal Research Centre at Chiengmai to conduct research which would provide a sound basis for the extension to the tribal areas of educational and welfare services and measures for the improvement of their economies. He suggested that as a first step the Government seek through international aid programmes the services of a qualified anthropologist to advise on the organization of the Centre and the planning of research.

The Australian Government asked if I would be interested in the position for a year or so and offered to support it out of its allocation for civilian aid projects. The reason for the invitation was that in public addresses to the Siam Society in Bangkok in both 1958 and 1962 I had argued the need for a more sympathetic appreciation of the situations of the tribal peoples and for an adequate understanding of their socio-economies before the introduction of any measures for social and economic development.

Several factors seemed to make such measures inevitable. Amongst the tribes themselves there was a growing desire for change which varied in intensity according to their circumstances. Some of the peoples, such as the Karen groups who were in closest contact with the lowlands, were said by those who knew them best to seek full integration into the Thai national system. The Miao retained a stronger addiction to self-determination but they were becoming increasingly aware of the superior status and services of the Thai in the lowlands in whose benefits they wished to share.

Irrespective of the tribespeople's own views of the desirability of change there were two other factors making alteration of their modes of life apparently inevitable. One was the increasing pressure on land, the nature of which is fully shown in this book. The other was the pressure upon the Thai Government to eliminate opium production, which to be effective would require basic changes in the Miao economy.

It was the inevitability of the changes and not any wish to advocate them that led me to accept the invitation. No anthropologist who has enjoyed the opportunities his profession offers him to experience cultural variety can welcome its diminution. No one who respected the Miao could wish to see change imposed upon them. No one who had come to know their stubborn independence could expect that outside direction, even if they had initially requested it, would not bring strain between them and the outside agents. But in a situation where measures affecting the people were going to be introduced in any case the difficulties and the loss could be reduced by knowledge of their social organization and sentiments. It was because I felt I knew the Miao and their opinions a little better than any other foreigner who was likely to be invited as advisor that I accepted the position.

During my stay at the Centre, and I believe subsequently, members of the staff were encouraged to regard their role as one of representing the tribespeople to the Government rather than the Government to the people. They did not engage in the promotion of developmental measures, which was the province of other sections of the Hill Tribes Division of the Department of Public Welfare. The lack of a positive involvement in planning by the Centre later brought criticism from some Thai authorities[1] but it did serve the purpose, in circles where its reports were read or its voice listened to, of attuning policy to the tribes' desires, and in the political troubles which came later to the tribal areas there were no instances of conflict between the people and members of the Centre.

I took up the position in July 1964, and in 1965 the Tribal Research Centre was established on the campus of the new University of Chiengmai. My recommendation and hope, like those of Dr. Manndorf before me, were that after the initial organizational phase the Centre would become a part of the University. But whatever its location in the Thai administrative structure—to which universities in Thailand also belong—it was from the start a wholly Thailand institution. Foreigners might be employed on contract to fill temporary gaps in expertise but the permanent staff were entirely Thai nationals. That they did not include at the senior levels any hill tribesmen was a defect which could be explained by the lack of literacy in the hills, although the centralism of Government departments might also cause problems in their employment.

In conjunction with Khun Wanat Bhruksasri, the Director of the Centre, a research scheme was developed which comprised basic socioeconomic studies, each to take two years, of the six main

[1] Bhanthumnavin Krachang, 'Overcoming the Problems of the Hill Tribes', *Spectrum*, S.E.A.T.O., Bangkok, Vol. 1, No. 1, October 1972, pp. 24–5.

tribes.[2] Because there were only two trained Thai anthropologists both of whom were required for teaching at Chulalongkorn University it would be necessary for foreign anthropologists to conduct the studies but each should be linked to a local national who should first act as field assistant and then be given opportunity for postgraduate study in anthropology. The anthropologist was to have complete autonomy in the conduct of his research and the free right to publish his findings independently. The Centre itself had no funds to employ the anthropologists but could offer those who did have independent means the services of a local assistant, the use of a small library donated by the British Government, and some logistic facilities in return for a copy of the research findings.

To initiate the scheme I began a more systematic study of the Blue Miao with Nusit Chindarsi, a Sooei (Kui) tribesman graduated from Thammasart University, as my assistant.[3] We chose the settlement at Meto because many of the people there were former residents of Pasamliem. Either Nusit or myself or both of us were present in the village for almost all the time between November 1964 and January 1966. After my return to Sydney Nusit spent long periods there until he too came to Sydney for postgraduate study in March 1968.

In November 1966 I returned to Thailand as a member of the United Nations Mission to enquire into the economic and social needs of the opium-growing tribes and in this connection revisited Meto briefly. The aerial photographs used in the detailed study of Meto agriculture in this book were obtained through the United Nations survey.

When the United Nations mission ended in March 1967 I again took up residence in Meto with my wife, remaining there until June. During this period, as well as collecting further economic data, I completed an ethnographic film subsequently edited under the title *Miao Year*. On this occasion the research was financed by a grant from the Australian Research Grants Committee, the main funding body for research in Australian Universities. I visited Meto briefly again in October 1968, when returning from the Eighth International Congress of Anthropological and Ethnological Sciences in Tokyo.

In September 1970 I returned once more to Thailand as a member of the second United Nations Mission to the opium-growing areas, this time charged with the task of drawing up a pilot plan for the

[2] A fuller description of the Centre is given in W. R. Geddes, 'The Tribal Research Centre', in *Southeast Asian Tribes and Minorities and Nations*, ed. P. Kunstadter, Princeton, 1967, Vol. 2. My ideas for the research scheme were derived from that composed for Sarawak in 1948 by Dr. Edmund Leach, a scheme in which I played a part.

[3] The Sooei, sometimes spelt Sooai and known also as Kui, do not belong to the Hill Tribe category as it is applied in Thailand. They are a Mon-Khmer people who in Thailand are located mainly in the Surin district near the Cambodian border.

replacement of opium in selected areas. Both before the beginning of the mission and during it I spent some time in Meto and in the village of Pa Khia, which was also populated partly by former residents of Pasamliem and to which some Meto residents had by now migrated.

Thus the fieldwork which provides the basis for this book spans twelve years and includes a total actual residence in Pasamliem and Meto of over two years. The fact that experience of the Miao was not confined to these two communities is the justification for the form the book takes. It is divided into two parts. The first part comprises a general description of Blue Miao society in Thailand. It should be appreciated that like all generalizations it evens out the differences and therefore it cannot be taken as a description of every Miao community, many of which will differ from the model in greater or less degree.

The statements are kept general in this first part of the book for two reasons. Firstly it would have defeated its purpose to load it with specific examples. Secondly it did not attempt to be a full statistical survey, and therefore to list instances confirming the model, which is based on Meto practices, could have created a misleading impression of certainty. On the other hand, exceptions where they were observed are noted. The generalizations are, however, based on a wide survey. During the two United Nations surveys I spent many weeks visiting by helicopter Miao communities in all Provinces where Miao live. Because the helicopter had to return to its base every night the investigations were superficial, but they did provide support for the statements made here. Further study may well prove some of these statements wrong as generalizations, but at least they were based on fairly extensive sampling.

The second part of the book provides the detailed validation of the generalizations in the case of Meto with comparative data from Pasamliem. It concentrates on analysis of the economy and does not give great detail on other aspects of the culture such as the religion. A simple reason for this is that otherwise the book would have been too long. A better reason is that Nusit Chindarsi who worked with me in Meto has completed a thesis on the Meto religious system which is to be published by the Siam Society.

The people of Meto knew that I was writing down for others to read all the information given in this book. When the film *Miao Year* was completed I took it back for a public showing in the village to be sure of their approval before it was released.

It is to the people of Meto and to those not amongst them whom I knew at Pasamliem that my first thanks must go for their co-operation, friendship, and the general pleasure of living amongst them and enjoying their countryside; particularly to Kalaow, Aitong, and the whole family of Bwotong. In the same special category as the Miao, who now treat him as one of their own, is my friend, companion in the hills, and colleague in the study, Khun Nusit Chindarsi.

To the Government of Thailand I am grateful for the complete freedom given to me to pursue my studies and express my opinions. My closest and most pleasant relationship in official circles was with Khun Wanat Bhruksasri, the Director of the Tribal Research Centre, but much help was received also from the Director and other officers of the Department of Public Welfare, particularly Khun Prasit Disawat and members of the Hill Tribes Division.

Most if not all the tribespeople living within the borders of Thailand recognize the supreme status of the King, whose position they generally regard as founded in the nature of the cosmic order and therefore independent of the actual functioning of government. The faith in his benignity has in the reign of the present monarch been justified in reality by a deep and growing interest in their welfare. Since this study was completed the King has made several visits to Meto and it has become a principal village in the programme of assistance to the tribes which he personally directs and largely finances.

Particular thanks are also due to the following organizations and people: the Rockefeller Foundation; the United Nations Narcotics Division; the Wenner-Gren Foundation for Anthropological Research for assistance in the cost of the film; the Australian Research Grants Committee; the Australian Embassy in Thailand and the Australian Department of Foreign Affairs; Mr. Donald Gibson, the British Consul in Chiengmai; Mr. Richard Wood, Mr. and Mrs. Wilfred Brown, Mr. and Mrs. Stanley Sewell, and other friends in Chiengmai. My wife spent much time with me in Meto aiding the study in very many ways. Mrs. Annelise Momoh, my secretary, and Miss Margaret Hamon were of great assistance in preparing the manuscript.

CONTENTS

NOTE ON THE NAME 'HMONG'

SINCE this manuscript was prepared for publication, a strong movement has developed amongst the people with whom it is concerned, especially those in Laos, for official recognition of their name as HMONG and for the subdivision of the people with whom the book deals to be called HMONG NJUA, for which they would wish the English translation to be GREEN HMONG. The origin of the term MIAO, and of its alternative form MEO, is discussed in Chapter One. We chose to use it in the text and in the title of this volume because of its long establishment in the literature, its international currency, and the fact that it is still the official name in Thailand. For the same reasons, we decided to use the translation of HMONG NJUA as BLUE MIAO. Amongst the Thai people with whom we worked, as indeed amongst the wider academic public for whom the book is intended, the name MIAO had no derogatory connotations, but linked the people to a recognized heroic history. Nevertheless, we support the wish of the people to become known by their own traditional name and hope that official classifications will recognize this desire.

LIST OF PLATES

LIST OF DIAGRAMS,
TABLES, AND MAPS

DIAGRAMS

TABLES

MAPS

PART ONE

THE MIAO PEOPLE

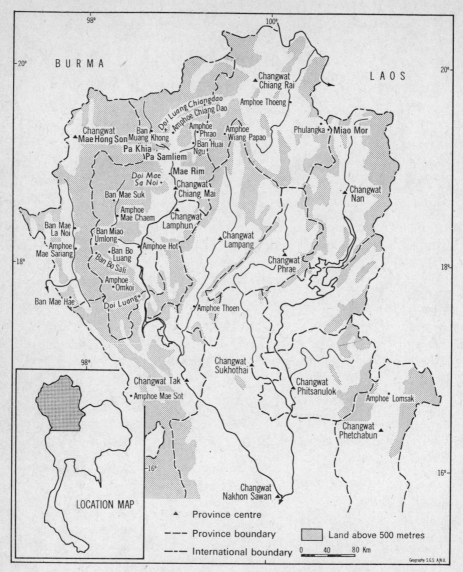

Within the map:

BURMA

LAOS

-20° 20°

Changwat
Chiang Rai

Amphoe Thoeng

Doi Luang Chiangdao
Amphoe Chiang Dao

Changwat
Mae Hong Son

Ban
Muang Khong

Amphoe
Phrao

Amphoe
Wiang Papao

Phulangka ⋅ Miao Mor

Pa Khia

Ban Huai
Ngu

Pa Samliem

Mae Rim

Doi Mae
Sa Noi +

Changwat
Chiang Mai

Changwat
Nan

Ban Mae Suk

Amphoe
Mae Chaem

Changwat
Lamphun

Ban Mae
La Noi

Ban Miao
Umlong

Changwat
Lampang

Amphoe
Mae Sariang

Ban Bo
Luang

Amphoe Hot

-18° 18°

Ban Bo Sali

Changwat
Phrae

Amphoe
Omkoi

Ban Mae Hae

Doi Luang

Amphoe Thoen

Changwat
Sukhothai

98°

Changwat Tak

Changwat
Phitsanulok

⋅ Amphoe Mae Sot

Amphoe Lomsak

16°

Changwat
Phetchabun

LOCATION MAP

16°

Changwat
Nakhon Sawan

▲ Province centre
- - - Province boundary
-⋅- International boundary

Land above 500 metres

0   40   80 Km

Geography S.G.S. A.N.U.

MAP 1: Northern Thailand Tribal Regions

CHAPTER ONE

THE ORIGINS OF THE MIAO PEOPLE

SAVINA begins his *History of the Miao* with the words:

From time immemorial there has existed in China a race of men whose origin we do not know. Living continuously on the heights, away from all other Asiatics, these men speak a particular language unknown by all those who surround them, and wear a special dress which is seen nowhere else.[1]

To most visitors the Miao do appear strikingly exotic, mainly because of the characteristics to which Savina refers. Except in dress, however, their distinctiveness is less than he suggests, and he himself proceeds to penetrate at least some of the mystery surrounding their origins.

The Miao are first mentioned in Chinese history, he says, about the twenty-seventh century B.C. when they were living in the basin of the Yellow River. Concerned at the rapid expansion of the Chinese, they attacked them. At first they had some success, but then the Chinese grouped together under Huan-yuan and defeated the Miao who were led by Tcheou-yu.

Huan-yuan later took the title of Hoang-ti, or the Yellow Emperor of China. Tcheou-yu, who Savina says was the leader of the Miao, was the person called by other writers Ch'ih-yu. This is the form of the name used by Lin Yueh-Hwa in his translation of a work written by Lo Jao-Tien in 1847 based upon a study of Chinese dynastic histories.[2] Ch'ih-yu, writes the author, supplanted the Emperor Yu and caused discord and degeneration in China before being defeated by the Yellow Emperor.

That Ch'ih-yu did have some kind of ancestral connection with the people who are today called Miao is indicated by the occurrence of his name in legends reported from several different Miao groups. Thus Hudspeth writes:

All the Miao people look back to a common ancestor chieftain Ch'ih-yu, who was defeated by the Yellow Emperor of China at a date prior to the days when Abraham went forth from Ur of the Chaldees to go into the land of Canaan. Of Ch'ih-yu these aboriginals still sing in their deeply moving

---

[1] F. M. Savina, *Histoire de Miao*, Société des Missions étrangères de Paris, 2nd ed., Hong Kong, 1930, p. vii (all passages from Savina have been translated by the present author).

[2] Lin Yeuh-Hwa, 'The Miao-Man Peoples of Kweichow', *Harvard Journal of Asiatic Studies*, Vol. 5, 1940. This gives a translation of the Miao-Man Section of the *Ch'ien-man Chin-fang chi-lueh* written by Lo Jao-Tien in 1847.

sagas of the sanguinary defeats inflicted on their ancestors by the Chinese.[3]

Thus the first reported location of the Miao was in the part of China which today constitutes the Province of Honan.

According to Savina the Miao continued to resist after their defeat by the Yellow Emperor.

They also refused [he writes] to recognise the Emperors Yao, Choun, and U the Great, and the two races continued to fight during the first centuries of Chinese history, now in the basin of the Yellow River, now in the basin of the Hoai. Towards the Twentieth Century people stopped talking of the Miao of the Yellow River Basin. The Chinese Annals imply that they were relegated to the bend of the Yellow River, near the present Chen-Si and Kan-Sou. Those in the basin of the Hoai crossed the Blue River, steered towards the lakes Tong-t'ing and Pouoyang . . .[4]

The Emperor Choun to whom Savina refers is the person whose name is more commonly written Shun. He is believed to have held power in the latter half of the twenty-fourth century B.C. As one writer has put it, Chinese history previous to Shun and Yao is regarded, 'even by the Chinese, as confused and fabulous'.[5] About this time reports appear of a group known as the San-Miao. Although Savina does not refer to them by this name, this must be the group which he says were driven from the basin of the Hoai (Hwai). There are many references to them by other writers. Lo Jao-Tien states:

In the reign of Kao-hsin a certain San-Miao chieftain seized the region between the lakes Tung-t'ing [now Tung Ting] and P'êng-li [now Poyang] and established a state . . . When Emperor Yao succeeded Kao-hsin . . . he commissioned Chung and Li to attack the San-Miao, and they subdued them. Afterwards, they rebelled again. When Emperor Shun was regent, he commissioned Yü to conquer and exterminate them. Yü drove their chieftain into San-wei and kept him there.[6]

The anonymous writer in the *Canton Miscellanie* of 1831 states that the earliest notice he has found of the Miao occurs in the *Sze-shoo* in the fifth chapter of *Mang-tsze*, or sayings of the celebrated philosopher Mencius, where it says: 'Shun . . . overcame and destroyed the San-meaou at San-wei . . .' He adds: '. . . the commentator on the Sze-shoo

---

[3] W. Hudspeth, *Stone-Gateway and the Flowery Maio*, Cargate Press, London, 1937, pp. 9–10.
[4] Savina, 1930, p. viii.
[5] Anonymous writer, 'Observations on the Meaou-Tsze Mountaineers', *Canton Miscellanie*, Vol. 3, 1831, p. 199.
[6] Lin Yueh-Hwa, 1940, p. 271.

explains the above by saying, "San-meaou is the name of a nation, obstinate and ungratefully rebellious, which would not submit. Shun defeated them and slew their King."[7]

Hudspeth says: 'From the Shu Ching (the Chinese Book of History) we learn that four thousand years ago the Miao-tzu were strongly entrenched in Hunan, where they occasioned considerable trouble to such historic figures as Shun and his redoubtable successor the Great Yu.'[8]

Lake Tung Ting is in Hunan Province and Lake Poyang in north-western Kiangsi. According to Lin Yueh-Hwa, San-wei was a mountain, the location of which is a matter of dispute. Thus, putting the various accounts together, it appears that the Miao were driven off the fertile plains of both the Yellow River and the Yangtze River some time between 2700 and 2300 B.C.

But does this mean that at the dawn of Chinese history the Miao were then driven into a rougher habitat? Or were they relatively recent incursors into the lowlands from mountain bases which they still held?

There are some accounts which suggest that they had come from the rugged regions of the west or north. An early Chinese work states that the San-Miao were 'a race who came from the Western wilderness, whose face, eyes, feet, and hands resembled those of other people, but under their arm-pits they had wings, with which, however, they were unable to fly'.[9]

Savina says that the folklore of modern Miao groups imply that they came from the north. He writes:

Miao traditions lead us within the polar circle to the country of snow, ice and days and nights of six months. We are ignorant of the time this people spent in the ice and darkness of the North and we are also ignorant of the date and reason of their leaving them. Nor do we know why and when they left them,

[7] The work referred to is more usually termed the *Ssu shu* or *Sze shu*: literally the *Four Books* a compilation of four early Confucian texts made by Sung scholar Chu Hsi (A.D. 1130–1200). The last book is *Meng-tzu* or *Mencius*, the sayings of the Confucian philosopher Meng-tzu (372–289 B.C.?), supposedly recorded by his disciples.

[8] Hudspeth, 1937, p. 10. The *Shu Ching*, or *Book of History*, is a collection of documents traditionally dating from the third millennium B.C. to the early Chou period (up to the 8th century B.C.) but containing forgeries of a much later date. It was probably compiled around the 5th–3rd centuries B.C., although traditionally ascribed to Confucius (551–479 B.C.).

[9] This quotation occurs in the K'ang-hsi Dictionary compiled in the reign of the Emperor Sheng-tsu (A.D. 1662–1722), the second emperor of the Ch'ing Dynasty, whose reign title was K'ang-hsi. The quotation in the Dictionary is taken from the *Shih-chi*, or *Historical Records*, compiled by Ssu-ma Ch'ien (145–90 B.C.) of the Han dynasty. The reference was first noted in the article in the *Canton Miscellanie*, 1831, p. 199, where it was attributed to the 'She-ke', a historical work of the 'Hea' dynasty. The exact reference was traced for me by Dr. B. McDougall of the Department of Oriental Studies, University of Sydney. I am indebted to her also for identification of other Chinese references.

what neighbours they had, or what track they took to reach the banks of the Yellow River.[10]

However, Savina says that the polar regions were not their first home: 'Their traditions say this. Traditions which lead us further towards the south. . . .' His only specification of the south is that it was 'towards the ruins of the Tower of Babel'.[11]

The theory of an ultimate southern origin is supported by Graham also on the basis of Miao folklore. He says that the traditions of the Ch'uan Miao, a group which he studied in Szechwan Province, point to their previous residence in a hot climate, and from this he concludes that they probably came from the torrid regions of India, Burma, or Tonkin into China where they migrated as far north as the Yellow River.[12]

Whatever the remoter origins of the Miao may have been, many of the writers assume that in earliest historical times they had become concentrated in the fertile basins first of the Yellow River and then of the Yangtze River, and that they moved into the mountainous regions from there. Savina says that after their defeat by the Chinese those in the basin of the Yellow River were 'relegated' to the borders of Shensi and Kansu. 'Those in the basin of the Hoai steered towards the lakes Tong-t'ing and Pouoyang (Lake Poyang), straggled through the present Hou-Pe (Hupeh), Kiang-Si, and Hou-Nan, then reached the mountain chain which separates the basin of the Blue River from the basin of the West River, and followed it up as far as Koui-Tcheou (Kweichow), from where the Chinese have never been able to dislodge them, and where they still are today.'[13] He believes that Kweichow was the base from which they then migrated into other provinces: 'From the Mountains of Koui-Tcheou, the Miao swarmed bit by bit into the neighbouring provinces, Louang-Si (Kiangsi), and Kouang-Tong (Kwangtung) in the south, Se-Tchouan (Szechwan) in the north and Yu-nan in the west.'[14]

Graham has them following a different route. He says that from the Yellow River they retreated south to Kwangtung and Kwangsi where some were taken captive and released in the highlands of Kweichow and Szechwan. He states that there is no evidence that there were any people ancestrally identifiable with the modern Miao in northern Kweichow or southern Szechwan prior to the Sung dynasty (A.D.

---

[10] Savina, 1930, p. 261. Koppers has suggested a possible connection between the Miao and the Tungus. (W. Koppers, 'Tungusen und Miao', *Mitteilungen der Anthropologischen Gesellschaft in Wien*, 60 (1930), 306–19).   [11] Savina, 1930, p. 261.

[12] D. C. Graham, 'The Customs of the Ch'uan Miao', *Journal of the West China Border Research Society*, Vol. 9, 1937, pp. 18–20.

[13] Savina, 1930, p. viii.   [14] Ibid.

960–1279), and that most modern groups there owe their origin to forced immigration in Ming or early Manchu times.[15]

Although differing in details regarding the supposed movements of the people, these accounts have in common the assumption that modern Miao groups in highland southern China and beyond derive from the populations of northerly river valleys 4,000 years ago. The concept is of a single migratory group of people who advancing out of the mists of antiquity met at the limit of the migration another group of people—the Chinese—who drove them from the valleys, causing them to scatter widely through the mountains. Yang, Beh, and Morse express this simple theory when they state that all the Miao are 'presumably the modern remnants of the San Miao whose original habitat, roughly speaking, was in the lower Yangtse River Basin'.[16]

The migratory behaviour of the Miao in recent times, especially their advance through Yunnan and down the Indo-Chinese mountain chains, is impressive, and it may have led to an oversimplified view of the nature of their movements. Savina states that their migration is 'one of the longest trecks that history has ever recorded, for it extends along almost fifty centuries',[17] and he speaks of the Miao as 'stranger and traveller for five thousand years in the middle of other peoples of China'.[18]

This can have poetic truth only. The striking modern movements of the Miao are not simple journeys onwards from place to place but a pioneering of new areas from bases which continue to be populated. Although of much greater complexity because of the presence of other different peoples, their movements may not be dissimilar to those which have led to the peopling of other continents within perhaps much the same time span. One of the purposes of this book is to seek an explanation of the modern Miao movement, and we shall later propose an ecological explanation in terms of their technology and environment.

The movement may have begun with their expulsion from the Yangtze River Basin. But at least equally likely is the possibility that their presence in the basin was a phase in a movement extending much further back in time—a phase which may, however, have been a high point in Miao culture because of the more settled mode of life and greater density of population which valley living would allow.

We have already referred to the Chinese legends which state that the

[15] D. C. Graham, 'Note on the Ch'wan Miao of West China', Man, 1939, Nos. 171–2, pp. 174–5.
[16] Stephen C. H. Yang, Y. T. Beh, and W. R. Morse, 'Blood Groups of the Aboriginal Ch'wan Miao of Szechwan Province, West China', Man, 1938, No. 66.
[17] Savina, 1930, p. viii. Perhaps, if present trends continue, after another fifty centurie Chinese history too will be assumed to have begun with a similar long march.
[18] Ibid., p. xi.

Miao came 'from the Western wilderness'. It will also be noted that Lo Jao-Tien's account, based on a study of the earliest Chinese written documents, refers to the San-Miao chieftain as 'seizing' the region between the lakes Tung Ting and Poyang. There are other indications of an early connection with populations in Kweichow. Lo Jao-Tien says that in ancient times the Emperor Yen married a daughter of a chief of an area in the south of Kweichow. It was this Emperor who is believed to have been supplanted by Ch'ih-yu, the legendary ancestor of the Miao, who may also have originated in Kweichow. Lo Jao-Tien also says that the influence and power of the San-Miao chieftain extended to the present provinces of Yunnan, Kweichow, Szechwan, and Kwangtung, and that 'all the people of these places followed his customs'.[19]

These statements suggest that right at the dawn of their recorded history the Miao were located in the southern regions and that even then their strongest concentration may have been in Kweichow. Certainly Chinese records do not support Graham's contention that people apparently identifiable as Miao came into Kweichow only during and after Sung times. Lo Jao-Tien refers to a kingdom of Tsang-ko in north-east Kweichow headed by a Miao which existed in the time of Chou dynasty (1122–256 B.C.).[20]

The identification of Miao groups in ancient times is complicated by the practice of Chinese conquerors of transferring leaders of peoples they had overcome earlier to be overlords of newly conquered groups. Thus it is said that at the time of the Warring States (481–221 B.C.) Chuang Chiao, a general of Ch'u, destroyed Tsang-ko. He then transported the clan of Ts-ai to be chiefs of the Miao there. Later Emperor Wu of the Han dynasty (140–87 B.C.) transported four great families of Szechwan, the Lung, Fu, Tung and Yin, to that region.[21]

A sequel to this event is referred to by Ch'en Ting in his account of his residence among the Chou Miao of Yunnan about A.D. 1667. He writes:

During the time of the Three Kingdoms, two Lung brothers followed Chu-k'o Liang [A.D. 181–234] against the southern barbarians. On account of his merit, the elder was made prince of Eastern Yunnan and founded the Lung clan. The younger was made prince of Southern Yunnan and founded the Feng clan. Each changed part of his written name. During later generations, these two clans were the chiefs of the Miao. They received their titles from the Shu Han dynasty . . . Even now their houses are palatial.[22]

[19] Lin Yueh-Hwa, 1940, p. 271.
[20] Ibid. The account is derived from the *Shi-chi* and the *Ch'ien-Han shu*.
[21] Lin Yueh-Hwa, 1940, p. 271.
[22] J. K. Shryock, 'Ch'en Ting's Account of the Marriage Customs of the Chiefs of Yunnan and Kweichow', *American Anthropologist*, Vol. 36, 1934, p. 531.

One may well ask whether the people whom Ch'en Ting refers to as living in Yunnan almost 2,000 years ago were really of the same ethnic stock as the people classified as Miao today. We shall discuss the general question of identification later and note the confusion which existed in Chinese classifications. Ch'en Ting appears to have encountered a mixture of peoples, probably because the noble family with which he dwelt had suzerainity over a number of groups. But there are distinct cultural resemblances between some of the people and Miao of today. Thus he says: 'The women wore short upper garments reaching only to the waist, and long skirts. These skirts were of a hundred or two hundred folds.' [23]

Graham may quite likely be correct in saying that ancestors of the Ch'uan Miao he studied in Szechwan near the border of Kweichow were brought by the Chinese as captives from Kwantung and Kwangsi, as this was a practice the Chinese had apparently followed for centuries. But long before this forced migration the Miao appear to have been widely dispersed in the mountainous regions of all the southern provinces.

Lo Jao-Tien gives an account of the formation of a group known as the Chung Miao in Yunnan. He writes:

During the period of the Five Dynasties (A.D. 907–60) the prince of Ch'u sent soldiers to garrison Nan-ning[24] and accordingly commanded them to keep its land from generation to generation. These groups were desirous of differentiating themselves from the Man people and accordingly took the surname of their commander as their designation and called themselves Chung people ... Therefore, at the present time, the Chung Miao by reason of their noble group still lord it over the Miao.[25]

In a footnote Lin Yueh-Hwa quotes S. R. Clarke as saying 'The term Chung-chia is Chinese. Chung possibly means the second of three brothers; chia ... means "Family" or "Tribe", and the term may be used to convey the idea that they are inferior to the Chinese and superior to the Miao.' [26]

Hints of an ancestral Chinese overlordship involving brothers also occur in the mythology of the Meto Miao. Every household honours a house spirit called Lau-tze.[27] It is said that he was one of four Chinese brothers to whom the people used to give offerings. One night he called out from the darkness that all his brothers were dead and that in future they should give offerings only to him. Although this was a lie, the people

---

[23] Shryock, 1934, p. 534.
[24] This is not the same place as Nanning in Kwangsi. It was in north-east Yunnan.
[25] Lin Yueh-Hwa, 1960, p. 277.
[26] Ibid. The work referred to is Samuel R. Clarke, *Among the Tribes in South-West China*, London, 1911.
[27] In the spelling we have generally used, 'Lowtsier'.

adopted him as their protective household spirit from then onwards.

The echoes from the past are sufficiently numerous and clear to indicate that people culturally identifiable with modern Miao were living in Kweichow and neighbouring provinces of China at least 1,000 years ago and possibly for more than twice that length of time. The preservation by the Miao of their ethnic identity for such a long time despite their being split into many small groups surrounded by different alien peoples and scattered over a vast geographical area is an outstanding record paralleling in some ways that of the Jews but more remarkable because they lacked the unifying forces of literacy and a doctrinal religion and because the cultural features they preserved seem to be more numerous.

Nevertheless the extent and constancy of their distinctiveness may easily be over-estimated. Physical and cultural interchange with neighbouring peoples must have occurred throughout their history. The concept of two groups—the Miao and the Chinese—meeting first on the Yellow River and each maintaining its original distinctiveness in all subsequent encounters is certainly an over-simplification. The Chinese who met the Miao on the Yellow River were probably much different in their ancestry and customs from those who defeated the San-Miao in the central Yangtse River area and very different again from the Chinese in contact with the Miao in recent historical times in Kweichow, Kwangsi, and Yunnan. The Miao, too, were probably different in each case, but quite likely the Chinese had altered more because they were a nation which expanded by absorbing many of the peoples they met on the frontiers of their growing power.

Today the term 'Han Chinese' is frequently used to distinguish the predominant people in China from the minority peoples. But even before the Han dynasty (206 B.C.–A.D. 220) from which the term derives, the Chinese were of composite origin. To quote a recent work by Moseley:

The empire of the Han dynasty, established on the basis of the unification of China achieved by the preceding Ch'in dynasty (221–206 B.C.), was already, it appears, a 'multinational state', for one of the former feudal states incorporated in it, the state of Ch'u in the middle Yangtze valley, is thought to have been inhabited by a T'ai people. The regionalism of the 'Han Chinese' is as old as this, too: for instance, the distinctiveness of the Szechuanese in the west can be traced to the State of Shu which had a quasi-independent existence prior to the Ch'in unification. Under the T'ang dynasty [A.D. 618–907] . . . the Cantonese area in south-coastal China . . . was welded into the empire; and under Ming (A.D. 1368–1644), Yunnan and the southwest were effectively incorporated.[28]

[28] George Moseley, (ed.), *The Party and the National Question in China*, The M.I.T. Press, Cambridge, Mass., 1966, pp. 11–12.

THE ORIGINS OF THE MIAO PEOPLE

The reference to Ch'u as possibly comprising a T'ai people is interesting, for it was said to have subdued the Miao kingdom of Tsang-ko. If this is true, it shows that not only the relationships between the Chinese and the Miao but also those between the Thai and the Miao have a very long history and that their character now is not so very different from what it was 2,000 years ago.

Amongst the peoples absorbed into the Chinese nation, or into the regional elements of it, there may have been some, or even many, Miao. Certain writers,[29] noting points of resemblance between the culture of modern Miao and that of the Chinese, conclude that this indicates that the Miao have become 'sinicized' in all these respects. The Miao must, of course, have been influenced by the millennia of contact, but there is no good reason to assume that the cultural influence was all in one direction. History, the handmaiden of patriotism, naturally reflects the Chinese view because the Chinese were the only people able to write it.

Whether the Miao who survived as a distinguishable people were merely those who, because they were living in remote areas, were less subject to contact and conquest, or whether they represented the bulk of the people whose way of life was preserved by a strong sense of ethnic identity, is a question which probably can never be answered satisfactorily. But if an answer could be given it would not be irrelevant to the modern situation in which governments are forming policies towards the Miao and other minority peoples. Edmund Leach[30] seems to imply that ethnic identities can change easily according to the dictates of economic and political circumstances. This theory, attractive to proselytizers and administrators of every faith and political persuasion, could be dangerous if it gave apparent scientific backing to a view which is incorrect. Therefore it is useful to speculate on the answer even if the result is only to preserve a measure of doubt.

Miao groups in China today do present gradations of similarity to Chinese in economic and, to a lesser extent, in cultural practices. But even in cases where the resemblance is closest there appears to be a strong sense of separate identity reinforced particularly by a lack of intermarriage. Nearly every writer refers to this factor. For instance, Mickey in her account of the Cowrie Shell Miao in Kweichow states that despite much intermixing with other peoples including the Chinese at markets the Miao marry only amongst themselves.[31]

[29] For example, Ruey Yih-Fu, 'The Magpie Miao of Southern Szechuan', *Social Structure in South-East Asia*, ed. G. P. Murdock, Chicago, 1960, p. 145.

[30] E. R. Leach, *Political Systems of Highland Burma*, G. Bell and Sons, London, 1954.

[31] P. M. Mickey, *The Cowrie Shell Miao of Kweichow*, Peabody Museum, Harvard, 1947, p. 9.

Ch'en Ting in his account of the Chou Miao written in mid-seventeenth century says: 'These Miao were never married to ordinary Chinese.'[32] The same feature is noted in Miao groups outside China. Thus Bernatzik, writing of the Thailand Miao, says: 'I could not find a single instance of a Miao who married outside his tribe.'[33] Savina records that the Miao of Tonkin explained their mountain living by saying: 'If we descend into the plains, our girls would marry people who do not belong to our race.'[34]

In a more general statement Savina says: 'The various people encountered by the Miao during the fifty centuries of their history are the I in the north and east, the Man, the Chinese, and the Thai in the south, and the Lolo and the Tibetans in the west. We have already seen that Miao beliefs are different from those of these peoples from whom they have borrowed practically nothing.'[35] Although this statement cannot be taken at its face value, it is indicative of the general view expressed of Miao independence.

That the Miao lived independently in the mountains at least for several centuries is indicated in the reports of the first European observers. The Jesuit missionary, Gabriel de Magaillans, who travelled over all the principal parts of China, arriving there in 1640 and remaining in the country until his death at Peking in 1677, wrote:

The independent mountaineers of Sze-chuen, Yun-nan, Kwei-chau, and Kwang-si, pay no tribute to the emperor, nor yield him any obedience, being governed by absolute princes, whom the Chinese call 'local or native lords', and 'local or native officers'. Their towns are, for the most part, environed with high mountains and steep rocks, as if nature had taken particular care of their fortification. Within these mountains lie extensive plains and fields, and many towns and villages. Though they speak the Chinese, they have a particular language also, and their manners and customs are likewise somewhat different from those of the sons of Han. Nevertheless, their complexion and the shape of their bodies are altogether alike, but as to their courage, you would think them to be quite another nation; the Chinese stand in fear of them; so that after several trials which they have made of their prowess, they have been forced to let them live at their own liberty, and to consent to a free intercourse and traffic with them.[36]

THE MEANING OF THE TERM 'MIAO'

Although some of the mountaineers whom Gabriel de Magaillans was describing were probably of the same cultural category as the modern Miao, it is unlikely that they all were. Often the term 'Miao'

[32] Shryock, 1934, p. 531.
[33] Bernatzik, H. A., *Akha und Meau*, Wagner, Innsbruck, 1947, p. 109.
[34] Savina, 1930, p. 174. [35] Ibid., p. 261.
[36] Quoted from W. Lockhart, 'On the Miautsze or Aborigines of China', *Transactions of the Ethnological Society*, London, No. 1, 1861, pp. 182–3.

has been used as a general name for all the mountainous people, or even all the non-Chinese, of the southern regions. Lin Yueh-Hwa says that since Ming times the term has become as broad as the term 'Man', embracing all groups of the barbarous people. He points out, however, that in earlier times the term was used with greater precision. The *Yuan shi lei pien* compiled by Shao Yuan-p'ing (A.D. 1662–1722) indicates that even during the Yuan dynasty (A.D. 1279–1368) it was applied to a distinctive group of people who were subdivided into the Hua (Flowery) Miao, the Pai (White) Miao, and the Ch'ing (Blue) Miao. During Ming times a fivefold division was made into Flowery, White, Blue, Black, and Red Miao.[37] This categorization was followed by Lao Jao-Tien in his work on Kweichow printed in 1847, from which we have drawn some of the preceding historical speculation.[38]

The term 'Miao' was used more than 2,000 years ago in both the *Shu Ching* and the *Shih Chi*.[39] Although the evidence is slender, we have given reasons why the people so designated may have been cultural ancestors of the modern Miao.

The character for 'Miao' in Chinese writing is generally said to be a compound term composed of one symbol meaning 'plants' and one meaning 'fields'. On this basis various interpretations have been made. Williams, writing in the *Chinese Repository* of 1845, says: 'The word *Miao* is a compound term, formed by the two words *tsau*, plants, and *tien*, fields; and Morrison in his Dictionary defines it thus, 'grain growing in a field; the first budding forth of any plants; numerous descendents etc.'[40] An implication here could be that it referred to the great number of barbarians encountered. Graves, writing for the *Chinese Recorder* in 1869, says that the term means 'grass springing up in a field' and hence designates 'wild uncultivated tribes'.[41] Frequently it is assumed to indicate that the Chinese regarded the Miao as autochthonous. For example Jamieson writes that the Chinese divided the peoples they encountered into four great classes—Man (meaning 'wild' or 'ignorant'), T'u, Miao, and Yao. 'Miao,' he says, means 'plant-shoot' and this indicates that the Chinese considered they were the product of the soil, 'which shows that they were there before the arrival of the Chinese'.[42]

Generally most writers have taken the name to mean aboriginal

[37] Lin Yueh-Hwa, 1940, pp. 278–9, n. 50.   [38] Ibid., p. 278.

[39] See above, p. 8. The *Shih Chi* was compiled by Ssu-ma Ch'ien (145–90 B.C.) of the Han Dynasty (206 B.C.–A.D. 220).

[40] E. W. Williams, 'Notices of the Miao-Tze or Aboriginal Tribes Inhabiting Various Highlands in the Southern and Western Provinces of China Proper', *Chinese Repository*, Vol. 14, No. 3, 1845, p. 106.

[41] R. H. Graves, 'The Miao-Tze', *Chinese Recorder*, Vol. 2, 1869–70, p. 1.

[42] C. E. Jamieson, 'The Aborigines of West China', *China Journal of Science and Arts*, Vol. 1, 1923, p. 380.

tribes with the added connotation of 'uncivilized'. This view, however, has been disputed by some writers. Lacouperie in his book on the languages of China before the Chinese has the following argument. 'Miao-tse', he says, was translated as 'son of the soil' by the old sinologists, but they had been led astray by the modern character analysis of Chinese writing. The character *Miao* has been regarded as composed of the particle 'herbs' and the particle 'fields'. If one takes 'tse' to mean 'child' or 'son', the interpretation 'son of the soil' can then be made. But in fact the ancient form of the character *Miao* represented a cat's head and meant 'cat'. This was probably because their strongly vocalized language seemed to resemble the miaowing of a cat.[43] Graham, too, although accepting the meaning 'sons of the soil', states that the word is similar to the Chinese word for 'cat' and suggests that it may have been related to the speech of the people.[44]

It is difficult to believe that Chinese seriously thought that there was any resemblance between feline utterance and Miao speech, which in most of its sounds resembles their own. There have been other cat associations made for the Miao, by outsiders or by themselves, which could account slightly more plausibly for the name if in fact it does bear any relationship to the symbol for cat.

In early accounts of the Miao there are frequent references to their having tails. Thus the Dictionary compiled under the direction of the Emperor in the reign K'ang-hsi (A.D. 1662–1722) states of the Miao that 'according to popular notion they are said to have tails'.[45] The belief persisted for a long time. Lockhart writing in 1861 says: 'One tribe, inhabiting Li-po hien, is called yau-jin, wild men, and although they occasionally come down to Canton to trade, the citizens of that place firmly believe them to be furnished with short tails like monkeys.'[46] Thwing, writing in 1896, says that he was told by the Cantonese that Miao children have tails which drop off when they are twenty days old.[47] The implication of the cat association therefore seems to be the

[43] Albert Terrien de Lacouperie, *The Languages of China Before the Chinese: Researches on the Languages Spoken by the Pre-Chinese Races of China Proper Previously to the Chinese Occupation*, London, 1887, p. 108. This is referred to by A. Schotter, 'Notes Ethnographiques sur les Tribus de Kouy-tcheou (Chine)', *Anthropos*, Vol. 3, 1908, p. 405. Schotter considers the term *Miao* as synonymous with *Yao* and, in a complicated explanation, suggests that there could be a connection with the ideographic sign for a cat's head in ancient writing.

[44] D. C. Graham, 'The Customs of the Ch'uan Miao', *Journal of the West China Border Research Society*, Vol. 9, 1937, p. 18.

[45] Quoted in Graves, 1869–70, p. 1. Graves refers to the work as 'Kang II'. K'ang-hsi is the reign title for the Emperor Sheng-tsu, the second emperor of the Ch'ing dynasty.

[46] Lockhart, 1861, p. 181.

[47] E. W. Thwing, 'A legend of the Ius', *China Review*, Hong Kong, Vol. 22, 1896–9, p. 781. 'Iu' is a name sometimes used for the Yao tribe, and the people of whom both Lockhart and Thwing were writing were probably Yao, but their use of the term *Miao* suggests that the belief had a more general application to all the tribes subsumed under the general term 'Miao'.

same as that implied by the other derivation of the name: the Miao were a wild species.

Sometimes the Miao associate themselves with a more formidable species. In Meto we were told by Lowtong, the head of the community, that all people have signs of tails, clearer in some cases than in others. The tails are a manifestation of the commonalty of species between men and tigers. All tigers are believed to belong to Miao clans and when one is killed divination horns should be cast to determine the clan to which it belongs, although there is no taboo on eating it.

The characteristics of the tiger–man category are believed to range from purely tiger to purely human qualities. Along the range individuals have greater or less potentiality to assume either the tiger or the human form. Not all men have been tigers or all tigers men but there is a danger of men turning into tigers after death, particularly the first and last born in a family. It is said that a tiger with five distinct claws instead of four is definitely human.

One explanation given in Meto of the Miao custom of wearing silver neck rings was that it kept persons human. It was said that once upon a time two people died. When the first was buried, tigers came to the grave to call the spirit to join them. People saw them and shot them. In the second case no one was around, so the spirit broke out of the grave. Although tiger hairs were beginning to sprout it still had the appearance of a human being and was still wearing its neck rings. The neck rings were irritating it so it begged a passer-by to take them off. When he did so it ran away into the jungle as a tiger.[48]

Belief in association between men and tigers has been reported from many Miao areas.[49] Several stories of the Ch'uan Miao in Szechwan recounted by Graham have lycanthropy as their theme.[50] At least three of the stories record a further transformation into a cat. In one the first cat possessed by a Miao family was said to have originated from half a tiger's liver.[51] In another a tiger wishing to capture a bad Chinese official transformed himself into a cat and the official into a

[48] Today tigers are uncommon in the Meto region. Only two were reported during our residence there. Both were believed to be people who had died. The second case was in 1965 just before Sitoa died. It was said that ten years before he had had a love-affair with a girl but her parents would not allow him to marry him. She later died. The sickness which led to Sitoa's death coincided with the appearance of the tiger, which was thought to be his lover calling him. When he died the tiger was seen no more.

[49] I. de Beauclair, 'Culture Traits of Nine Chinese Tribes in Kwei-chow Province, South-West China', *Sinologica*, Vol. 5, Zurich, 1956, p. 33. He says that in the high mountains of south-east China the 'Raw Miao' (believed to be the same as the Black Miao) believe the dead may change into tigers and attack people to eat their blood.

[50] D. C. Graham, *Songs and Stories of the Ch'uan Miao*, Smithsonian Institute, Washington, 1954.

[51] Ibid., p. 16.

mouse so that he could carry him off from his house without alerting the guards.[52]

MIAO AND CHINESE CLASSIFICATIONS

The general term which the Miao use for themselves, whether in China or beyond, is 'Hmong', or some close approximation to it. A secondary word or words indicates the sub-grouping to which they belong. Savina lists ten sub-groupings, or 'tribes', and says 'this is about all.'[53] He adds. 'As one can see, we are far from the fifty or hundred tribes and dialects of the Miao which supposedly exist in Koui-tcheou, but which, in reality, have never existed except in the imagination of the Chinese.'[54]

Chinese accounts do indeed often show a multiplicity of names.[55] Lo Jao-Tien lists fifty-three sub-divisions in Kweichow but states that there were five major groupings to which many of the others were subsidiary: the Pai (White), the Hua (Flowery), the Ch'ing (Blue), the Hei (Black), and the Hung (Red).[56] Analysing Lo Jao-Tien's account, Lin Yueh-Hwa concludes that the fifty-three sub-divisions, which include some peoples other than Miao, indicate that the Miao proper comprised ten groups[57]—which interestingly is the same number as given by Savina, although comparison of the names is difficult because Lo Jao-Tien gives the Chinese terms whereas Savina uses the Miao dialect names.

Most frequently the Chinese distinguished the various groups by the colour of their clothing, as in the case of the five major groupings listed by Lo Jao-Tien, but a variety of other characteristics were used also, such as geographical location, topography, items in use for decoration and exchange, habits or physical attributes often of an uncomplimentary kind, making up a weirdly exotic list: the Western Miao, the Eastern Miao, the Steep Slope Miao, the Trumpet Miao, the Robe-Wearing Miao, the Pot-Ring Miao, the Iron-Making Miao, the Tooth-Knocking Miao, the Dog-Ear Miao, the Horse-Saddle-Flap Miao, the Crow-Sparrow Miao, the Magpie Miao, and so on.[58]

The assumption that the names which Miao groups apply to themselves are also based on the colour of their clothing has probably been a cause of confusion because it is at best only sometimes true. When the Miao do use a colour term it may not refer to their clothing. Even if it

[52] Ibid., p. 139.   [53] Savina, 1930, p. xv.   [54] Ibid.
[55] Lin Yueh-Hwa, 1940, Appendix A, p. 328, summarizes Chinese classifications which have as many as 82 groups.
[56] Ibid., p. 278.   [57] Ibid., p. 283, n. 62.
[58] All the names except the last are from Lo Jao-Tien's list (see Lin Yueh-Hwa, 1940, pp. 279–83). The last is from Mickey, 1947, who states (p. 5) that in Kweichow there are as many as 80 or 90 different names in use locally by the Chinese.

does, it is not necessarily the same term which the Chinese have chosen to designate that group because the costumes of many Miao are multicoloured. One writer has described them as 'marvels of barbaric beauty'.[59] Therefore choices of names tend to be arbitrary. For this reason it cannot be assumed that a group called by a particular name in China is identical with a group called by the same name elsewhere.

In the case of the Blue Miao of Thailand, with whom our study deals, the identity of name cannot therefore be regarded as strong evidence that they belong to the same group of people as those whom Chinese writers have called Blue (Ch'ing) Miao. The brief descriptions of the Ch'ing given by Lo Jao-Tien and others suggest that they do not. Can we then discover a more likely identification for them?

In his *History of the Miao*, Savina writes: 'The Miao dialect which is most different from the others and which is also the widest spread is that of the green Miao, Hmong ngioa, whom the Chinese, for some reason or other, call red Miao, Houng Miao.'[60] The name by which the Blue Miao of Thailand call themselves is *Hmong njua*. Savina's term 'ngioa' is probably a different rendering of this term. The exact translation of 'njua' is open to debate because the Miao system of colour classification differs slightly from the European system. The term can be applied to certain ranges of blue, such as the blue of the sky, but most frequently it designates green. Lyman translates 'Hmong njua' as Green Miao.[61] The translation Blue Miao has been used here simply because that is the established name for the group in Thailand, probably because of an assumption that it refers to the basic colour of the costume.

In the statement just quoted Savina identifies the group with that called by the Chinese the Red Miao, or 'Houng Miao'. However, Lo Jao-Tien's description of this group, called by Lin Yueh-Hwa in his translation the 'Hung Miao', and of its sub-division the 'Hung-t'ou Miao' does not suggest great similarity.

Of all the groups described by Lo Jao-Tien the one which has most points of similarity with the Blue Miao of Thailand is the Chung-chia Miao. He says:

The women cover their rolls of hair with flowery cloth. Their skirts are long and minutely pleated with more than twenty pleats. Their upper garments

---

[59] B. G. Tours, 'Notes on an Overland Journey from Chungking to Haiphong', *Geographical Journal*, Vol. 62, No. 2, 1923, p. 125.

[60] Savina, 1930, p. xv.

[61] Thomas A. Lyman, 'Green Miao (Meo) Spirit-Ceremonies', *Ethnologica*, Neue Folge, Band 4, Brill, Cologne, 1968, p. 1. Also personal correspondence. The Thai may refer to the group as Meo Khiaw, which is usually translated as 'green' but may be translated as 'blue', or as Meo dam, meaning 'Black Miao'.

are very short. They wear at their waists a piece of coloured cloth, like a sash, which is pieced with blue cloth. By nature they are diligent in weaving. They take the twelfth moon as the beginning of the year . . . Each year in the first month of spring, the 'Moon Dance' is held. Out of coloured cloth they make small balls called coloured balls. Aiming at their favorites they throw them . . . In mourning they slaughter cattle and summon their kindred and friends . . . They use large jars to hold wine . . . In burial they use coffins . . . When sick, they take no medicine, but prefer (to rely on) witchcraft and ghosts.[62]

With very minor differences all these features occur with the Blue Miao of Thailand but are not found in combination in other groups which we have seen described. The resemblance is reinforced in the accounts of the Chung-chia Miao by other writers. Sainson makes reference to the 'sailor collar' which is a feature of the costume of Blue Miao girls in Thaliand: 'Les femmes se couvrent la tête avec de la toile noire à la façon d'un bonnet de bonze et y cousent des coquilles marines: elles ont une veste et une jupe en toile de diverses couleurs.'[63] Their characteristic skirt of many pleats is mentioned in *Yen-chiao chi-wen* written by T'en Ju-ch'eng in A.D. 1558.[64]

Chinese manuscripts of unknown origin purchased by Playfair in Peking and reviewed by him in 1876 describe some customs of the 'Chung-chia' or 'Chung Clan' living in the area mentioned by Lo Jao-Tien. We are told that the women wear pleated skirts and gay-coloured sashes. At the beginning of the year they have a dancing festival at which 'they make balls of coloured cloth; any one of the dancers may throw this at the person best liked of the opposite sex. Without further ceremony the two set out on a honeymoon trip without being subjected to any interference.'[65] This is a truncated but nevertheless unmistakeable description of the courting ball game at the New Year festival at Meto.

The same manuscripts describe close neighbours of the Chung Miao called 'Hua-miao' or 'Embroidery-Weaving Miao' saying that they make hair-dresses of horse-hair and mark their cloth with wax before dyeing which when removed leaves the designs apparent. Several of the clan names mentioned, such as Chang, Li, Ma, and Yang, are the same as clan names at Meto and elsewhere in the Blue Miao area of Thailand today.[66]

[62] Lin Yueh-Hwa, 1940, pp. 292–3.

[63] Camille Sainson, *Nan-tchao ye-che, Histoire particulière de Nantchao*, Paris, 1904, p. 185. Lin Yueh-Hwa, 1940, p. 292, n. 133, also notes this reference.

[64] Quoted by Lin Yueh-Hwa, ibid.

[65] G. M. H. Playfair, 'The Miaotzu of Kweichow and Yunnan from Chinese descriptions', *China Review*, Vol. 5, 1876–7, p. 94. See also W. Geil, *Eighteen Capitals of China*, Constable, London, 1911, p. 132, for reference to the ball game amongst the Chung Miao.

[66] Playfair, 1876–7, p. 95.

The Chung-chia as a whole cannot be identified with the Miao. They are normally classified as a sub-category of the Chuang group, which includes the Tai peoples. In China the Chuang form the largest nationality after the Chinese, numbering approximately 7 million. The Chung-chia, also called Puyi by the Chinese, are the largest of the sub-groups with a population of about 1¼ million located in south-west Kweichow and Yunnan.

Amongst the Chung-chia, however, there appear to be some groups which have had intimate connections with the Miao. Bruk remarks that in the central part of Kweichow they 'live together with the Miao'.[67] Lin Yueh-Hwa refers to the 'Chung-chia Miao' although, on the basis of Lo Jao-Tien's statements, he differentiates them from the 'Miao proper' whom he concludes consist of ten groups (some of which are subsidiary to others): the Pai Miao, Hua Miao, Ch'ing Miao, Hei Miao, Hung Miao, Shan Miao, Ch'ing-t'ou Miao, Hung-t'ou Miao, La-pa Miao, and Kao-p'o Miao. The Chung-chia Miao, he says, may form an independent category.[68] Other writers have mentioned cultural features of the Chung-chia not shared with the Miao of Thailand—such as building their houses on piles—and it has been suggested that their language belongs to the Thai-Shan group.[69] Lo Jao-Tien says that they are a noble group founded by Ma Yin, Prince of Ch'u, who migrated with five other families from southern Kwangsi during the time of the Five Dynasties[70] (A.D. 907–60) and that they still lord it over the Miao.

This statement may hold the key to the situation. Although there are probably many Chung-chia groups who have little or no Miao connection, there may be other groups formed from a Miao population subjected to a Chung-chia overlordship resulting over the centuries in a unique cultural blend. Chinese contact—using the word Chinese in its broadest sense—and probably Chinese overlordship at various times in their history, has clearly left marks on many Miao groups. In Thailand the Blue Miao commonly attribute to the Chinese certain cultural elements, such as the titles given to sons to indicate their order of birth,[71] and their household gods. Although they seem to be without

[67] S. I. Bruk, *Peoples of China, Mongolian Peoples Republic and Korea.* (Naseleniye Kitaya, M.N.R. i Korei) Moscow, Academy of Sciences, U.S.S.R., Institute of Ethnography imeni N. N. Miklukho-Maklay, 1959; translated by U.S. Joint Publications Research Service, No. 3710, Washington, D.C., 1960, p. 26.

[68] Lin Yueh-Hwa, 1940, p. 283, n. 62.

[69] V. K. Ting, 'On the Native Tribes of Yunnan', *China Medical Journal*, Vol. 35, 1921, pp. 163–4. This and references to later similar classifications are noted by Lin Yueh-Hwa, 1940, in Appendix A, p. 328.

[70] Lin Yueh-Hwa, 1940, p. 291.

[71] The birth order titles are: Laotow, Laolier, Laosang, Lowsier, Laowu, Laoliu, Laochi. The term 'lao' would appear to be the common Chinese term for older person and the suffixes, except apparently the first one, variants of terms for numerals in Mandarin.

any sense of subservience to the Chinese as people, they respect them as traditional teachers and regard Chinese culture, in a way, as a 'father culture'.

Part of their regard is no doubt due to Chinese literacy. The Miao frequently inscribe by careful copying Chinese characters denoting ancestral names on the small silver plates which are attached by silver chains to their neck rings. They do not, however, consciously accept their own illiteracy as an aspect in which they are inferior to the Chinese. At Pasamliem I was told by some of the people that long ago, when they were still in China, they had a book like the Chinese. But one day it got cooked up and was eaten by them with their rice. The implication of this story was not, as I at first thought, that the Miao thereby lost access to the knowledge in the book. On the contrary, it indicated that they no longer needed the book because they had absorbed the knowledge.[72]

MIAO LANGUAGE AND ITS DIALECTS

More detailed information of the various Miao groups in China, particularly in regard to language, is necessary before we can decide which is the most likely cultural parent of the Blue Miao of Thailand. But whatever the parent group—whether it be Hung, or Ch'ing, or Chung or one of the other major sub-divisions—it is almost certainly not derived in the main from Chinese stock. If the Miao groups had been formed from various intermixtures of peoples occurring at widely separated times in history, their languages might also have been expected to show wide diversity. But this is not the case. Although there are dialect differences between the groups, their speeches are mutually intelligible so that we may speak of a general Miao language.

The correct linguistic classification of the language has been the subject of much debate. It now appears to be fairly generally agreed that the language belongs to the Sino–Tibetan group, although exactly how it should be classified within the group remains uncertain. Haudricourt[73] says that there is a strong Chinese overlay in the language but that the form of the words in this overlay shows that they are recent borrowings. Another part of the vocabulary has strong affinities with Burman, a member of the Tibeto–Burman branch of the Sino–

---

[72] A story in similar vein is reported by Graham from the Ch'uan Miao. In earliest times the Miao and Chinese were all one family. The Miao were descendants of the older brother and the Chinese of the younger. But in the centuries that followed the Chinese became more powerful and denied their common ancestry, so that now the Miao are the younger and weaker brothers and the Chinese the older and stronger. (D. C. Graham, 'More notes about the Chwan Miao', *Journal of the West China Border Research Society*, Vol. 3, 1926–9, p. 112).

[73] A. G. Haudricourt, 'Introduction à la phonologie historique des langues Miao-Yao', *Bulletin de l'École française d'extrême-orient*, Vol. 44, 1947–50.

Tibetan family. On their map of ethno-linguistic groups of mainland South-East Asia, Le Bar and others provide a separate classification within the Sino–Tibetan group for Miao–Yao.[74]

It appears also as if the major sub-divisions of the Miao came into being at a fairly early stage because the dialect distinctions are preserved over a wide area. Savina writes: 'All the Miao dialects have this in particular and that is that they do not vary from place to place. Thus the white Miao, or the black or yellow Miao of Laos and Tonkin speak exactly the same language as their fellows in Yunnan, Se-tchouan and Koui-tcheou. It is the same with all the other Miao.'[75] Although we are having difficulty in identifying the exact affiliations in China of the Blue Miao, the other main group in Thailand, the White Miao, appear to have very close dialect affinities with the Pai (white) Miao of China.[76]

THE MIAO AS ONE PEOPLE

Despite the differences in dialect and other cultural features between the major sub-divisions, or 'tribes' as they have sometimes been called, the Miao do have an over-all sense of being one people *vis-à-vis* all the non-Miao in the world. At least in the case of the Blue and the White Miao in Thailand this sense of unity is reflected in the fact that inter-marriage between them is quite common whereas it almost never occurs with different ethnic groups.

The sense of unity exists even though there are normally no political unions wider than villages or village clusters. Indeed this may be a reason for it. Tribal lines in territory or political organization appear never to have been drawn. The wider temporary alliances which have come into being in response to outside threats have lasted only as long as the threats, and in any case have often included portions of different dialect groups. Therefore the unifying forces of common language and general common culture could operate without political impediment to create a sense of being one people. Thus when the word 'tribe' is used, as it is in Thailand, to describe all the Miao people it is not without meaning, although it may be regarded anthropologically as a loose usage of the term. If the word is so used to designate all Miao then the major sub-divisions, such as the Blue and the White Miao, may be called 'sub-tribes'.

That there is a general cultural resemblance between Miao groups from widely separated areas is indicated in the descriptions of various

[74] Frank M. Le Bar, Gerald C. Hickey, and John K. Musgrave, *Ethnolinguistic Groups of Mainland Southeast Asia* (Map), Human Relations Area File, New Haven, Conn., 1964.

[75] Savina, 1930, p. xv.

[76] Broadcasts from Communist radio stations somewhere north of the Thailand border were using this dialect in 1965.

writers. One of the best accounts of a group in China is that by Ruey Yih-Fu of the Magpie Miao in southern Szechuan. I quote from his description at some length in order that the parallels may be seen with our later description of the Blue Miao community at Meto in Thailand.

The Magpie Miao live in villages, occasionally compact but normally consisting of a cluster of separate hamlets. Unlike most of the Thailand Miao, they have some wet rice 'raised in padi on the rare stretches of level ground, along the river banks, and behind terraces laboriously constructed on the lower slopes of the mountains', but they also grow other crops by 'slash-and-burn techniques on the higher mountain slopes'. Cloth is woven from hemp, is dyed dark blue or patterned by batik, and is sometimes elaborately embroidered.

The case of the Miao hamlet [writes Ruey], or occasionally of an entire village, is a localized patrilineal kin group, consisting mainly of the families of men who bear the same surname . . . the normal residential unit is the patrilocal extended family of the small or lineal type . . . not infrequently . . . extended families of considerable size do occur. These seem, however, to reflect the influence of the Han Chinese family organization.[77]

Ruey attributes several basic features of Magpie Miao social structure to Chinese influence—not only the extended family but also their patrilineal system and their system of patrilocal residence. These, however, are general features at least of all the Blue Miao groups in far-away Thailand. If they were adopted from the Chinese, they must have been adopted long ago and are now fully established in Miao culture.

THE ORIGIN OF PEOPLES IN THE MIAO VIEW

The Miao sense of tribal integrity is supported not only by similarities of language, custom, and social structure which facilitate inter-personal and inter-group relationships, but also by similarities of mythology. For example, in widely separated areas the story the people give to explain their own origin is roughly the same.[78]

Savina's version of the story, presumably collected in Tonkin, follows:

After the creation of the heavens and the first man, people had lived on the earth for 9,000 years. That year two brothers who worked in the same field noticed that someone was coming at night to undo all they had done in the day. They waited and watched and saw an old man who filled in the furrows they had dug. The elder of the brothers wanted to kill him but the younger told him they should first ask him why he was doing this. He told them that

[77] Ruey, Yih-Fu, 'The Magpie Miao of Southern Szechuan', in *Social Structure in Southeast Asia*, ed. G. P. Murdock, Chicago, 1960, pp. 144–5.

[78] There are other stories also common to many different areas explaining the creation of the heavens and the first man, events which occurred ages before the flood described above. The story is also reported from Kweichow by Geil (Geil, 1911, pp. 127–8).

it was because they were working in vain as a flood was coming to cover the whole surface of the earth. The two brothers realised that he was the Lord of the Sky and asked him what to do to escape drowning. He told the elder, who had a violent character, to build an iron boat. He told the younger, who had a gentle nature, to build a wooden boat in which he was to take his sister, a male and female of each animal species, and two seeds from each species of plant. In the seventh month the rain fell for four days and four nights. The iron boat of the older brother sank, but the boat of the younger brother floated up to the sky. When the Lord of the Sky saw the earth was flooded he sent a dragon in the shape of a rainbow to dry it out. The brother then wanted to marry his sister. At first she refused but after various tests proving that it was the will of the Lord of the Sky they married. The child of the union had neither head, hands or feet. 'This child is an egg', they said to each other. 'Let us cut it open.' The egg contained no child but as they cut it apart, the pieces which fell to earth became children. Seeing this, they cut it into the smallest pieces possible. Thus they had an infinite number of children and the earth was once more populated.[79]

The version given by Graham collected from the Ch'uan Miao of Szechuan is as follows:

Two brothers went daily to plow a field. At night Ye Seo came and turned the soil back. Then one night the two brothers went to watch. They saw the old man come and turn the soil back. The two brothers ran and seized the old man. The older brother said, 'Let's beat him.' The younger brother said, 'Do not beat him but ask why he is doing it.' The old man replied, 'The older brother is not a good speaker. Let him go and make an iron barrel. The younger brother speaks well. Let him go and make a wooden barrel. Do not do any farming. A deluge will come and submerge the field and the earth.' When the flood came the younger brother with his sister got into the wooden drum and it floated. The iron drum sank and the older brother was drowned. Ye Seo saw all this, and took the wooden drum into the sky. He used a 4-pronged iron weapon, and dug deep pits into the ground, and the water receded down these pits. Ye Seo sent the brother and sister down to earth and wrote their names in a book. The sister was unwilling to marry her brother. But after various tests (which are described) they realised that it was the will of heaven and became husband and wife. The next morning the wife gave birth to a son. It was like a piece of wood. They cut it into pieces and from these pieces people arose.[80]

In Meto I collected several versions of the story which, in summary, were as follows:

Joser, the Spirit of the Sky,[81] knew that a great flood was coming and sent two spirits to warn the people of it. Some people weeding in their fields

---

[79] This is an abbreviated version of two stories given by Savina.

[80] Graham, 1954, p. 180. The above is a condensation of two stories given by Graham.

[81] I have used this spelling to be consistent with that used by Nusit Chindarsi in his account of the religion of the Meto Miao. The actual sound of the word makes it almost certain that

found that the weeds were present again every morning. They watched and caught the two spirits who were replanting the weeds just before dawn. One man wanted to shoot them but his companion said they should ask the spirits why they were replanting the weeds. The spirits said that they should not be weeding the fields because a great flood was coming. Instead they should be preparing drums. Only one man followed the advice. When the flood came he placed his two children, a brother and a sister, in the drum and they floated up to the sky. The children were beating on the inside of the drum. Joser heard them and looking down saw that the earth was flooded. He took a long stick and punched holes in the earth to let the water run away. This accounts for the unevenness of the earth's surface. When the surface of the earth was dry the drum with the children in it rested on it. Joser asked which child was the older and found out that it was the boy. He told them to marry as there were no other people on earth. When they had married the girl gave birth to a baby which had no head, legs, or arms. It was just like a marrow. The parents complained to Joser. He told them to cut the baby up and it would give rise to many people. He told them to cut it into many pieces and to throw the pieces in every direction. Each piece gave rise to a different people—the Chinese, the Thai, the Miao, and the other peoples in the world.

Another version of the story says that the pieces of the child formed the different Miao clans and does not mention them as accounting for the different peoples of the earth.[82]

The variations in the story can be accounted for by lack of written records and its adaptation to the local environment. In Szechwan Ye Seo (or Joser as we have rendered his name) was interfering with a ploughed field and in Meto with a swidden; appropriately in the former place he used a fork and in the latter a digging stick to let the water out. But in both places he was the same deity doing the same general things and thereby helping to establish a common tradition for the Miao.

THE NUMBER OF MIAO IN CHINA

According to Chinese sources the Miao population of China in 1957 was estimated to number 2,680,000.[83] In 1959 Bruk, on the basis of a total population estimate of 2,511,000, listed their provincial distribution. His figures are given in Table 1.

---

it is the same god as that referred to by Graham as Ye Seo. He is the main protective deity of the Meto Miao. The thunder is his voice and the lightning his sign.

[82] A third version collected by Nusit Chindarsi brings in the four spirits who carry the earth on their shoulders, causing earthquakes when they shift their burden. When Joser looked down and saw the earth flooded he called out to these spirits to punch holes in it to let the water out. A further version I collected says the man who heeded Joser's advice got into his drum himself with his own sister.

[83] Moseley (ed.), 1966, Appendix A, p. 162. The figures are derived from *Jen-min shou-ts'e* (*People's Handbook*), Pekin, 1965, pp. 108–16.

TABLE I

Distribution of Miao in China by provinces

Kweichow	1,425,000
Yunnan	360,000
Kwangsi	204,000
Hunan	378,000
Szechwan	84,000
Kwangtung	16,000
Fukien	14,000
Chekiang	28,000
Hupeh	2,000

THE MOVEMENT OF THE MIAO BEYOND CHINA

Savina describes Miao as an 'eternally footloose people' and suggests that their migrations could be traced all over the main mountains of China.[84] Their reputation as travellers, however, seems to have come mainly from their movement beyond China's national borders or beyond the Chinese mainland. Whatever may have been the nature of their movements within China, this was demonstrably a migration because it was into areas where they were previously unknown and for which the testimony of many writers and administrators is available.

It has been suggested that their presence in the south-western area of China itself is also quite recent. Thus Major H. R. Davies, who travelled extensively in western China between 1894 and 1900, wrote:

The Miao or Miao-tzu, as they are called by the Chinese, give themselves the name of Mhong. The Shans call them Meow or Hka-meow, and in some districts also speak of them as Che-hpok, 'white chinamen', from their white clothes. The real home of the Miao is in Kuei-chou province and they probably extended into Hu-nan. In fact many of the Chinese of these two provinces have doubtless much Miao blood in their veins. In Yun-nan and western Ssu-Ch'uan they are comparatively recent arrivals, and many of them only left their original homes in Kuei-chou three or four generations ago. They are certainly not numerous in either of these provinces.[85]

Although it is clear from accounts which we have quoted previously that Miao were in fact in Yunnan much longer ago than the author believed, his report does provide some support for the theory that the movement which took them beyond the borders of China was a continuation of a process occurring within China, and that it may have

[84] Savina, 1930, p. 230.
[85] H. R. Davies, *Yun-nan: The link between India and the Yangtze*, Cambridge, 1909, p. 370.

started as a comparatively recent wave from the Miao heart-land.

An uncertainty also exists concerning a Miao movement into the island of Hainan. Several writers have reported their presence on the island. Swinhoe, writing in 1871, says they were brought by Chinese from the provinces of Kwangsi and Kweichow to act as buffers between the Chinese residents of the island and its indigenous mountain tribes known as the 'Le'.[86] De Beauclair disputes this.[87] Quoting in support several other writers, including Savina who states that a Yao group he studied in Annam are represented on Hainan, he says that the so-called Miao on the island are really Yao. He writes that the Government of the People's Republic of China has perpetuated the error by naming the autonomous region on Hainan the Li-Miao Autonomous District.

This is indeed a curious error in view of the intensive studies of minority peoples carried out by anthropologists of the Central Institute of Minorities in Peking.[88] In view of his erudition, de Beauclair is probably right. But a measure of doubt may remain pending an opportunity to carry out a thorough field investigation. De Beauclair bases his opinion on the grounds that Miao have never been recorded in Kwangtung province (whence some of the authors he quotes state the Miao on Hainan to have come), that Yao patterns in batik and embroidery have been ascribed to Miao, and that an important motif in Yao folklore, the dog ancestor myth, has also been ascribed to Miao who do not have it.

None of these particular arguments is completely convincing. Writers we have quoted earlier, for instance Graham, do report Miao in Kwantung and we must note that Swinhoe said that the Hainanese Miao did not come from there in any case but from Kwangsi and Kweichow. Moninger also assigns a Kweichow origin for them, stating that they went to Hainan at the time of a big famine in their old home.[89] Photographs of the people accompanying Moninger's account appear to show likeness of costume to the Miao. The description given by Gilman in 1891 also seems to fit the Miao better than the Yao: 'Their dress [of the women], which is also blue, consists of a jacket with narrow sleeves, and reaches almost to the knee, and under this is a

---

[86] R. Swinhoe, 'The Aborigines of Hainan', *Journal of the Royal Asiatic Society, North China Branch*, No. 7, 1871–2, p. 32. The 'Le' are termed by other writers 'Loi' or 'Li'.

[87] I. de Beauclair, '"Miao" on Hainan Island', *Current Anthropology*, Vol. 2, 1961, p. 394. Also *Sinologica*, Vol. 5, 1956, p. 22.

[88] W. R. Geddes, 'The Chinese Institute for National Minorities', *Journal of the Polynesian Society*, Vol. 65, No. 1, 1956, pp. 83–5.

[89] M. M. Moninger, 'The Hainanese Miao and their food supply', *Lingnan Science Journal*, Vol. 11, 1932, p. 521.

rather narrow skirt reaching to the knee. Both the jacket and skirt have a conventional pattern in white, printed on the cloth before it is dyed.' [90]

The dog ancestor myth is certainly more characteristic of the Yao. But although we have come across no reference to the Miao treating dogs as actual ancestors they are important in the spirit cults of some Miao groups. Writing of the Miao of Tonkin, Bigot states 'un chien est attaché par une patte à la main droite du défunt et est censé devoir guider ses pas errants dans l'autre monde,' [91] At major spirit ceremonies of the Wang clan in Meto a dog is sacrificed as well as a pig.

In his *Histoire des Miao* Savina explicitly mentions Miao on Hainan Island:

The Miao tribes who retired to the island of Hainan, to escape the civil war in the south of China, defend the central massif they occupy with ferocity, and all the Chinese who have tried to force a passage have been pitilessly massacred. These tribes know that in fact, when the Chinese manage to make themselves masters of these mountains, that will be the end of their freedom. [92]

This statement is interesting in view of the fact that de Beauclair quotes another article by Savina in support of the claim that the Hainanese 'Miao' are really Yao. Perhaps here lies a clue to the real situation. The mountain people of Hainan may include both peoples. After all, Mouly, one of the authors who believes they are Yao, entitles his account: 'Hainan, l'île aux cent visages'. [93]

Their number on Hainan, whatever they really are, is said to be about five or six thousand. [94]

THE MOVEMENT INTO INDO-CHINA

Whether or not they went to Hainan there is no doubt that they went southwards into Indo-China. The date of their first arrival there is uncertain, but most writers believe it to have been within comparatively recent times—not much less than 200 years and probably not more than 400 years ago. [95]

[90] Frank P. Gilman, 'The Miaotze in Hainan', *China Review*, Vol. 19, No. 1, 1891, p. 60.
[91] A. Bigot, 'Ethnologie Sommaire de L'Indochine Française', *L'Indochine Française*, Hanoi, Nov. 1938, p. 56.
[92] Savina, 1930, p. 234.
[93] R. D. Mouly, 'Hainan, l'île aux cent visages', *Bulletin de l'Asie Française*, 1946.
[94] Ibid., p. 47.
[95] Janse writes that they 'have entered northern Indochina in the last few centuries' (O. Janse, *The Peoples of French Indochina*, Smithsonian Institute, War Background Studies, Washington, 1944, p. 24). Bigot, 1938, p. 47, says: 'Leur pénétration au Tonkin est récente et si au début, elle fut pacifique, elle n'alla pas sans violence à la fin du XVIII° siècle et au XIX° siècle (1860).'

Savina sees it as part of a continuous migration:

From the mountains of Koui-Tcheou, the Miao swarmed bit by bit into the neighbouring provinces . . . The Miao of Tonkin are all originally from Yu-nan and those in Laos are originally from Tonkin. The latter are still pushing towards the south and they have now [i.e. 1924] reached the twentieth parallel, on the Annamite chain.[96]

This statement may give the impression of a single company of migrants journeying steadily southwards. But the process is surely more complex because in every area of Indo-China where they are present at all there are more Miao to the north than there are to the south, just as there are apparently more in Kweichow than there are in Yunnan. The first group of people who came from Yunnan may indeed be the same people, generations later, who have reached the furthest south today. But other groups would have come more recently from Yunnan also.

A simple analogy might be the waves of the sea. The first waves seem to be pushed along by those coming from behind. But this is not entirely correct because each wave also proceeds from its own force, the waves behind serving mainly to hinder its return when its force is spent. This at least seems to be the nature of the process as we have observed it within the limited area of Thailand. The Miao, as Savina says, are indomitable pioneers. But they are not nomads and they are not driven to travel by an innate compulsion. Our observation suggests that every Miao, if asked, would say that he prefers to be settled.

The force which takes him along is his desire for productive land. Whenever he settles he farms the land intensively until its productivity falls below that which he believes he can find elsewhere. Then, unfrightened by the prospect even of journeying far, he moves off to find it. He knows that the old place will probably regain its fertility with the passage of the years, and if it remains unoccupied it could come back on his list of possible settlement sites. But he knows also the law of the mountains which says that land which is not under settlement is everybody's land and, there being more people behind than in front of him, he is prepared to keep moving onwards.

The people who do follow behind may have a lower range of expectations because they are usually farming land which has already been occupied. Therefore those in the vanguard tend to stay there because they have the greater incentive. Opportunity, too, is greater at the frontier. Those behind may have to adapt to longer periods of settlement, and modify their farming practices accordingly, because of lack of opportunities to better themselves. Although we lack the facts to

[96] Savina, 1930, p. viii.

prove it, we suspect that the further from the frontier the more stable the settlements.

The Miao are conditioned to adventure, however. They appear to have little attachment to places as such. If they are 'sons of the soil', they are not sons of any particular soil. Their folklore links them to distant places and not to their present abodes in the south. Land is to be exploited and its local spirits are placated not worshipped. They seek always to maximize their opportunities. Therefore if a new territory appears before them their migration speeds up according to its potentialities.

The potentialities depend upon many factors—the total size of the area, how well the terrain suits Miao preferences, the amount of competition from other peoples, the political circumstances, and above all the types of crops which can be grown and their profitability. The conditions in Indo-China led to the growth of the sizeable but not huge Miao population. In 1944 it was estimated that there were 40,000 Miao in upper Tonkin and 20,000 in Laos.[97] These figures were probably an under-estimate at the time. Certainly the population is very much larger now. In Laos recent estimates have ranged from 150,000 to 300,000. No reliable information has been obtained on numbers in Vietnam.

As the Miao moved south of the Chinese border they acquired, in the parlance of foreigners, a new name. In writings on both Indo-China and Thailand, and in the official English rendering of their name in Thailand, they are called 'Meo', which Janse says is a Sino–Annamite rendering of the Chinese word 'Miao'.[98] Regardless of foreign idiosyncrasy, they continued to call themselves 'Hmong'.

It is generally believed that they reached Thailand only at the end of the nineteenth century. Writing of his experiences in 1894, McCarthy who travelled widely in the hill areas of the north, says that they had crossed the Mekong river only in the last eight years.[99] But some Miao, including the ancestors of the main group at Meto, appear to have come via south-eastern Burma, and as the oldest men at Meto all say they were born in Thailand,[1] this migration may have been at a slightly earlier date. However, some of these men say that their parents had lived in Burma, so we are probably quite safe in concluding that all the Miao have come into Thailand within the last 100 years.

The entry into Thailand has been continuous over this period. As recently as 1965, when border restrictions were being more strongly

[97] Janse, 1944, p. 24.   [98] Ibid.
[99] J. McCarthy, Surveying and Exploring in Siam, John Murray, London, 1900, p. 149.
[1] In 1964 in the village of Doi Kam in the Hot District of Chiengmai Province I saw an old man who villagers said was over 100 years old. He was too feeble to be questioned but members of his household said he had been born in 'China'.

applied, a group who entered Chiengrai Province from Laos were turned back. In earlier years there were few serious attempts to control immigration into the tribal regions. The rate of the Miao migration and its fluctuations over the total period are not known.

The southernmost group of Miao have now reached an area only 300 kilometres from Bangkok. They could not proceed further south in Thailand without leaving the hills.

THE MIAO AS MOUNTAIN-DWELLERS

In what appears to be the earliest description of the Thailand Miao, McCarthy notes three important features of their way of life: they prefer to live on mountain tops; they move elsewhere when the soil is exhausted; and they have 'wide stretches devoted to poppies'.[2]

Throughout their migration down through Indo-China and into Thailand the Miao, with very few exceptions, have kept to altitudes above 3,000 feet. Various reasons have been assigned for this. Janse says it was because the valley floors were already occupied.[3] A 1962 Thailand Government Report states: 'As a typical cool-climate population the mountain peoples have difficulty in becoming acclimatized to a tropical surrounding, which may be one of the reasons why they have stuck to altitudes around and above 1,000 metres throughout their history in Southeast Asia.'[4] Both factors could have operated to inhibit any moves to change their mode of life in South-East Asia, but conditions in South-East Asia cannot explain why they followed the same mode of life in the northern areas from which they came. The ethno-linguistic map prepared by Le Bar and others makes it strikingly clear how, even in China, the Miao are scattered widely in the southerly provinces often in comparatively small groups the size of which was probably determined by the availability of suitable terrain.[5]

When we survey the Miao scene as a whole, the two most striking features are their mountain-dwelling and their wide-ranging movement. Savina writes:

The normal and natural habitat of the Miao is the mountains. Only in the heights are they in their element and elsewhere they are at a loss and ill at ease. Fish in the water, birds in the air, and the Miao in the mountains, they say. In fact, as far back as one follows them in history, right up to pre-historic times, one finds them everywhere and always in the heights . . . Even in our time one would look in vain for Miao settled in the plains.[6]

Savina says the people gave him many reasons for their mountain-

---

[2] McCarthy, 1900, p. 42.   [3] Janse, 1944, p. 24.
[4] *Report on the Socio-Economic Survey of Hill Tribes in Northern Thailand*, Department of Public Welfare, Bangkok, 1966, p. 8.
[5] Le Bar *et al.*, 1964.   [6] Savina, 1930, p. 173.

dwelling but the real reason, he believes, was one which was unspoken—
that they were forced into the mountains by the hostility of other
peoples who occupied the plains:

Beaten by the Chinese they had to give way . . . That is how the Miao became
mountain men, in spite of themselves, some four thousand years ago, and that
is how too they were always able to keep their independence in the middle of
other peoples, keeping intact, along with their language and their customs,
the ethnic character of the race.[7]

Whether or not it is true that they were originally lowlanders who
were forced into the mountains, factors which would tend to hold
them there are not hard to discern. One factor which would become
of increasing importance as time went on would be the presence of
other peoples in the fertile valleys below them. Janse, as we have seen,
gave this as the main reason for their keeping to the mountains in
Indo-China. Savina expresses the same view of their situation more
generally:

These people have stayed too long on the heights and there is no longer any
place for them on the plains. Everywhere they stop to raise their tents, they
find someone telling them 'this is my land, keep on moving and return to
your mountains.' . . . That fine rice they see growing at their feet in the plain
will never ripen for them. 'tarde venientibus . . . montes!'[8]

He goes on to say, however, that 'Far from showing any desire to leave
these arid mountains where they know they have been pushed, kept
apart and watched over by the races which surround them, they show
themselves, on the contrary, very attached to them . . . This is their
country and they know no other.'[9]

This is surely the crux of the matter. The Miao may yearn at times
for what they believe is the easier life of the lowlanders. 'Each year',
says Savina, 'when these painful jobs [clearing the fields] come round,
the Miao, in spite of their love for their mountains, cannot help
glancing with envy on the neighbouring plains in which, they say, it is
enough to lead buffalo to make the rice grow, whilst they are obliged
to water their maize fields with their sweat.'[10] In October 1970 I stood
on the top of Chiengdao mountain with a Miao whose maize and
opium field was just under the lip of the crater. As we looked down six
thousand feet at the cars moving along the road to Chiengmai he
remarked that he would like to die and be born again so that he could
live as a lowlander. But envious though they may sometimes be of what
seems the soft life of the plains, they are tied to the mountains by their
whole way of life. Love of their countryside may play a part. Their

[7] Ibid., p. 175.   [8] Ibid., p. 175–6.   [9] Ibid., p. 176.
[10] Ibid., p. 180.

physical constitution may do so also. Competition for land and political circumstances certainly do. But most important is their ecological adaptation worked out over hundreds, and possibly thousands of years. They have developed an economy suited to their mountain environment, which acts as the core of their total culture. Very many aspects of their way of life—their folklore, their religion, their songs, their costume, and the nature and conduct of their social interrelationships—depend on the economy or bear reference to the mountains which are its setting. This is why my Miao friend thought that to change would mean having to be born again.

Their wide-ranging movement may be seen as a consequence of their commitment to the mountains. Simple population pressure could produce this result. In many places the areas of land on the mountains suitable for agriculture are quite small, and therefore when the population got above a certain size some would have to move. The effect of this factor would be accentuated by their mode of cultivation, again largely dictated by their mountain environment. Savina writes:

When the Miao settle on a mountain the first thing they do is to cut down the trees in order to prepare the ground for cultivation. Since they do not have an inch of land on the plain, if they did not do this they could grow nothing and would be condemned to die of hunger on their mountains. Thus they clear the trees out of necessity: 'primum vivere.' The area that is thus cleared of trees grows each year and at the end of some time all the forest has gone. Thus the Miao are a people of wood cutters. They are the ones who cut down the majority of the old forests of Asia. The few groves of trees which have escaped their axes lie on the edge of streams and in places that cannot be cultivated.[11]

This slash-and-burn method of agriculture—or swiddening as it is now generally called—is an old-established feature of Miao economy. It has probably been followed continuously by many of their groups ever since they first became acquainted with agriculture many thousands of years ago, although the first clear description of the Miao use of the method which we have come across is in *Miao-fang pei-lan* written in 1820: 'In agriculture, the Miao men and women work together. They have more mountain farms than irrigated fields. Burning the thorny trees and decomposing plants and exploiting the mountain slopes, they plant sesamun, millet, rice, wheat, beans, calyx grain, Kao-liang, jungle-wheat—all these various crops.' [12]

The slash-and-burn method is followed by millions of people throughout the world. It has been argued that it is the only possible method

[11] Ibid., p. 179.
[12] Yen Ju-yii (1759–1826), *Miao-fang pei-lan*, 1820, 8.8b–9a. This is quoted by Lin Yueh-Hwa, 1940, p. 289, n. 112.

of cultivating many mountain slopes especially in monsoonal areas. Certainly alternative methods would require developed technology or far greater labour. The Miao, however, practise a variation of the method which, although not entirely confined to them, is not typical of shifting cultivators in South-East Asia, and could significantly effect their pattern of movement.

Most practitioners of the method cultivate the ground for one, or at most two, seasons and then leave it fallow so that new jungle growth can restore its fertility while other areas are utilized in other years. The method is cyclical. Each portion of a village territory comes under cultivation only perhaps once in every seven years or in ideal circumstances at longer intervals. By following this method a village may remain stable indefinitely. The cultivations shift but not the people. The only threat to its stability is population pressure on the land which may reduce the fallow period to a level at which fertility cannot be maintained.

The Miao practice is often different. They do not operate according to a cyclical system which will forestall decline of fertility but instead continue to cultivate an area until actual decline makes further effort unrewarding. Savina comments on this:

They grow the same crop on the same pieces of ground until the harvest becomes too small. At that point they let the plots rest. They leave them fallow, in total fallow, which they call *tê phàng*. The fallow period is never fixed . . . at the end of a certain number of years they can no longer feed those who cultivate them. This is the main cause for the Miao migrations . . .[13]

We believe that the Miao behaviour is largely due to the types of crops they grow. When they are cultivating hill rice, which is the main crop of most of the people who follow the cyclical method, they too tend to follow it. But cash crops of various kinds induce a different pattern. This is especially the case with the opium poppy. We suspect that it is their devotion to the opium poppy which makes the Miao shifting cultivators in the complete sense of the term—not only the cultivations but the people themselves shift. The main purpose of this book is to show why this is so.

But in case we blame the poppy too much, we must note that the rudiments of the method appear to predate the appearance of the poppy in the Miao economy. The *Miao-fang pei-lan*, which does not mention the poppy, states: 'Having cultivated for three or four years, they relinquish the old land and exploit new places because the land becomes poor after intensive cultivation. After lying fallow several years, when the soil is rich again, they continue to cultivate. . . .'[14] Therefore the

---

[13] Savina, 1930, p. 214.   [14] Lin Yueh-Hwa, 1940, p. 289, n. 112.

poppy may merely have accentuated a pre-existing pattern. The traditional mode of agriculture made the poppy readily acceptable into it. In turn this reinforced the traditional mode. The Miao are thus involved in a different kind of cycle—one which has sent them circling, sometimes slowly, sometimes more rapidly, out of China, down through Indo-China and now into Thailand.

The Miao have been called nomads. But may they not, after all, really have been peasants who took to the hills? Their mode of farming, despite the movements it causes, is in essence much closer to settled agriculture than that of most shifting cultivators who populate the hills.

In South-East Asia opium production has been the main sustenance of most Miao groups. In descriptions of the people it has often not been accorded the importance it deserves because the illegality associated with it shrouds it like the mountain mist, but Savina lists it among the reasons the people gave him for keeping to the hills: 'We don't want to go down into the plain because we could not grow opium, maize or fruit trees there.'[15]

As we have seen, there are other reasons too—their love of independence, their suspicion of other peoples, the competition for land, and their general cultural adaptation to the mountain environment. Opium production reinforces all these factors and adds its own dynamism, pushing the people ever further abroad in search of new uplands where the poppy will bloom in renewed or greater splendour.

[15] Savina, 1930, p. 174.

CHAPTER TWO

THE MIAO POPULATION IN THAILAND

PENDLETON[1] and others have classified the geographical regions of Thailand as follows: (1) the Central Plain; (2) the South-East Coast; (3) the North-West Plateau; (4) the Central Highlands; (5) the North and West Continental Highlands; and (6) Peninsular Thailand. The Miao are found mainly in the fifth region and in a small part of the fourth.

The 'North and West Highlands' are subdivided by Pendleton into the 'Northern Hills and Valleys' and the 'Western Mountains'. The Miao are present in both areas but are more numerous in the former. The Northern Hills and Valleys are a montane region, physiographically a southern extension of the Shan Highlands of Burma. From the Daen Lao range on the northern border parallel ridges extend southwards, including the peaks of Doi Inthanond (8,452 feet) and Doi Chieng Dao (7,100 feet). Four main tributaries of the Chao Phraya, the central river of Thailand, flow north to south between the ridges—the Ping, Wang, Yom, and Nan. The great majority of the Miao live on the ridges. In the Western Mountains sub-region, the Miao are in the north-west strip of the central cordillera along the Burma border. The streams off this ridge flow into the Chao Phraya or the Salween.

The Miao in the Central Plains regions are confined to a small montane area north-east of the Central Valley and north-west of the Korat Plateau.

In terms of the administrative sub-divisions of the country, the Miao occur in eight different provinces (changwad). In preparation for the visit of the United Nations Team to study the economic and social needs of the opium-producing areas of Thailand, the Thailand Government carried out a survey of Hill Tribe population and agriculture.[2]

[1] R. L. Pendleton, 'Thailand, Aspects of Landscape and Life', *American Geographical Society Handbook*, New York, 1962. Amendments to the classification have been suggested by Santhad Rojanasoonthon and F. R. Moorman in *Soil Survey Report No. 8*, Land Development Department, Bangkok, 1966. The classifications are discussed by John Phillips, in *Report of the United Nations Survey Team on the Economic and Social Needs of the Opium-Producing Areas in Thailand*, Bangkok, 1967.

[2] This report, which we shall hereafter refer to as the *Thailand Government Survey of 1965*, was published in Thai and English in Bangkok in 1965. It is not easily available, having been prepared primarily for the information of the United Nations Survey Team. In addition to the published report, a number of detailed tables were prepared and it is from these that many of my subsequent figures are drawn.

On the basis of head counts in sample areas combined with the identification of all villages from aerial photographs, the total Miao population was estimated to be 53,031, distributed in provinces as shown in Table 2. There was a sampling error of 11 per cent. A complete census,

TABLE 2

Distribution of Miao in Thailand by provinces

Phetchabun	24,681
Nan	9,454
Chiengrai	5,728
Tak	5,609
Chiengmai	4,725
Phitsanulok	1,790
Maehongson	858
Lampang	186
TOTAL	53,031

which has never been taken in tribal areas, would no doubt lead to an adjustment of the figures, but the estimate is probably a fairly close approximation to actual numbers.

Table 3, also derived from the *Thailand Government Survey of 1965*, shows the relative position of the Miao compared to the other main tribes. It can be seen from this table that of the so-called tribal peoples

TABLE 3

Villages, households, and populations of the Main Hill Tribes in Thailand

Tribe	Number of villages	Number of households	Total population of tribe
Miao	364	7,634	53,031
Karen	1,457	24,550	123,380
Yao	200	2,094	16,119
Lahu	176	2,748	15,994
Lisu	110	1,726	9,440
Akha	48	1,021	6,442
Others and unidentified	362	8,350	50,843
TOTALS	2,717	48,123	275,249

the Karen are by far the most numerous, with 54.5 per cent approximately of the 226,405 persons who were tribally identified. Their actual number in Thailand is even greater because the survey took account only of people living at a height above 600 metres and some Karen are settled on valley floors.

The Karen differ from the other tribal peoples in three interrelated respects. They have been in Thailand longer; the bulk of them live at a lower altitude; and they form a more cohesive population block, being found only in the Western Mountains region. They can be seen, therefore, as a more settled people. Although some of them have moved into their present locations in Thailand in comparatively recent times, they are not a migratory people in the same sense as the other tribes. They may be said to be living within or adjoining their homeland of at least recent historic times.

Of the other tribes, comprising 45.5 per cent of the total, the Miao are the most numerous, relative proportions being:

Miao	22·5%
Yao	7·1%
Lahu	7·1%
Lisu	4·2%
Ahka	2·4%
Unclassified	2·2%

Thus, although one of the latest arrivals in Thailand—only the Ahka apparently being more recent—the Miao have either come in greater numbers or shown a greater natural increase.

In average numbers per household, the Miao are exceeded only by the Yao, the figures for all the tribes being:

Miao	6·9
Yao	7·5
Ahka	6·2
Lahu	5·8
Lisu	5·5
Karen	5·0

Another interesting conclusion from the *Survey* data is that the Miao, equalled by the Ahka, have a larger average number of households per village than any of the other tribes, the figures being:

Miao	21
Ahka	21
Karen	17
Lahu	16
Lisu	16
Yao	10

The Miao live at an altitude which, on the average, is probably higher than that of any other tribe in Thailand. Saihoo[3] gives a schematic representation of residential heights which, in respect of the six major tribes, is shown in Table 4. Relatively few Miao villages,

TABLE 4

Residential altitudes of main tribes in Thailand

ALTITUDE IN FEET	TRIBES
5,000 and over	Lisu, Miao
4,500	Lahu Nyi/Na, Akha
4,000	Lahu Shehleh
3,500	Yao, B'ghwe Karen
3,000	Lahu Shi
below 2,000	Karen (P'wo, Skaw)

however, are above the height of 5,000 feet and it would be more accurate to say that the majority of them lie between that height and 3,500 feet. The same is probably true of the Lisu.[4]

There are some major cultural distinctions amongst the Miao in Thailand. Gordon Young[5] states that there are three main subdivisions—the Blue Miao, the White Miao and the Gua M'ba Miao. The Report of the socio-economic survey carried out by the Department of Public Welfare in 1962 gives a more detailed classification: 'The main divisions are: (1) The White Meo (Meo Khao), and (2) The Blue Meo, who in their turn subdivide themselves into the Black Meo (Meo Dam), the Striped Meo (Meo Lai), and the Flowery Meo (Meo Dawk). There is, moreover, a third division which is very small in number, the Gua M'ba Meo, who are becoming more and more absorbed by the Blue Meo ... the Meo call themselves H'moong.'[6] Gordon Young estimated that there were only 200 Gua M'ba Miao in 1961. If they still exist in their distinctiveness, they are not a significant

[3] Saihoo, Patya, *The Hill Tribes of Northern Thailand*, Typescript published by SEATO, Bangkok, 1946. A fuller diagram giving the estimated heights of several smaller groups also appears on p. 12 of the publication.

[4] Some Yao villages, too, are at heights above 3,500 feet.

[5] Gordon Young, *The Hill Tribes of Northern Thailand*, Siam Society, Bangkok, 1962, p. 36.

[6] *Report on the Socio-Economic Survey of Hill Tribes in Northern Thailand*, Department of Public Welfare, Bangkok, 1966. The anthropologist largely responsible for the conduct of the survey, which was carried out in 1962, and for the preparation of the excellent report was Dr. Hans Manndorf, then a United Nations expert attached to the Department and later at the University of Vienna.

group in Thailand. The Black, Striped, and Flowery classifications appear to be Thai categorizations and, although occasionally echoed by Miao, do not seem to be meaningful to them.

We may say, therefore, that there are two main divisions of Miao in Thailand today—the Blue Miao and the White Miao. Young estimated their 1960 populations as: Blue Miao 26,400, White Miao 19,200. The total numbers are greater now but their relative proportions may be the same. The 1966 Survey, being based upon the aerial identification of villages, was not able to distinguish between the two groups.

The most noticeable differences between the divisions are in dress and language. Blue Miao women invariably wear deeply pleated hempen skirts, dark blue in colour, with a superimposed lighter blue patterning above a band of highly coloured silken embroidery. White Miao women may wear skirts also, but are commonly seen in loose trousers. It is their skirts, however, which have given them their name amongst the Thai. They are of undyed white cloth above the embroidered band.

More study is required to determine the exact nature of the linguistic differences between the two groups. Most Blue Miao can understand White Miao, although not perfectly, and apparently the reverse is true also. But there has been much contact and some inter-marriage between them in Thailand and the mutual intelligibility could be due to partial learning of each other's language.

There are other differences, too. For instance, the White Miao house is of a slightly different shape from the Blue Miao house and usually has two doors, whereas the Blue Miao house has only one. To what extent differences also occur in social structures and economies cannot be stated until studies of the White Miao have been published.

The Blue Miao appear everywhere to call themselves Hmong Njua, the significance of which name we have discussed in the previous chapter.

THE MOVEMENT OF THE MIAO IN THAILAND

There is no doubt that frequent movement is typical of the Miao in Thailand and that therefore conclusions about their socio-economy drawn from the special study of the Meto community which follows are likely to have a fairly general validity. I have visited one long-settled village—Ban Miao Mor in Chieng Dao Province—which had been stable for at least forty years, but such villages are relatively few.

Practically everyone who has written on the Miao remarks on their residential instability. Bernatzik says: 'The Meau as well as the Akha of Thailand are semi-nomads who change their residence sites every

couple of years . . . compelling circumstances induce them to undertake the undesirable labour of moving a village.'[7] It is clear, too, that
it is a pattern they have carried with them into Thailand, for Halpern,
writing on the people of Laos, says: 'In most regions where the conventional economy is followed, the Meo move every decade or so once
they have cut over all the land within walking distance of the village . . .
[they] tend to migrate as family groups . . . quite extensive migrations
may be involved. Meo in northern Laos recall moves from Xieng
Kouang to Luang Prabang, Sayboury, and Vientiane Provinces.'[8]

There are two forms of Miao movement, which probably accounts
for apparent confusion in the reports of some writers, such as Bernatzik,
who will tell us at one time that the movement occurs about every two
years and at another time that it takes place about every ten years.
The first form of movement is that which is covered by his statement:
'In general, if there is no compelling reason such as war, epidemics,
crop failure as a result of rice diseases, and the like, a migration is never
further than half or at most a full day's march from the old village.'[9]
In this form of movement it is not the cultivations which are shifting
but the people to catch up with them. The cultivations have moved
earlier, perhaps creeping forwards, or crossing valleys within the same
region. Later comes the stage when, as Bernatzik writes, 'After four to
ten years, all the cultivable land in the vicinity of a village is
exhausted . . .',[10] and then both people and cultivations must move
together. The Miao do not progress through a country steadily; nor do
they wander as we would expect nomads to do; they move by hop,
step, and jump, and some of their leaps may take them to mountains
far away and across numerous intermediate people. We must note,
however, that not all the jumps are so big, and Halpern shows insight
when he writes:

Migration patterns of the Meo, Khmu and Lao need more study. Although
over the generations some of these people may move long distances, their
short-term circular patterns and reusing of certain areas suggests a possible
intensive–extensive *hai* cultivation that may become more important as the
population in the mountain areas increases.[11]

In Thailand it does not take even one generation for the Miao to move
long distances. Nevertheless a circular pattern is discernible in the case
of some groups and is currently being manifested by some of the Meto
Miao.

The typicality of movement and its frequency is indicated by data

[7] Bernatzik, 1947, p. 259.
[8] Joel M. Halpern, 'The Natural Economy of Laos' (typescript), University of California,
Los Angeles, 1960, pp. 23–4.
[9] Bernatzik, 1947, p. 260.   [10] Ibid., p. 259.   [11] Halpern, 1960, p. 48.

collected during the course of the Thailand Government Survey of 1965. Households in the sampling areas were asked how long they had been in the present place of residence and the answers were projected to give a table covering the total population (Table 5). In considering

TABLE 5

Number of years Miao households have been in location of present residence

TIME	NUMBER OF HOUSEHOLDS
Less than 1 year	606
1 year	2,639
2 years	626
3 years	1,513
4 years	1,193
5 years	1,099
6—10 years	794
11—15 years	452
16—20 years	188
20 years or more	15
Never migrated	69
Unknown	58
TOTAL	9,252

this table it must be noted that the figures cannot be taken as an exact, or even fairly accurate, record of the situation. The question put to the people was supposed to be how long had they been in their present 'province' (changwad) of residence. Clearly, there could not have been so much movement actually between provinces as the table indicates. Probably many people interviewed interpreted it as movement of any kind, especially as numbers of them would be unfamiliar with exact provincial boundaries. The projection from the samples to the total population may also have involved considerable error. Finally, we must note that there is a discrepancy between the number of Miao households given in this table with the number given in Table 4.

But however inaccurate in detail, the figures can at least be taken as evidence of the generality of movement. The frequency of their movement compared with that of other tribes is shown in Table 6, in which in order to reduce the probable errors in details we have used wider time-divisions.

The results of the survey become even more striking when the

TABLE 6

*Number of years households of different tribes have
been in present location*

	Under 5 years	6–10 years	11–20 years	Over 20 years	Never moved	Unknown	Total
Miao	7,676	794	640	15	69	58	9,252
Karen	3,640	757	1,074	22	12,642	838	18,973
Yao	1,231	487	317	295	—	—	2,330
Lahu	1,452	365	117	—	435	3	2,372
Lisu	270	714	216	—	113	10	1,323
Akha	627	112	761	100	—	1,518	3,118

figures are converted into percentages of the total number of households surveyed in each group (Table 7). The Miao stand out as the tribe with the least stable residential pattern. According to the survey, 92.1 per cent of households have moved within a ten-year period. Well beneath them on the scale are three tribes with figures closely approximating one another—Lahu (76·7 per cent), Lisu (75 per cent) and Yao (73·7 per cent). There is a further substantial gap to the Akha with 46·2 per cent, and at the bottom of the scale are the Karen with 24·4 per cent of households reported moving within the ten-year period.

Among the factors which may influence the differences in residential stability of the tribes are the altitudes at which they live and the dates of their migrations into Thailand. Neither factor, however, can account for all the differences. In regard to altitude it is true that cultivation areas tend to become more circumscribed the higher one goes and, on the upper mountain slopes, there is very little opportunity

TABLE 7

*Percentages of households which have been in same locations for various
time-periods*

	Under 5 years	6–10 years	11–20 years	Over 20 years	Never moved	Total number of households
Miao	83·5	8·6	7·0	0·2	0·8	9,194
Karen	20·1	4·3	5·9	0·1	69·7	18,135
Yao	52·8	20·9	13·6	12·7	—	2,330
Lahu	61·3	15·4	5·0	—	18·4	2,369
Lisu	20·6	54·4	16·5	—	8·6	1,313
Akha	39·2	7·0	47·6	6·2	—	1,600

for the irrigated rice-growing which helps keep the Karen stable. But altitude cannot explain the differences between the Miao and the Lisu or between the Lisu and the Akha. The earlier migration date of the Karen may be one reason why they are the most stable—they have had a longer time to settle down; but all the other tribes are such recent immigrants that relative date of arrival is unlikely to be an important factor.

A difference between the tribes which does accord much more closely with their various positions on the scale of stability is in the amounts of opium they grow. The Karen at the bottom of the scale grow very little. The Akha, next on the list, grow only a small amount. There are grounds for suggesting that the positions of the other tribes, all of whom are substantial opium producers, are in accordance with the amounts they grow or, if not with the absolute amounts, at least with the relative importance of opium in their economies.

The major difference in residential stability amongst the tribes producing opium on a large scale is between the Miao and the rest. There is a lack of clear evidence that the Miao produce more opium per head of population than any other tribe, although we believe it to be probable. Young implies that they are in more or less equal place with the Lisu, saying of the Miao: 'The vast majority are poppy growers',[12] and of the Lisu: 'The Lisu are second to none in the vigorous pursuit of opium cultivation. They rank with the Meo of the northern areas in the size of opium fields per family.'[13] No accurate figures have been produced to determine the issue on a tribal scale. The 1965–6 Survey was not able to produce from the analysis of the aerial photographs a breakdown of the total area under poppies into tribal ownerships and provided only an estimate of production figures, based upon answers to a questionnaire, which were clearly inaccurate.[14] In the absence of reliable statistics one can go only on impressions gained by oneself and reported by others. Everyone would agree that opium is a prime crop of the Miao. We ourselves in the course of two extensive aerial surveys and during expeditions on foot have seen no other tribe with such large areas of poppy.

Whether or not it is true that the Miao actually produce more opium per head of population than any other tribe, it is almost certainly the case that it is of greater relative economic importance to them.

[12] Young, 1962, p. 41.   [13] Ibid., p. 31.
[14] The results of the questionnaire gave the following figures for production in kilogrammes per head of population: Lahu, 0·54; Miao 0·31; Lisu 0·25; Akha 0·14; Yao 0·06. No observer could agree that Akha produce more than Yao. The figures are out of accord with the total production indicated by the aerial photographs. Opium is an illegal crop and the questionnaire was administered by Government officers who were strangers to the people. Possibly the people who grew most were the most adept at concealing the amount.

Amongst the Miao, Yao, Lisu, and Lahu opium is the main cash crop. Secondary cash crops, however, appear to be more common at least among the Yao and Lahu than among the Miao. The detailed study described in this monograph demonstrates that at least in the case of the Meto Miao opium is not merely a cash crop but the main, and often exclusive, objective of their agriculture. Generalizing more widely on the basis of this study and wider evidence we shall argue that opium-growing has been the principal factor accounting for the frequency of Miao migrations within Thailand.

CHAPTER THREE

SOCIAL RELATIONSHIPS AND GROUPINGS

It can be said that there is a general concept of Miao society as designating a field of potentially intimate social relations. Miao may visit Miao anywhere and expect to be received with courtesy, not as strangers but as belonging to the same brand of humankind. Subject to clan restrictions, they may seek marriage partners anywhere within the field, whereas marriages outside it are not favoured. The sense of society extends beyond the Blue Miao with less intensity to include the White Miao as well.

Within this field each person belongs to a widening series of residential, local, and dispersed groups. The situation is represented in truncated form in Diagram 1, the double lines indicating the residential groups, the single unbroken lines the local groups, and the dotted lines the dispersed groups. A person also has his or her own individual set of relatives which will differ from the sets of other persons and which will extend across group boundaries.

We shall leave the consideration of residential groupings until the next chapter. In this chapter we are concerned with the more general types of relationships which we shall discuss in what appears to us their order of importance in the daily lives of the people. It is indeed their relative importance which is our main classificatory principle, as is appropriate in a book concerned with economic behaviour.[1]

The main relationship categories which we shall distinguish are the family, the immediate relatives of the family, the house relatives, the lineage, and the clan. As they are all parts of a total system the meaning of each can be fully understood only when the whole is described.

FAMILY RELATIONSHIPS

The family is obviously the primary area of relationships because it is the procreative and nurturing institution of the society. It includes

[1] For this reason our categories differ in some respect from those often used in structural analyses by anthropologists. We are less concerned with abstract or logical distinctions of relationship type, as for instance between affinal and consanguineal connections, than with the frequency and utility of the relationships. The former type of analysis may be better for comparing kinship systems morphologically, but it may obscure the realities of social life.

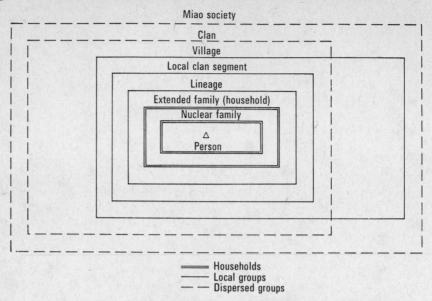

DIAGRAM 1: Social Groupings of the Blue Miao

the specific relationships of husband–wife, father–son, father–daughter, mother–son, mother–daughter and brother–sister. It would require more space than we could give to it here to discuss their exact meanings according to differences of circumstances. Some of them too are given special loadings by the lineage and clan classifications yet to be described. But we may say of them all that in normal circumstances they are the strongest relationships of the Miao, and as we shall see from the examples given in Chapters 7 and 11, any of them may be a factor in bringing about resettlement.

A common feature of these relationships is that there are no intermediate links defining them. It is this feature which has led us to include the marriage relationship in the one fundamental category with the parental and sibling relationships. The procedure could be justified on practical grounds. Although marriage may be impermanent whereas the other relationships endure so long as both parties live, it is usually stable and the tie which one has with one's marriage partner possibly affects more moments of one's life than any other tie. But it is the characteristic which it shares with the others of being an immediate link to the next range of important relationships that is the main justification for our categorizing it with them. Indeed it is consistent with its basic role in this regard that Miao culture through the institution of bride-price stresses the importance of marriage and generally ensures its permanency.[2]

The second most relevant category of relationships embraces all relationships one degree removed from the nuclear family circle. Let us call these second-degree relationships. Specific ties are, inter alia, grandfather–grandson, father's brother, father's sister, brother's wife, wife's brother and daughter's husband. As it is rather unusual in anthropological analyses, the combining of all these relationships in the one class may be thought to require some justification. It is true that there would appear to be a good reason for subdividing the category into consanguineal and affinal sets in that ties with one's grandfather and one's father's brothers are often stronger than with one's wife's brother or one's sister's husband. They are not always, however, more significant in determining practical choices in such matters as where to live; and where it does exist the superior strength of the consanguineal ties can be better accounted for by the operation of the lineage and clan principles, which as we shall see later are not explained in the Miao ideational system by a simple concept of blood descent.

Our chief reason for designating all second-degree relationships as a single category is to make clear that they stand as an area of relationship independently of the clan and lineage system although they overlap with it. Each person has, to a greater or less extent, this range of close relatives, many of them made through marriages, which provides him with individual opportunities to vary his life and seek improvement of his condition beyond his birthplace and the confines of his clan.

The choices made vary greatly. One man may decide to migrate to the land of his brother's wife, another to that of a nephew and so on. Close analysis would show that from a variety of causes some types of relationships are more significant than others. For instance, sisters of the wife or of the mother occur comparatively rarely in the examples we have collected of relationships affecting migration. Such ties are undoubtedly of importance to women, and a reason for their general scarcity of mention in our records is that we have looked at the society from a man's point of view. Another reason, however, is that from the Miao man's point of view they are, for practical purposes, more distant relations. Major decisions altering the circumstances of living, such as moving to a new area, are taken between men. Therefore a

---

[2] In some Thailand Miao communities, including Meto, marriage breakdown, although still at a very low rate compared to western industrialized society, appears to be increasing. The people themselves associate this with a general weakening of traditional cultural values including proper adherence to the bride-price system.

decision to go to live in the neighbourhood of one's wife's sister means an agreement with the wife's sister's husband, who is one degree more removed than the brother of one's wife.

The importance of the category of second-degree family relatives must be seen in the light of the migratory pattern of the Miao communities we have studied. A kinship system provides various potentialities. In a settled state the Miao may place a more exclusive emphasis upon lineal connections. The flexible system we have described facilitates their freedom to range over a wide territory both of clansfolk and other folk related to them in a variety of ways.

The importance of non-clan ties mediated by women is symbolized in ritual. For instance, at the funeral of a man his daughters should jointly present one ox as a sacrifice, which should be killed by a son of the eldest daughter. The brothers of his wife and his sisters should give smaller offerings of rice, paper money, alcohol, and joss sticks as well as carrying out ceremonial actions. The oxen which sons should give should be killed by the brothers of their wives. When a bride-price is received by the father of a bride he should, while retaining the bulk of it himself, give portions not only to his father, his brothers, and his sons but also to his wife's sisters and his father's sisters. During a marriage the husbands and sons of the sisters of the bride's father should be given places at the ceremony at her house, and the husbands and sons of the sisters of the bridegroom's father at the ceremony at his house when the bride is received.

Relationships do not stop at the second-degree range, but those beyond it are generally less important. One reason is that normally as children marry new second-degree relationships are constantly being made. Older people who are no longer forming them and whose range of second-degree relationships is dwindling have usually passed beyond the age of family independence. Secondly, ties beyond the second degree have less strength to compete with clan ties, so that a man finding himself resident amongst only remote relatives is likely to move to an area where he can feel more secure amongst clansmen. Thirdly, the number of such possible connections could be very large, necessitating some means of discriminating among them if they are to have any value as providing special bonds in the general social world.

THE FAMILY LINE

One form of discrimination is made by a conception expressed in ritual form which we may call the 'family line'. In a sense it provides a link between the pattern of individual relations and the clan categorization.

When a family makes offerings to the spirits, which most families do frequently to secure their welfare in one respect or another, the spirits honoured are those shown in Diagram 2. The invocation is as follows.

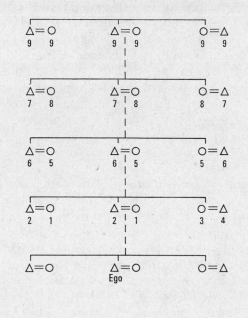

1 Na
2 Sier
3 Nyang
4 Sier Gier Yer
5 Pu Nyang
6 Yor
7 Yor Gong
8 Pu Nyang Gong
9 Lao Sier Gong

DIAGRAM 2: Categories of 'ancestral' spirits invoked at ceremonies

We have indicated the generation levels, beginning with the first ascending generation, by the use of semi colons:

'Na hor, sier hor, Nyang hor, sier gier yer hor; pu nyang hor, yer hor; yer gong hor, pu nyang gong; lao sier gong—come back to eat and drink.'

The spirit titles may be translated as follows. To understand the translation note should be taken of the wider denotation of the terms as shown on the diagram:

'Spirits of my mothers, spirits of my fathers, spirits of my father's sisters, spirits of my father's sisters' husbands; spirits of my grandfathers; spirits of my great-grandfathers, spirits of my great-grandfathers' wives and sisters; all ancient spirits.'

The full justification of this translation would require more space than can be given to it here but we may make reference to certain key words in partial explanation. 'Hor' (or 'haw) means 'spirit of deceased person'; 'na' is the term for mother; 'Nyang' (which could be rendered 'ngang') is that for sister; 'sier' (which could be rendered as 'zer' and is the same word that other writers have rendered as 'jeu') is the term for father and it may be extended to father's brothers and to the same categories of persons in ascending generations. It may also be extended, apparently with a subtle tonal variation, to 'husband'. The more usual variant for 'husband' is 'yer' but either variant may in certain contexts be used for a general classification which includes both 'fathers' and husbands. Precise identification when necessary can, of course, always be made by descriptive terminology.[3] 'Gong' indicates a spirit of remote generations.[4]

The line extends back in time the basic principle of family linkage. It has several interesting features:

At all generation levels brothers of the father are classified with the father as also are wives of these fathers' brothers with the mother, although distinctive terms for them are normally used in daily life. Their classification in the ritual context as fathers and mothers can be seen as a symbolic expression of the parental type of status which they have and of the roles they may actually exercise in many families. For the sake of simplicity we have so far spoken of the family as though it comprised only true parents and children. In fact most Miao spend at least part of their lives in extended families which include two or more married sons of the family head, and in such families the parent–child relationships, although usually closer between actual parents and children, are diffused over all the members of the respective generations.

A fully extended family would include not only married brothers of the true father but married sisters as well. It is noteworthy that in the ancestral line shown in the diagram married sisters and their husbands are thus included. In Miao practice, however, the family is extended only patrilineally. It is consistent with this practice that at the first ascending generation in the ancestral set father's sisters and their husbands are not classified under family terms but are described in terms of their ritual relationships. At this level distinction is significant because they are a category of persons, closely associated with the family but always outside it as a domestic unit, with whom practical

[3] Miao kinship terminology is complex. In general the system at Meto was in many respects similar to that described in detail by Ruey Yih-Fu, 1960, pp. 146–55. Full analysis of the details of difference, taking account of tonal subtleties, would require longer study and greater linguistic competence than I or Nusit Chindarsi achieved during our time together in Meto.

[4] Lyman says that the 'Spirits of Ancestors' are called 'pu yaw tsi tsong', which may be shortened to 'pu yaw'. As he translates 'tsi' as 'father' or 'male', this could mean 'female and male ancestral spirits' (Lyman, 1968, p. 27).

relationships will be of a different order from those within the family.

At high generation levels distinction is not likely to be significant. It should be borne in mind that we are discussing the line in the context of an ancestral ritual. The person carrying out the ritual—ego in the diagram—will be the oldest man in the family, or someone acting on his behalf. It would be a rare circumstance for him to have grand-parents or their siblings living, and if they were the organization of contemporary relationships would not involve them but their more distantly related descendants. Therefore classifications become more general at the second and third ancestral generations, and termino-logical distinction disappears entirely at the fourth generation from the living.

The line is not a complete family tree because parents of the mother are not included. Nor, as we have seen, is it a simple patrilineal line. What, then, can be its rationale?

The line comprises the people who, had a family house endured through many generations, would have lived in it. Wives come from outside but are incorporated into the family. Daughters move away on marriage but, as they have once been members, the family retains a kind of residual interest in them and members of the separate family lines into which they have been incorporated will constitute a special class of remote and remoter relatives closer than others in the vast range which the passage of years creates.

The ancestral cult symbolizes the spiritual unity of the family household. Husbands of daughters are included because they are directly linked to persons who have shared in the communion. On the other hand wives who join the group participate in the communion only after they have separated from their relatives who thus have no direct link with it and are therefore not included. The total class of relatives associated with the family line we may call the 'house relatives'. It will not be a significant form of relationship more than three or four generations from the living.

Within the general class of house relatives we may distinguish group-ings of a closer order which we shall call lineages.

THE LINEAGE

Within the family line as shown in Diagram 3 there is an important distinction between the persons in the centre and left-hand columns and those in the column on the right. Whereas all the persons shown on the diagram may be worshipped as ancestors, the worshipping group itself includes only those in the first two columns. Persons in the right-hand column will belong to different worshipping groups although there will be an overlap of one or more ancestors in the sets honoured.

For want of a better word we shall call persons in the first two columns, so long as they remain a cohesive group and acknowledge common ancestral spirits, a lineage. In using this term we are diverging from its classical use in anthropology because in the present case the group comprises not only patrilineal descendants but their wives as well.

This is not merely a definitional matter, as it could be said to be if patrilineal descent were the group's main criterion and the wives were admitted simply as affiliated members. As in the case of all Miao social groups patrilineal descent is of only limited relevance. The lineage is a spiritual community united by the fact that all its members worship the same set of ancestors. These ancestors no less than other levels of the line include women, and after a very few generations they become grouped together in a manner which eliminates the sex distinction.

If we consider only the ancestors shown in Diagram 3 it is obvious that lineages cannot be of greater depth than two generations from the living because after that there is no further specifying of the patrilineal ancestors. In fact the Miao commonly recognize two orders of association—that between brothers and their families, and that between this group and their father's brothers and *their* families. But it will be understood that lineage membership may extend over more generations than two because we are speaking only of the most senior men among the living.

The only other way in which a lineage could be extended would be by the recognition of a named ancestor. This is unlikely to happen to any significant extent because of the nature of the ancestral cult. Particular ancestors may be called upon by name. But the occasions when the ritual is employed are usually when sickness or misfortune has occurred. It is believed that both may be caused by an ancestor's running short of food or money in the afterworld and his indicating his need for an offering. The identity of the ancestor may be determined by the head of a household or a priest studying signs, such as the appearance of the skull of a chicken killed for the purpose, or by casting divination horns. The ancestors most likely to be troublesome are the more recently dead. Therefore they are the ones most likely to be remembered in the ancestral ceremonies.

It is true that sometimes an ancestor who is almost certainly more remote is remembered by name and serves as a recognized link between quite a large group of people. Even so, in all the cases we have recorded, the genealogy linking him to the living is never longer than two generations. Diagram 5 in Chapter Five illustrates a case of this kind. This type of grouping differs from the kind we are now considering. There is no cult of the ancestor concerned and no knowledge of the precise ways in which the living are related to him. We shall discuss such groupings later under the heading of sub-clans, although even in them the genealogical link is not the crucial criterion. The existence of such cases can be taken as indicating a patrilineal bias in the society but it is not a major structural principle, a fact which is shown in this instance by the very abbreviated genealogy.

The spiritual structure of the lineage accords with its practical value as a contemporary organization providing mutual support for its members. Its personnel may be conterminous with a large extended family living in one household, although in the descriptions of Meto society which follow we shall in the interests of clarity use the term 'extended family' for persons still sharing the one household and 'lineage' for the types of association now being discussed which extend beyond one household.

Each family is the embryo of a lineage. The foundations of its practical meaning are laid in the co-operation of a common household. The continuity of the household group is symbolized by the practice when families leave a house to set up new houses of their taking with them some ash from the big fireplace to deposit in the fireplaces of their new homes, thus transferring the fireplace spirit. A symbolic connection with the old house is also maintained by the practice of burying the placenta of a boy beside the central post. It is believed that when he dies his spirit will return to the site to resume the placenta before returning to the spirit parents in the other world.[5]

When a section of a household moves to a new area and sets up its own household it will usually encourage other sections of the household to move with it or to follow. The maintenance of lineage ties is especially valuable while the new households are small. The households of brothers usually maintain close links. Although the households usually work their fields alone, they may assist one another when there is a need for extra labour or at times of sickness. They may care for one another's children. They will attend and assist at major ceremonies in any of the houses. They will participate in marriage arrangements. They will jointly contribute to the welfare of their parents if they are alive and manage their funerals together. Socially, there is a great deal of visiting between the households. Thus the ideology and practical co-operation of a household persists in an attenuated form after it has dispersed into a lineage.

The principle on which lineages are formed is that of the family extended through its male members. Of particular importance are the bonds between father and children and between brothers. So long as either of these bonds persists, all the descendants in the male line of the

[5] The placenta of a girl is buried beneath the bedroom floor. We did not record whether or not it was resumed.

persons so linked will consider themselves to belong together in a group with special obligations to one another.

It follows that there will be lineages within lineages. Obviously the categories will appear differently for different persons in the groups according to their generation level, and even if we consider only persons of a single generation, the practical relevance of their lineage associations will change as time increases the number of their own descendants. Thus two brothers may initially have close working relations. By the time each has become a father or grandfather with, say, ten sons each of whom may have sons of his own, the newer closer family ties outclass in importance the earlier ones and the brothers association, from being originally important economically, passes into a largely sentimental association accompanied quite often by a wide separation in space.

The situation is flexible. Larger lineages break down into smaller ones, which then expand and break down again. There are many intermediate situations. Sometimes persons belong coincidentally to a wider, largely ritual association and to a narrower, economically co-operating one. Sometimes they participate only in a small lineage. Sometimes brothers continue to co-operate in a comparatively wide group because their own families are too small or too immature to fulfil their economic needs.

When the father of the originating family of the lineage dies, his widow may serve as the focus of the group. After her death the eldest of her sons may provide a focus.

As a lineage widens and its economic roles tend to pass to narrower subsidiary lineages, unity may be preserved through the expression of ritual bonds in ceremonies additional to the ancestral rites. For instance, in the cases of the widest lineages in which there are adult members in the third descending generation it is usual for there to be periodic ceremonies in which the male members of this generation may make obeisance to the originating couple or to one of them if only one survives.

Even after both have died similar ceremonial may be carried out by junior members of the lineage under the direction of the eldest of the surviving sons, who is now the lineage head. In this case the obeisance may be made to his wife's parents or to one of them if only one is alive. Although the person honoured is not a member of the lineage, the ceremonial still unites the lineage members in common ritual action.

It also has other meanings. It expresses the important Miao value of respect for age and it reminds the junior members of the lineage of the connections they have with other clans through female members of their family line.

THE CLAN

The Miao are divided into a number of clans. Just how many there are amongst the Blue Miao in Thailand is uncertain but the number is usually said to be about twelve. We have encountered eleven: Tang, Wang, Yang, Jang, Tong, Goo, Kloo, Mow, Jow, Her, and Tchai. Some reports of greater numbers may have been confused by the fact the Miao often have two names for the same clan, one used amongst themselves and the other when talking to outsiders. Lyman[6] says that this is the case with all clans but we have noted it only in the following cases: Tang to outsiders becomes Hang, Yang becomes Ma, Kloo becomes Tow, Tchai becomes Lee and Mow becomes Song. The Miao name may be prefixed by the Miao term for clan, which is Hmong, and the outside name by the Thai term, which is Seh. Thus Hmong Tang becomes Seh Hang. Miao were unable to give us any explanation of this double name except to say that it was traditional. It may derive from ancient times in China when Miao were associated in States with Chinese or Tai, as in the principality of Ch'u.

As with our use of the term 'lineage', we are using the term 'clan' for want of a better, although in this case there is also the additional excuse that most other writers have so designated the named sub-divisions amongst the Miao. They have done so, however, with stronger reason because they have regarded the groups as patrilineal. Thus Lyman writes: 'Miao kinship structure is based on twelve exogamous patrilinear clans. . . .'[7] Following German usage in which 'clan' is reserved for matrilineal groups, Bernatzik prefers the term 'sib' and states: 'Among the Meau . . . the family is organized strictly by father right.'[8] Hudspeth, on the other hand, writing of the Miao in China calls their divisions 'surname groups', and in our view he is closer to the social reality.[9]

It is true that if the genealogical structure of a clan over several generations could be determined it would be patrilineal in character. It is true also that in any generation a majority of the members will be patrilineal descendants of previous generations. It is a fact, further-more, that children may be expected generally to belong to the clans of their fathers. To this extent the term 'patrilineal clan' is justified and it is a convenient short-hand term to use.

There are, however, important qualifications to the statements just made. The genealogical structure of a total clan over several generations is never known. Small sections of it may be aware of their genealogical links but rarely to any great depth. In any generation up to half of the

[6] Lyman, 1968, p. 3.   [7] Ibid.   [8] Bernatzik, 1947, p. 30.
[9] Hudspeth, W. H., 'The Cult of the Door Amongst the Miao in South-West China', *Folk Lore*, Vol. 33, 1922, pp. 400–10.

adult members may not be patrilineal descendants of previous generations. These are the wives, and as there is a high rate of polygyny in many groups the percentage of married persons who are not in the patrilineal category may be higher than of those who are. Finally, although generally children may be expected to belong to the clans of their fathers, a number of them will belong to the clans of their mothers.

The truth of the matter is that the recruiting principle of the clan is not patrilineal descent but marriage. The fact that marriage is virilocal —that is to say, that wives join their husbands' group—gives the groups their basically patrilineal appearance.

Therefore it is no oddity in the Miao case that wives become members of their husbands' clans. It is the crux of the system.[10] Children are born to mothers; fathers (and father's clan) acquire the women; therefore they acquire the children. If fathers do not establish property rights over the mothers by marrying them in the proper manner then the children belong to the clans of the mothers.

In the Miao belief system children are not reincarnations of the fathers or the mothers. Although the Miao know that sexual intercourse is a necessary precondition of birth and men can be penalized for their part in a pregnancy outside marriage, they believe that the soul of a child comes from the afterworld where the souls of all the dead are waiting to be reborn. The child may not have belonged in its previous existences to the clan into which it is born but to another clan, or another race, or to a lower level of the animal kingdom.

The singling out of patrilineal descent as the criterion of Miao clans could lead to a misunderstanding of the character of the groups and of Miao social attitudes and behaviour. It may be regarded as implying a concern with genealogies and an orientation to the past foreign to Miao concepts as we understood them.

Certainly the clan sub-divisions to which they belong come to them as a heritage from the past, but, for the very reason that they are part of the nature of things, there is little need to bother about their history, especially as they have no landed property over which there could be dispute as to the original title. The clans are contemporary associations serving current interests and thus they are oriented to the present and future, not to the past.

[10] This practice is characteristic of all Miao groups on which we have read reports. Graham (1937, p. 26) says of the Ch'uan Miao of Szechuan that on marriage a girl changes membership from her parents' family to that of her husband. Hudspeth (1922, pp. 405–10) says of the Miao he studied in Yunnan and Kweichow that the daughters are not allowed to take part in the sacrificial meal to the door spirit of their household because later they will marry and become part of another clan. Partaking of the meal would attach their souls to their parental household thus causing their marriages to be unsuccessful. Bernatzik (1947, p. 30) says '... married women belong absolutely to the family of their husband ... the married woman ... loses every connection with the sib.' These are only a few of the references.

The interests which the clans serve are security and prosperity in the wide world of natural and supernatural forces. They do so by providing combinations of persons united in spiritual strength and co-operating in mutual help. In their mundane aspect the clans may be likened to clubs and in their religious aspects to sects. As their religious aspect is fundamental to their conception, we may define the clans and their sub-divisions as essentially religious associations conferring rights of community upon their members through the spiritual bonds between them. Anyone admitted to the association has these rights irrespective of whether he is linked to the others by blood descent.

The property of a clan is its members and the more people who belong to it the stronger it is conceived to be. In a ceremony which we witnessed at Meto in 1965 carried out by members of the Tang clan in order to subdue a spirit called 'Suter Sublong' who periodically harasses the people, part of the spell chanted by the leader was:

Let the Tang clan be so numerous that when they walk the sound will be like thunder. Other clans will then say that the Tang are so many that they make a great commotion walking. Our clan will grow and spread like the forest, and none will die like the trees in it.

To increase its strength, or even to maintain itself, a clan must acquire new members. It could do so by children being born to women who have themselves been born into the clan. But this rarely happens because sexual relations between clan members are incestuous and cohabitation within her parental house between a girl and any man offends the house spirits. Thus the only effective way for a clan to keep up its membership is to obtain women from outside thereby acquiring rights not only over them but also over their children.

MARRIAGE AND BRIDE-PRICE

The women are brought in as wives and their transfer from the clans where they were born to those of their husbands is effected by the payment of bride-price.

The rights which a husband's clan then has over a woman whose price has been paid are entitlements to retain her and her children as members of the clan. If her husband dies his younger brother has a superior right over anyone else to take her as a wife without the payment of bride-price. If she is not remarried within the clan, consent of clansmen should be obtained before she marries outside and bride-price should be paid to the near relatives of her former husband. In this respect her position is similar to that of a clan daughter.

Relative to the Miao economy bride-price is high. It is calculated in

Indian silver rupees[11] and must be paid in silver, either as rupees or ingots or neck rings made from melted silver. The price appears to be fairly standard averaging in marriages we studied about 350 rupees, equivalent in United States currency to approximately $200. There are other costs too. The bridegroom's party should provide chickens for sacrifice in the bride's house, and rice, alcoholic drink, a pig, and more chickens to feed spirits and guests on their return with her to the house of the bridegroom. The total expenses would be more than the savings of most households for at least one and possibly several years.

To persons who are not anthropologists familiar with such systems the high bride-price may give the impression that women are bought and sold like chattels. In fact the transactions are not aimed at economic gain, nor do they yield it to any extent. In the first place the price is offset to some degree by the fact that, according to the best Miao traditions, the bride's father should give her a dowry of an ox, a pig, silver neck rings, and a new embroidered costume. Secondly, the need for women is reciprocal so that what a clan receives for its daughters is more or less counterbalanced by what it has to pay out for its wives. Thirdly, the amount gained for a girl by a family is not usually equal to the loss of her value as a worker.

The high price serves a number of social ends in addition to marriage itself. It displays the status of a family which can amass the bride-price. Some families are unable to achieve this status by the time of the marriage, and have to offer promises along with part payment. It gives a family temporary prominence and its head leadership in the small circle of clansmen who are called upon to help in arranging the marriage. It bestows prestige on the bride and her family. It cements friendships in a party atmosphere. In short, once subsistence needs are provided for, it offers one of the most satisfying uses of wealth.

The main utility of bride-price, however, is the symbolization it gives to a new creative act in the Miao social universe. The symbolization is both general and particular. There is probably significance in the fact that the price should be paid in silver and not in ordinary money, thus setting it apart from a commercial transaction and relating it directly to the traditions of Miao culture. The most precious metal, the material of ornamentation as well as wealth, symbolizes the most important occasion and celebrates the worth of the woman. The way

[11] These rupees, bearing dates from the reigns of William IV to Edward VII but mainly Victorian, still circulate in the hills of Burma and northern Thailand where they are used mainly in traditional exchanges but also as standards of weight and for making ornaments. In 1958 they could be bought from Chiengmai Indian traders for 8 baht apiece. In 1965 the price was 11 baht so the cost of traditional exchanges, such as in marriages, had actually risen in terms of ordinary currency. During the period of this study one American dollar was worth approximately 20 baht.

the price is contributed by a group of the husband's relatives and distributed to relatives of the wife gives particular significance to the new relationships brought into being. These are not only clan ties, although they are our present concern. Marriage is the creative act at the centre of almost all new kin relationships, which otherwise can arise only rarely and through misbehaviour and are therefore more limited in scope.

These symbolizations might, of course, be achieved in other ways than by a bride-price, for instance by the type of reciprocal exchange which occurs in many societies, or simply by a celebration party. In attempting to set the Miao bride-price in its wider symbolic context, therefore, we do not wish to argue away its meaning as a price. Miao clans are exclusive groupings in several respects and women are important assets to them. Through marriage, a clan gains new spiritual adherents and its constituent households mothers, housekeepers, and workers in the fields. It is appropriate that these assets should be paid for to validate the transfers in the public eye.

That the women are not treated simply as property to be bought and sold is further evident from the fact that they do not lose their integrity as persons. The claims which clans and their constituent units exercise over any of their members, men or women, are limited. Miao society is not autocratic. The concept of individual rights is strongly embedded in the culture. One of the earliest indications of this is the right of a new-born baby to its mother's milk. No other being can share in this so long as the child lives, and if milk drops accidentally from the mother's breast on to an animal it should be killed.

The rights of the child in respect to the mother are reciprocated by the rights she has over it. In the first instance it is her child and unless a bride-price is paid for her the father has no rights over it and it will remain within her clan. Even when a husband has acquired rights by payment of the bride-price the primacy of the mother's rights remains so long as the child is immature. If a marriage breaks up she may take her children with her provided arrangements are made to compensate her husband for their loss.

The nature of these arrangements varies as they are subject to disputation and negotiation. If the woman remarries into another clan and takes with her all the children her full bride-price should be paid back. Sometimes it is argued that an additional price equal to half the bride-price should be paid for each child taken. If she leaves children behind, the bride-price to be returned is reduced. We heard different opinions in Meto as to what the reduction should be. One was that the price should be reduced ten rupees for each child left; another that if any child was left no bride-price need be returned. In practice no attempt would be made physically to restrain a woman from taking her children even if no price had been paid, although this would inevitably lead to dispute between the new husband and the old.

A woman is not obliged to remain with her husband if he physically maltreats her, and in such an event she can return to her parents' home, although her husband may raise objections to her remarrying unless the bride-price is first returned. It is a rare event because husbands know that if they get a reputation for ill-treating women they may find it impossible to gain other wives. Also, although a younger brother has the right to an older brother's widow, she may refuse to allow him to exercise the right. She may not marry elsewhere unless a price is paid to him, but she cannot be forced to cohabit with him against her will.[12]

It is only young children not often above the age of seven who would be involved in transfers from their father's group. The Miao have no rites of passage marking the transition of a child through stages of immaturity to adulthood, but each passing year further establishes the father's claim over it in virtue of his contribution to its upkeep. Also in the extended family pattern of the Miao the diversification of bonds quickly strengthens the child's attachment to its natal group, to break which against its will would be an infringement of its own individuality. In extremely exceptional circumstances even an adult may may change his clan affiliation, but normally a person's own identification with a particular clan and that which others make for him render change impossible after the early years of childhood.

SEX AND CLAN MEMBERSHIP

From the above discussion it will be clear that in respect of clan membership there is a difference between men and women in that men remain members of the same clan all their lives whereas women normally change from one clan to another. This has some practical consequences.

Although we have said that a woman changes clan membership upon marriage this statement requires some slight qualification. Her position is in fact somewhat ambivalent. It appears that her natal clan never entirely relinquishes interest in her or she in it. We have noted earlier that sisters of the father and grandfather appear in the lists of spirits which are honoured by families. Surveying the family line in the other direction we can distinguish the same enduring interest in the female members expressed in the custom of child betrothal which, although not a regular practice, is also not uncommon.

It occurs between a boy and his father's sister's daughter. It is

[12] A case occurred during our stay at Meto.

dependent upon the agreement of the father of the girl and his superior rights are symbolized by the boy's father giving to him articles of fine clothing for her, a bottle of alcoholic spirit, and four silver rupees. The eldest brother of a family has the first right to betroth his son to his sister's daughter and thereafter the right descends to younger brothers in order of seniority. When the age for marriage is reached either party may opt out of the arrangement, but if one does it must pay to the other the sum of forty silver rupees. If the marriage does take place no bride-price is required.

The residual bond between a woman and her natal clan is shown too by the fact that if a marriage ends she may return to it.

The ambivalent status of women compared to the certain status of men in respect of clan membership also supports the political dominance of men. A widow may sometimes become the effective head of a large household, and although we encountered no cases of women as village leaders amongst the Blue Miao, we did do so in the case of one large White Miao settlement. As shamans, too, women may exercise considerable influence upon community affairs. But generally women's voices are limited to the private deliberations of the family circle. Public debates and inter-group negotiations, such as the arrangement of marriages, are the preserves of men.

None of the qualifications we have just mentioned alter the truth of the statement that once bride-price has been paid for her a woman belongs to her husband's family and clan. She can only return fully to her natal group with their agreement and usually only after compensation has been paid to them. The residual interest in her which we suggested was indicated by the custom of child betrothal can only be expressed in this form with the agreement of her husband.

But most of all her new clan membership is manifested in her changed spiritual allegiance. When a bride is first brought to her husband's house she is introduced to the house spirits. Thereafter she participates in all the ceremonies of the clan and its sub-divisions. If she falls ill, it is the guardian spirits of her husbands' household or clan who are appealed to and not those of her own birth group. If she is visiting her parents, takes ill, and is believed to be dying, an effort should be made to take her back to her husband's home, and if this is not possible she should be taken to another house. When she does die, her spirit joins those of her husband's clan.

THE COHESION OF THE CLAN

Membership of a distinctive spiritual community is the criterion of clanship. Admission is by birth to a clan member, by marriage, or by adoption. In fact all may be seen as forms of adoption because the

children themselves are gifts of the gods and may have been linked to
other clans in other times. Membership is signified by a distinctive clan
name and expressed by adherence to particular ritual observances.

The ritual distinctions which mark off one clan from another may be
only small differences in procedure in ceremonies which otherwise are
common to all clans. In his description of 'The Cult of the Door' among
the Miao of south-west China, Hudspeth says that there are very
definite variations in the forms of the ceremony associated with each
surname. Some of the differences are in the types of animals sacrified,
others in the way offerings to the spirits are laid out, and others in the
way invocations are rendered. Surnames 'Hmao-tang' and 'Hmao-
chih', he writes, open and close the door three times saying: 'May we
come to be rich. May our children be numerous! May our cattle
multiply!' [13]

Amongst the clans we encountered in Thailand there were similar
variations in ritual practices. A full description of the differences would
take more space than we can devote to it but we may mention some of
the more general types. Frequently the differences concern the 'house
spirit'. Every Blue Miao household has a shrine for this spirit, both
shrine and spirit being called 'Sier Klang'. It is a white paper about
nine inches square to which red neck feathers or white breast feathers of
fowls sacrificed to it are stuck with blood from the sacrifice. Some clans
have the shrine on the wall immediately opposite the door of the house;
the Tang clan has it on the wall just to the right of the door.

Some clans sacrifice a dog in major ceremonies as well as pigs and
chickens, and eat portions of the cooked body. Others sacrifice a dog
but do not eat it. With other clans, such as the Tang, dogs have no
place in the ceremonies.

Many, if not all, clans acknowledge the existence of the harassing
'Suter Sublong' spirit but differ in the details of how they deal with it
and in the timing of their ceremonies.

Slight mythological differences as well as actual distinctions in ritual
procedure may also mark one clan off from another. The Tang clan
in Meto explain the origin of the Sier Klang[14] spirit by a story which
says that there was once a family with seven sons, all of whom helped
each other in the fields except the fourth son who was very lazy. His
brothers disliked him, would not help him when he fell sick, and when
he died held no funeral ceremonies but threw his body away in the
forest as food for the wild animals. The brothers then fell sick and their
animals began to die. They consulted a shaman who told them their

[13] Hudspeth, 1922, pp. 406–10.
[14] A literal translation of 'sier klang' might be 'father spirit', but he is not considered a
Miao ancestral figure.

fourth brother's soul was very angry at his body's being cast away like that of an animal, and that they should hold a ceremony to apologize to him. They were to light joss sticks for him, offer him paper money, sacrifice a cock to him, and ask him to stay in the house as their protective spirit.

The story of the Jang clan is different. It says that there was once a family which was very poor. Its members sickened and their animals died. So the head of the family went to the Chinese to ask what was the matter. The Chinese told him how to hold the ceremony to invite the 'sier klang' spirit to take up residence in the house.

The ritual distinctions mark off one clan from another. By doing so they contribute to clan identity, but the inner strength of clanship comes from the relationship members conceive they have to one another. Persons come into the clan in the context of a family, and the rules and sentiments of clanship can be seen as the widest extension of the family. Of course, as we are dealing with an on-going cultural system, we are not suggesting that they are so derived in each individual case, but rather that clan and family conform to the same paradigm and because of this mutually reinforce each other, the family forming an early model of behaviour and the existence of the same rules in a wider context strengthening its authority.

As the families display the incest taboo so do the clans, which are therefore exogamous. Respect for the household gods is duplicated by respect for the clan gods. Mutual help and protection, friendship, recognition of the decision-taking role of men, respect for age, and to some extent common property rights are the basis of the moral code in both.

It is true that the clan as a whole appears to diverge from the family pattern in that it has no single head. Partly this can be explained by the fact that the paradigm is not that of the nuclear family, which as we have seen is not a Miao ideal, but the extended family in which authority is less strongly particularized. An over-riding reason, however, is that the clan as a whole is a dispersed group some of the members of which may be in China and others scattered throughout all the mountains to the south where the Miao pause in their migrations. In its group functions clanship operates through lesser sub-divisions, and the smaller and more localized these become the closer the approach to a leadership pattern. But before discussing these sub-divisions let us try to assess the over-all role of clanship.

THE SOCIAL VALUE OF THE CLANS

We have already said that clanship operates as a general area of reciprocity. At the widest clan level this amounts to little more than a general friendliness and a willingness to render help provided it does not conflict with narrower interests or closer liaisons between kinsmen or sub-clan members. Reference was made also to some conception of common property rights. Although land under use or intended for use is individual or household property, clansmen will usually recognize a right of fellow clansmen to settle within a general territory which they might otherwise try to preserve for themselves. Thus clan ties can be an important aid in migration.

In its most general sense clanship enlarges the social horizon, allowing each person a wide range of social contacts which he may use to his personal benefit. The dispersed nature of the clans and the fact that they are associations of mutual aid not dependent on specific ties between members make them of high value to people who frequently move over long distances. The mere possession of a common clan name is enough to ensure a friendly reception amongst people who would otherwise be strangers. Not all the journeys are for the purposes of resettlement. They may be to explore, to seek marriage partners, or to visit relatives. The wide scatter of clansmen provides staging posts over much of the countryside.

The horizon is not limited only to members of one's own clan. Links with other clans through marriage also facilitate entry to communities. Diversification of clan ties is encouraged by the Miao belief that it is bad practice for more than two marriages to take place between the same families. Inter-clan ties, however, are of less intensity than common clanship; they usually involve only those of the other clan who have been co-resident with or are close relatives of the families which provide the links, and they tend to evaporate with deaths of the generations which created them. In a general sense, too, clanship enhances the moral strength of the lesser groups within its span by placing them in the context of a wider, more powerful, if vaguer, union.

Their dispersed nature precludes the clans from operating as unified groups. They never come together in assembly and they have no political organization. This does not mean, however, that they have no roles as groups. On the contrary, their very lack of total political organization means that their local representatives can be regarded as representing the whole.

Through the clan system many Miao social events, instead of being the affairs of individuals and families, become the interests of larger sets of people. We have already spoken of the value of this in creating inter-personal ties. Equally valuable is the enrichment it gives to social life by bringing people together from far and near, producing variety, excitement, and the general warmth of greater social intercourse, and providing scope and rationale for diversified ceremonial.

The group functions resulting from differences in clanship are most clearly evident in marriages. On most other important occasions the clans are represented in some roles as distinctive groups. For instance at funerals the body should be washed and clothed by the children and grandchildren, male and female, of the deceased person. Although they perform this particular duty in virtue of their family relationships they almost always comprise members of two or more clans. In the assignment of other special duties clanship is the primary criterion. Special shoes for the corpse should be made by men of a different clan from that of the deceased. The chanting may be performed by an expert of any clan but he should be accompanied by representatives of the clans into which the deceased and his or her spouse were born. The cooking of the funeral feast should be supervised by two persons only one of whom should be from the clan of the deceased, and other duties—the coffin-making, the cutting of firewood for cooking the food, the dish-washing, the firing of the gun to salute the soul—should be given to men of different clans. The grinding of rice for the feast should be done by at least two women of different clans, and a man belonging to a different clan from the deceased should arrange the payment of any outstanding debts on behalf of the deceased's sons upon whom the responsibility devolves.

THE SUB-CLANS

Within the clan there are associations of persons who regard themselves as more closely linked with one another than with other members of the clan. These groupings we shall call sub-clans. Their uniting principle is the same as that in the clan: they are spiritual associations symbolized by the same ritual practices and the same mythology. It is the differences they display from the otherwise common ritual pattern of the clan that mark them off as separate groupings. Unlike the clans, however, they do not have names to perpetuate their distinction. They exist as single groups only so long as the ritual of all their members remains the same. Separation by time and distance causes divergences so that sub-clans may sub-divide into further sub-clans and there may be various degrees of association between them.

Because they are based on known or presumed former family associations, perhaps in ancient times, the sub-clans are extensions of lineages with sentiments of the same type uniting their members but becoming less binding the more distant the relationship is regarded as being. Persons encountering strangers of the same clan may inquire into their ritual practices to determine how close is their association.

The ritual differences which mark off the sub-clans are various. Different names for the spirit honoured in the ceremony for the door spirit of the house indicate a considerable separation, but generally it appears to be the number of differences rather than particular items which count. Common differences are the manner in which oxen sacrificed in ceremonies to cure sickness are divided up; variations in the forms of respect shown to the house spirits; and in the times of the year when ceremonies are held.

The sub-clans are most important locally. Within a settlement area they have considerable significance as providing circles of friendship and co-operating bodies in ritual. Members of a sub-clan are expected to live in close harmony. For instance, before a head of a household carries out the ceremony for the spirit of the central post of his house, which he should do every three years if the household is to prosper, he should ensure that he has good relationships with the members of every other household in the sub-clan, and he should invite them all to the ceremony. Often members of the sub-clan will farm together in the same part of the village territory, and they can call upon one another for help should occasion arise.

On the local scene the sub-clans are usually distinguished from one another by the names of principal members, often by that of the man most socially prominent in each, although as they have no organized political roles *vis-à-vis* one another, and decisions within the group depend largely on consensus, there is no emphasis on particular leadership.

The sub-clans also have potential significance beyond the local area as aid in resettlement. Clansmen in general, but sub-clansmen in particular, should extend hospitality to one another and allow newcomers to settle amongst them, providing them with land whenever possible. The difference appears to be that whereas members of other sub-clans will be accepted into the local community if they so request, members of one's own sub-clan may be actively invited to join it. This frequently happens in the early phase of a settlement when the pioneers seek the company of those most close to them in the clan in order to increase their security and perhaps improve their status in relation to other groups in the neighbourhood.

Because of the value of wider ties of sub-clanship members of a dispersed sub-clan may seek by ritual means to preserve their sense of union. The longer the separation, however, the greater the likelihood of divergence which could ultimately lead to sub-clan division. On the other hand small groups in long association may tend to coalesce. The extent to which either separation or combination occurs will depend much upon circumstances, as intra-clan behaviour appears to be fairly adaptable to immediate needs. In a large congregation of clansmen minor ritual differences may be emphasized because there is value in circumscribing interest groups, and also because a diversity of groups permits a more varied ceremonial life. Small groups entering a new situation where they are faced with larger combinations may find common ground for union. The embrace of common clanship makes such rearrangements easier.

As an illustration of the workings of sub-clans in the ritual sphere we shall describe in a little detail one of the ceremonies concerning the Suter Sublong spirit, which we attended at Meto in 1965. We have already referred to this spirit as one which most clans believe to harass them. The name means 'the fire and blood spirit'. It may burn down houses, make the blood flow from wounds, and cause other forms of sickness. Therefore at one ceremony it must be trapped and beaten, and at another it must be burnt and drowned. It revives and the sequence starts again.

Most clans and sub-clans hold the first type of ceremony every year for three years in succession followed by the second type of ceremony for each of the three subsequent years. The various sub-clans within a clan may differ in the dates for the ceremonies. Thus within the Jang clan the sub-clan of Tungsang holds them on the last day of the new moon in the seventh month but the sub-clan of Jusu on the last day of the new moon in the sixth month. In the case of the Tang clan all the sub-clans hold a ceremony every year on varying dates except the sub-clan of Yaitong which holds it every three years on the last day of the new moon in the twelfth month. In every sub-clan and clan all members must refrain from work on the day when a ceremony is held, and all males should participate.

The sub-clan of Yaitong now carry out only the first ceremony—the trapping and beating of the spirit. Each time a different house is selected as the ceremonial place so that eventually they will all have had the spirit driven from them. Early in the morning every male in the sub-clan within walking distance should come to the house. Females of the sub-clan may come if they wish. All the members of the sub-clan must be careful not to handle knives or guns on this day because if they injure themselves they will bleed to death.

A member of the household who is either a first- or last-born son will have been chosen to lead the ritual. First he goes all around the inside of the house chanting and scattering rice to attract the spirit. Over his shoulder he carries a leafy sapling of a certain species of tree favoured by the spirit which has tied to it flaming wooden torches to direct the spirit to it. When it is considered that the spirit has had time to settle in the leaves, he carries the sapling outside, where all the clansmen now assemble and are surrounded by a band of white cloth to separate them from the spectators and to symbolize their common bond. In front of them are piled all the agricultural implements and all the weapons belonging to the household.

Many times the man circles the group and the implements, uttering a chant which in part says:

'This is not the day for prayers for wealth, or for the old people, or for the house or for the children, but the day for the prayer to Suter Sublong. If he comes to the doors of our houses he eats the women; if he goes to the working places he eats the men. Today I shall kill Suter Sublong. Whoever believes I have not killed him will die; he will die down like the fire. Today will be a good day!'

Thereafter follows the part of the invocation we have already quoted on page 57. As he continues his chant he directs his words to particular localities. None of these is higher than the village in which the ceremony is taking place, for which the reason given is that water flows downward to the village from higher places. This suggests that the evil spirit follows the stream upwards from the lowlands, and perhaps, therefore, it is a symbolic representation to Miao minds of the dangers which threaten the tribe from the alien powers in the plains.

At Meto the man carrying out the ceremony repeats his chant for the following localities in descending order of altitude: 1. Bo Sali (the headquarters of the tambong, or administrative sub-district); 2. Hot (the headquarters of the amphur, or administrative district); 3. Chiengmai (the headquarters of the changwad, or province); 4. Bangkok (the national capital); 5. the sea. He prays that the spirit, if it is in the forest, the trees will fall on it; if it is on the plains, the wind will blow it away; and if it is on the sea, a sea serpent will eat it.

When the chanting is completed, the sapling is planted in the ground. Suddenly, the man leaps towards it and severs the base of it with a knife so that it falls to the ground. The cloth is unwound from the assembled clanspeople. In front of them an arch is made by the man holding from one side the knife used to fell the sapling and by another person on the opposite side holding a cross-bow against the knife. The clanspeople file beneath the arch to end the ceremony.

The disposal ceremony is similar in many respects. A first- or last-born son officiates, the clanspeople assemble as witnesses and are surrounded by a white cloth. Three samplings of the proper species, one for each year the spirit has been trapped, are tied together with red cloth and are held in a fire while prayers for the destruction of the spirit are chanted. They are then taken to a stream, submerged, and covered with stones.

When members of this particular sub-clan migrated to Meto they left behind at Pasamliem other members of the same sub-clan. In an effort to preserve their sub-clan unity in the face of the long distance separating them an agreement was made before they parted that on the same day every three years those at Meto would carry out the trapping ceremony and those at Pasamliem the disposal ceremony.

Other events which occurred at Meto in 1965 illustrate the opposite situation—the relative weakness of bonds when intra-clan relationships are not considered to be close. Having heard a report that good land was available at Meto six Tang households from a place in Chiengrai Province more than 500 kilometres away arrived at the village and sought the help of the predominant Tang clan in settling there. Inquiry showed that the name of their principal spirit was different and there were several major distinctions in ritual. They were received with courtesy, permitted to build their houses near those of the other Tang clansmen, and were given land.

However, the land they were given comprised fields which had been abandoned after long cultivation by the Tang people already resident in the village. There was no ill-will towards them in this. In more favourable circumstances they would have been more actively welcomed as co-residents. But Meto was already at the end of its reserves of new land and for the Tang clansmen to give them better fields would seriously have reduced their own ability to stay much longer in the area, a sacrifice to which the distant clan relationship did not induce them.

While the new arrivals stayed at Meto they were treated with the respect due to fellow clansmen but their Tang brethren did not appear in general to develop as close an intimacy with them as they had with the sections of different clans with whom they had been co-resident for many years and with many of whom they have inter-familial relationships. The situation may have changed in time and clan ties asserted themselves more strongly, but after harvesting their first crops, which were poor, the Chiengrai settlers abandoned their new-built homes and returned whence they had come.

CONCLUSION

The example just given draws us back to the opening remarks of this chapter—that each person has a range of possible relationships of different types the degrees of importance of which are determined principally by the extent to which they serve life interests. The categories which we have defined are the immediate family (including the family of birth and the family of procreation); the immediate connections of the family; the family line; lineages of up to four generations' depth in which at various stages of his life a person may occupy any of the generational positions; the clan and the sub-clan.

It will be noted that the categories are not exclusive. The family itself is part of the clan and so are some of the immediate connections of the family and most members of the family line. On the other hand the categories do not constitute a hierarchy of inclusive groups. Many of the family connections and some of the family line are outside the clan groupings.

The situation is explained by the dual nature of the family. It is part of the clan system but it is also the nucleus of new relationships arising out of the alliances which form it. The alliances formed within one generation continue with lessening force into the next generation thus creating the concept of the family line.

There is no contradiction in principle between clan and non-clan alliances because they follow different principles and fulfil different needs. Recognized connections of kinship and affinity radiating from the family offer a suitable basis for many of the inter-personal relationships useful in daily life. They cannot, however, offer a suitable basis for clanship because they exist only so long as they are recognized, and memory of them must weaken as the number of intermediate links increases. Clanship, on the other hand, is based on the concept of an enduring group unaffected by generational distance or spatial dispersion its value being that it provides a spiritual association of a wide order between people, increasing their security in the material and immaterial worlds. The aspect of the family which serves as the model for the clan is not that of the family as the nucleus of radiating contemporary relationships but that of the family as a unitary household group worshipping its house spirits.

In discussing the family line we said its central core comprised people who would have lived in a family house had the house endured. We also described it as a link between the pattern of individual relationships and the clan categorization. At the limit of fading memory it symbolizes the parting of the ways.

Thereafter persons who were once in the house—that is, daughters who married—are forgotten. The house then comprises only those born into it or who come into it through following the rule of patrilocal marriage. They worship the same distinctive spirits and jointly perform the same distinctive ritual. All that would be necessary to make them a clan would be for the house to have a name and for them to have no memory of ever having been a part of another house.

There are therefore two basic principles which determine the practical ties which people will have with one another—the degree of relationship, whether it be affinal or consanguineal, and their clan affiliation. Let us call them the principle of relative immediacy and the principle of clanship.

Analytically, there might seem better sense in distinguishing categories not as we have done but according to whether the relationships are by lineal descent or by marriage, a practice which is much more usual in anthropological analysis. If we disregard Miao ideology—a big step to take—it could be said that all ties within the clan area— other than those with wives and mothers—are lineal ties, and it is true that generally they are stronger than those with non-clanspeople. But such a categorization would obscure the fact that within the clan area the principle of immediacy operates also, and that its operation outside the clan area may offset the strength of clanship. It is the operation of the two principles in conjunction that determines the categories which we have set forth above.

If both principles come together, as they do within the family, the extended family, and the lineage, the ties are especially strong. In the case of the wider lineage, however, and sometimes within the narrower lineage if its membership is dispersed into several houses, the bond of clanship may be offset by the greater distance of relationship so that a relationship, say, to one's wife's brother may be utilized in preference to one with one's father's brother's son. Within the total range of close relatives personality and practical advantage also often play decisive roles in determining choices. With increasing distance of relationship clanship becomes the predominant principle. The principle of immediacy then operates within a restricted sphere in determining closer ties with sub-clansmen than with other clansmen.

Clanship also has group functions which individual relationships cannot fill. Therefore although a person in his daily life may associate more with non-clansmen than with clansmen, and although he may utilize a non-clan tie to gain entry to a settlement, he will seek some association with fellow clansmen, for otherwise he will be an outsider in ceremonial life, be insecure in the spiritual world, and lack a reliable group of allies in wordly competition and crises.

The importance of different categories of relationships will depend very much upon the social interests concerned. In listing them in the order given above we had in mind mainly economic affairs which are the subject of this book, but a different viewpoint, as for instance that of religion, might yield another order. The roles of the relationships can be assessed only in terms of cultural contexts and the particular circumstances in which the people are situated. This is the case with all so-called social structures, but it is very clear in the case of the Miao where there is considerable flexibility in social behaviour. With regard to settlement arrangements, for example, there appears to be only one compulsory principle: that marriage may not be matrilocal. It may be virilocal but the effect of the rule, in the Miao cultural context and in the situations of the groups we studied, is to make it generally patrilocal. Otherwise there is no certain pattern. Clansmen tend to congregate in settlements but their representation in a particular settlement may be as low as a single household.

Relationships are constantly being varied according to contemporary circumstances. In the migratory way of life the younger generations are the pioneers and therefore the new relationships which they make become the focal points of new alignments, convenience in the present being of greater importance in many cases than association in the past. The social system is suited to this condition. As we have seen, in neither the clan system nor the pattern of individual relationships is blood descent significant. The creative principle is marriage. It will connect a girl not only to a new set of clanspeople, and her old clanspeople to the new people, but also her blood relatives to all the relatives of her husband's family; and her children, legitimized by the marriage process, will perpetuate the clan.

CHAPTER FOUR

THE HOUSEHOLD AND THE VILLAGE

THE HOUSEHOLD

THE primary local group in Miao society is the household comprising the people resident in a single dwelling. It may consist of one person, although this is extremely rare, a married couple, a simple family of parents and children, a polygynous family, or a patrilineally extended family which may or may not have polygynous extensions.

The largest household we saw was in a village in Tak Province which had forty-four members in five families some of which were polygynous. The largest household at Pasamliem, which was larger than any at Meto, had twenty-six members comprising the household head, his wife, his six sons and an unmarried daughter, the two wives of his eldest son the first of whom had two sons and three daughters and the second of whom had one son, the wife of his second son who had one son and three daughters, the wife of his third son who had a daughter, and the wife of his fourth son who had a son. Households of more than twenty persons are not uncommon. The most frequent household form is that comprising a simple family, but the majority of such families have previously been part of a larger extended family household and will develop into another such household before a further separation occurs. Although the Thailand Government Survey quoted in Chapter two gave the average household size for the Miao as 6·5 persons, the average in the villages we studied was 7–8 persons.

The household is the basic socio-economic and religious unit. It is a property-sharing group in which the interests of its individual members are qualified by the interests of the whole. Its material property is its house, its padi fields, its pigs and chickens, and its common food stocks; its immaterial possession is the protection offered by the house spirits. Padi fields are worked conjointly, there is a single cooking-place and common meals, and all the members participate in the ritual which secures their collective welfare.

Order and authority in the household are maintained by respect for age tempered by recognition of capacity. Through the kinship terminology, through the birth-order titles, through the attitudes encouraged in the children, respect for age is constantly emphasized. Younger brothers respect their older brothers, sons respect their fathers, and nephews respect their fathers' brothers in order of their seniority of birth. Therefore, nominal authority in the household belongs to the senior man in it. If he dies, a measure of his authority may pass to his widow.

Miao, however, do not tend to cling to the direction of affairs once they cease to be leading actors in them. Such a situation would not be consistent with their migratory pattern because, if a man clung to the rigid control of his household's affairs right through old age, the easy household segmentation which facilitates migration would not be possible. One informant stated that 'when a man gets to thirty years of age he becomes a child again'. This was an exaggeration, due probably to the fact that there is no accurate reckoning of chronological age, but it is true that once a man gets well into the grandparental phase of his life, his effective leadership passes to the most senior man of the most active generation. There are intermediate phases, too. As men's families grow, they tend to have more say in the general affairs of the household which functions very much as a co-operative organization, sufficient order being given to it by the presence of the old man to act as counsellor or, very occasionally, as arbiter.

In a large household comprising an extended family, the families of married sons are subsidiary units in which each controls its own part of the economic proceedings concerned with the acquiring and expenditure of wealth. It has its separate poppy fields, it conducts its own trading activities, it stores its own silver, and it disburses its wealth to its own members or contributes it separately to the general needs of the household. Fathers have the first say in the marriages of their children. There may also be some ritual distinction in that where two or more fathers are each qualified to perform rites for the ancestral spirits they may have separate altars on the house wall. But the families are not self-contained units because a good part of their labour goes for general household purposes, they will help the head of his household with his poppy fields, and part of their opium or silver is used to buy household food or to pay for its ceremonies. When one of the two or more qualified persons carries out ancestral rites he always does so on behalf of the household as a whole.

The differences in the organization of the cash and subsistence activities of a household should be seen in the light of the changes which a household may face through time. The activities which are concerned solely with its maintenance in the one place are joint affairs. But those which will be involved in its dispersion are the affairs of the subsidiary units which may divide from it. Padi fields are important for food only, as rice is not normally traded. House repair and ritual activities are tasks which keep the common venture going. But when a component family is migrating away, neither the padi fields nor the house can be taken with it, and at most only a small quantity of rice can be carried. On the other hand money, or the wealth which can be converted into it, is needed to provide for the family during its migration and until it can harvest fresh fields. Therefore, the separate management of its cash affairs by each family in a large household preserves a measure of independence for it which will enable it to migrate more easily.

There is, also some distinction between groups of mothers and children within a polygynous family, but it is too slight for them to be considered as subsidiary units. In some polygynous systems elsewhere in the world, the wives each have their separate dwelling places and the husband will visit each of them on different occasions, so that the situation is in effect a number of nuclear families with a common father. The Miao situation is by no means so clear-cut. The wives do not have separate dwelling places. They do not even have separate beds, but share a common bed with their husband. All immature children will sleep in the same place or in unpartitioned portions of the house. As we have said, infants are fed from their own mothers' milk, and generally mothers spend more time with, and have a closer attachment to, their own offspring. But there is a considerable merging of maternal care, especially as the children get older. The fact that the father is present all the time and has an equal link with all the children further modifies the separation. Between half-siblings the distinction of relative age is more important than distinctions of maternal parentage.

The ritual unity of the household

Household unity is given moral sanction by religious beliefs and practices which play an important part right from the time a household is formed.

When a site has been selected for a new house, a small hole is dug in the ground and a grain of padi is dropped into it for each person who will live in the house. The hole is covered for the night. The next morning it is uncovered. If any grains have disappeared, the site will be abandoned and another selected because the disappearance means that there will be sickness and perhaps death in a house built there.

In addition to the house spirit, Sier Klang, mentioned previously, there are four other spirits important to a household—the spirit of the door; the spirit of the central post; the spirit of the big fireplace where food for the animals is cooked and other large cooking tasks, such as the making of maize spirit, are carried out; and the spirit of the small fireplace. Except on special occasions as when a house site is being abandoned, the fireplace spirits are not the subject of special ceremonial, but the first two spirits are honoured at regular intervals.

The ceremony for the spirit of the door, Klang Kla Chong, should be carried out every year. Some households may fail to hold it in some years because of shortage of animals for sacrifice, but a special effort to carry it out should be made within the year a new house is built, if ill-fortune is to be avoided.

The atmosphere of the ceremony is almost conspiratorial.[1] It must be held at night and is normally attended only by close relatives of the same sub-clan. Married daughters are excluded. The main sacrificial animal must be a sow, which is accompanied by chickens. When the pork is almost cooked the head of the household shuts the door saying: 'I have shut the door not to keep out money, silver, and gold, but to feed the door spirit.' When the offering of cooked pork has been arranged in the correct manner, he pours juice from the pot into specially made bamboo cups, saying: 'The souls of money, silver, gold, pigs and chickens, and the souls of everybody in this household, please come to stay inside this house.' After the people present have eaten he opens the door, saying: 'I open the door, not to let diseases in or the souls of money, silver, and gold go out, but to let the souls of money, silver, and gold, and good fortune come in.' After the ceremony has ended and relatives have left, only members of the household are permitted to enter the house for three days.

The ceremony for the central post should be held every three years, although sometimes, at the risk of ill-health or misfortune, it may be longer delayed. The mythology supporting the ceremony is that during the migration of the Miao from north to south they were attempting to cross a large river when their raft became stuck in the middle. They got free by promising the spirits of the river a human sacrifice. The leader sought a child for the sacrifice from several men but when all were unwilling to render it he asked a poor woman for her only son. She yielded him on condition that the leader would care for her now that she was losing her only future support. Before he died the boy, called Esor Jineng, said he would come to eat a large sow every three years. He would first sit on the roof of the house and then enter it by the central post.

Each year at the time of the New Year Festival a ceremony is held for the Sier Klang, the protective house spirit. It must be carried out by the head of the household. Standing in front of the shrine of the

---

[1] Faitei (House 10) carried out this ceremony in May 1967. I was not present in the village at the time but Nusit Chindarsi witnessed it. He was allowed to attend on condition that he spoke only Miao while it was in progress. The reason Tang clansmen give for the secrecy is that an ancestor wishing to carry out the ceremony had no pig and was forced to steal one. He insisted that the ceremony be carried out at night and only Miao speech be used so that strangers would not become aware of the theft.

spirit and holding a cock he calls upon the house spirit to look after the members of the household and their animals. He then kills the cock and affixes some of its small feathers with its blood to the paper hanging on the wall which constitutes its shrine. The fowl is cooked and along with paper money offered to the spirit with a further request for protection for the household and its animals. The head of the household then casts his 'divination horns' until they show, by one falling on its face and the other on its back, that the spirit has given its assurance.[2] Only members of the household are permitted to eat the fowl. It is believed that if any non-member did partake of it the household would become unhappy and beset by misfortune.

On New Year's eve—that is on the day before the moon reappears in December—the souls of all the household members together with the souls of animals and crops are summoned to the house where they are enjoined to stay at home for the three following days of festivities. When households can afford the number, a chicken is sacrificed for each human soul; in other cases one or two chickens are offered for the souls of male members and the same number for female members; when resources are lacking even for an offering of this extent, eggs may be substituted for chickens. The offerings, with burning sticks of incense, are placed just inside the door of the house. The head of the household stands behind them looking out the door and intones: 'Today the New Year is about to come. The old year is going to pass. All souls please come home. We have plenty of food for you. Please do not believe those who are trying to persuade you to go elsewhere. Come and stay until you are old, until your hair has become white as silver. All the souls of horses, cattle, pigs and chickens please come home.'

On this day too sacrifices are made to spirits of the family line. Two or more chickens and paper money to a nominal value of 1,000 rupees, conveyed by burning, should be presented to them conjointly with a request for their help in the protection of members of the household and its crops. Similar ceremonies to cure or prevent sickness are carried out by most households once or twice at other times during the year. If there is a member of the household qualified as a priest he will conduct them. Otherwise a close relative who is a priest will be called

---

[2] The 'divination horns' are 4–5 inches long, curved, and with one side convex and the other flat. They are either of bamboo or of buffalo horn. Lyman says that the bamboo specimens are imitations of buffalo horn (Lyman, 1968, p. 12). Nusit Chindarsi says that Miao told him they were originally made from the roots of bamboo and that buffalo horn was adapted later when it was found to be more durable. They are used to determine the will of spirits on many different occasions and the interpretation of the way they fall differs according to the context of the ceremony and the questions asked. In certain ceremonies only bamboo specimens are used and must be destroyed afterwards.

on. It is said to be possible for women to become priests of this cult, but it is rare and all we have known were men.

We were present at a typical ceremony in the house of Yaitong in Meto in 1964. His eldest son, Wang, had developed a swelling in his neck. He was first treated by a Chinese trader with an injection of penicillin, which failed to show any effect. One evening shortly afterwards, his father, carrying a chicken as an offering to the ancestral spirits and a burning joss stick to attract their attention, uttered a chant, calling on Wang's soul to return to him, first at the entrance to Wang's sleeping compartment and then at the doorway of the house. The chicken was sacrificed. The ceremony was repeated at dawn the next day. The tongue of the sacrificed chicken and the colour of its skull were studied for signs of the cause of the sickness, and Lowtong cast the divination horns to find whether the ancestors had been responsible. The signs made it clear that they had. The chickens, together with an offering of paper money, were considered sufficient in the meantime, but Lowtong promised an ox when his opium harvest had been completed. He also treated his son by skin puncture learnt from Chinese. Wang recovered rapidly. The ox was not sacrificed and the failure to do so could provide an explanation for a future case of sickness which, if serious, might occasion the sacrifice.

Another class of ceremonies carried out by households are those conducted by shamans. The role of shaman is much more difficult to acquire than that of priest as it requires special characteristics to begin with and longer learning periods. The performance is more exacting because it involves not only memory of complete incantations but spirit possession. The possessing spirits do not belong to the 'ancestral' category described above; they are familiars of the shaman living in the supernatural world and they can act as his agents there. The shamans are as powerful as their familiars. They differ in their ratings, assessed by their degrees of success, but all are believed to have powerful influence. Women as well as men become shamans but generally the male practitioners have higher prestige.

Shamanistic ceremonies are more elaborate and costly than most priestly ceremonies. They are therefore engaged in by households less often, but all households wish to hold them at least every year or two. Their capacity to do so will depend upon their resources because at least one pig must be sacrificed as well as several chickens. Although the reason for a ceremony is usually a serious sickness or a specific threatening circumstance of some kind, advantage is taken of the presence of the shaman to drive away all evil influences from the household. In the secular world the ceremonies provide visible evidence of household wealth.

The marriage process

Marriage is a precondition for the formation of a new household, although it does not usually lead to it immediately because most new families begin their existence within established households from which they may separate later.

Marriages are the concern of whole families and, less intensely, of the clan groupings of which the families are parts. Their arrangement therefore follows the pattern of authority and respect within the family, based upon age and sex, but also takes into account individual rights and the desirability of achieving general agreement.

A father has the right to propose marriages for his sons and to judge upon those proposed by them or proposed by others for his daughters. He should pay regard to the opinions of older sons, especially those who are already married. Women of the family generally have less say in the matter because a wife is expected to accept her husband's decision in household affairs and the daughters are in any case almost always junior members of the household who will leave it upon marriage.

In a large household where the father himself is the son of the household head he should consult with this person, to whose opinion he should pay particular regard. Although we have no instances to confirm the practice it appears that he should do so even if the household head is not his father but his father's widow who is his mother. He should also consult with his brothers. But he has the ultimate right to decision because in matters of marriage, as in all other matters concerning family future, the subsidiary families within a household manage their own affairs.

The wishes of the person to be married are also an important consideration. This is clearer in the case of a boy than a girl, because male status is generally higher, but rarely are marriages made against the wishes of either. On occasions the couple may assert their own wishes by eloping, and will not be forcibly returned to their families. Such unions, however, cannot be regarded as marriages until bride-price has been paid, and the dependence upon the father for bride-price usually makes agreement between father and son essential.[3]

A girl is expected to accord more readily with the wishes of her family. This does not mean that her own inclinations do not often play a part because a boy is not likely to be attracted to an unwilling partner.

[3] Sometimes marriage is delayed by the inability of father and son to reach agreement. A case occurred in Meto in 1965 while we were in the village. Wang, the son of Yaitong, the village headman, was in love with a local girl of whom his father disapproved on the grounds, so he said, that her family were poor and lazy. He took his son on a visit to a village in Tak Province where he maintained there were several suitable girls. Wang looked them over and declared that all were ugly to him. Lowtong was very angry with Wang but, after a year, allowed him to marry the first girl.

If for some reason a marriage is wholly against her will she may be permitted to avoid it. Such cases are rare, but we shall refer to one which we recorded because it also illustrates an unusual form of marriage arrangement recognized by Miao custom.

It is a form of 'marriage-by-capture'.[4] A girl of another clan may be seized by a group of men as a bride for one of their clan. She may be captured only when outside her village environs. She will be taken to the house of her intended husband and the following day emissaries will be sent to present her father with the *fait accompli* of cohabitation and to negotiate bride-price. Marriage of this type will rarely be attempted with a girl from a family of secure status in a village because it will place the family at a disadvantage in bride-price negotiations and thus arouse the anger of its members and their near clansmen. It happened, however, at Meto in 1965. Pai, the pretty daughter of Bwotong of the Wang clan, was seized as she was walking to her fields by men of a Tang sub-clan including Yaitong, the village headman, and his brother Ger, as a bride for Ger's son Tong. Bwotong was the only member of his sub-clan living in Meto and was also an opium addict with little wealth. Pai was taken to Ger's house and put in a sleeping compartment with Tong, but in the evening she made an excuse to go outside and ran home. Although the Tang sub-clan demanded her return, Bwotong refused, causing Yaitong to declare that in future his clansmen would not enter into marriages with members of the Wang clan related to Bwotong wherever they lived.[5]

In marriages which follow the regular course the intention to make a proposal should be communicated by the father of the boy to all near clan relatives and ideally to all accessible members of the clan. A group of clansmen led by the father will visit the home of the girl to initiate arrangements. The girl's father will be the chief representative on her side, but his consent to the marriage should also be conditional upon that of his own family, his close clan relatives, and ideally of all accessible clansmen.

The age of marriage

It is difficult to determine the average age of marriage in a society where there is no precise reckoning of chronological ages. Some informants said that it was the girl's qualities—especially her industry and her kindness to visitors—that mattered, and her age relative to that of the boy was of no importance. Others said that boys usually

---

[4] This form of marriage is reported by Graham as occasionally occurring amongst the Ch'uan Miao of Szechuan Province in China (Graham, 1937, p. 36).

[5] Bwotong's family continued to have an unhappy history caused both by Bwotong's addiction and its relative isolation. Pai, who never did marry, took her own life by swallowing opium in 1970.

married when 15 or 16 years old and girls at about the age of 20 years. In cases we observed the boys did appear about 16 years old and the brides at least two years older. This situation accords well with the polygynous system of the Miao. Second and later wives are rarely older than their husband. The relative age seniority of the first wife gives her greater status in a society which in many ways emphasizes respect for age, and assists her in her role as the leading woman in the household.

Marriages within and outside the village

Men must marry outside their clan. This does not mean that they must necessarily marry outside their village, or village area, since most local communities are multi-clan in composition. Yet extra-local marriage is regarded as preferable. The reasons for the preference are related to the character of Miao society, which outside marriage helps to perpetuate.

There are some inducements to marriage within the local community and advantages resulting from it. The close proximity of the potential partners provides greater opportunity for courtship. Although the bride-price is usually much the same for a girl close at hand as for a girl who is taken from a strange village, in the latter case it must be paid in full before she is allowed to go whereas in the former case promises alone may suffice and be long delayed in fulfilment.

Other marriages may result from pregnancies. Love play is a permitted and highly popular game of the young unmarried men and women of different clans. Although it usually takes the form of small groups of men laying siege to one or two girls and is confined for the most part to teasing, a girl may agree to go off alone with a favoured partner, and no criticism is made of her if she does. Although it is a stated ideal of the Miao that a girl should maintain her virginity until marriage, it is also a code amongst the young that she should not resist intercourse for more than two such private meetings with the same boy-friend. The number of pregnancies resulting from the liaisons seems to be small, but they probably do precipitate some marriages.

For these reasons there are many marriages within local communities, especially when they are large and comprise several different clans. There are also factors which might appear to discourage marriage into outside communities. In such cases the receiving family will be introducing a stranger. For a girl who leaves her home to join her bridegroom in a distant place the breach is severe. She is losing the clan membership which has given her security, comfort, and companionship all the years of her life to become possessed by strangers. Many Miao songs have as their theme the sadness of a girl at departing from her relatives and village, and her fear of the servitude and loneliness that may await her. The spectacle of her leaving, as she weeps and is half-dragged away by her girl friends in the bridal party, seemed to us to express not merely a cultural mode but genuine distress.[6]

Given the advantages and the inducements to intra-village marriage and the strains associated with marriage outside the village why then do men so often seek brides further afield; why are they encouraged to do so by their families; and why do girls and their families so often oblige them?

The reason seems to be that the benefits of marriage outside the local community outweigh the disadvantages. The benefits are both short-term and long-term. Firstly there is economic advantage to a family which can gain the whole bride-price at one time, and doing so will make marriage arrangements for its sons easier. Secondly the payment of the total bride-price is an assurance to the girl that she will be highly valued, and hence probably well treated by her husband's family.

Generally marriages outside the local community are more prestigious for all the parties concerned. To seek and be sought from afar elevates the status of both boy and girl. It might also be suggested that it is more exciting. The status of the families, too, is enhanced by demonstrating wealth and the power to attract it.

The greatest long-term benefit from extra-local marriages is that they increase the range of social relationships for the marriage partners and their relatives. Not only do the new connections provide occasions for inter-visiting, thereby adding to the interest and variety of life, but more importantly they promise greater possible opportunities for resettlement, an important asset to the Miao who are constantly seeking more productive land.

Communities which are largely endogamous are often poorer communities to begin with, and their endogamy tends to perpetuate their relative poverty. The poverty plus the endogamy probably accounts for the fact that poorer communities tend to be more residentially stable than the richer communities.[7] A poor community tends to stay

---

[6] Savina, describing the bride in her new home before her friends leave, says '. . . . as she is crying she sings to her girlhood friends who are trying to console her, the touching "song of the bride" . . . part of which is "attracted by the song of the treacherous decoy, the poor forest bird is caught in the trap. Shut up in a cage, he looks with sorrow at his companions flying by. Such, alas, is my sad fate . . . Tomorrow when you leave . . . go up the slope slowly so that I can see you the longer from the bars of my prison."' (Savina, 1930, pp. 227-8.)

[7] The hypothesis does require further testing, but it appeared to be confirmed by investigations we made in Ban Meo Mor in Chiengrai Province. According to the residents, the community had been at its present location for over forty years. It was almost entirely endogamous and the reason given was that persons could not afford the bride-price for outside marriages.

stable because it does not have the wealth to make wider connections. On the other hand a wealthy community has the means to make wider connections which allow its members, when the productivity of their land begins to dwindle, to escape into richer environments. At first sight there may seem to be no reason why once they are in such an environment they should not remain as stable as any other community. The fact is, however, that the wealth and the exogamy which got them there will also tend to drive them out.

In the first place the Miao usually seek to exploit their resources to the limits of opportunity. Land in excess of subsistence needs will be planted with opium poppy, and if their means and location permit they will employ outside labourers to increase the area which they can work. Secondly, the wider connections which they have through marriages can also be utilized by others to join them in their rich environment. Their coming will be encouraged because generally the Miao favour large communities, and this is especially so when they have wealth which can give them prestige in the eyes of neighbours. Thirdly, their wealth enables them to practise polygyny, bringing more women than average directly into the community, increasing the number of children, and further widening the connections which tend to swell their numbers. When density of population and exhaustion of land make a further move imperative if standards of wealth are to be maintained, their exogamous connections provide outlets to new areas where the process may be reduplicated.

It is not to be wondered at, therefore, that marriage outside the community is favoured. It facilitates success in the geographically expanding economy which the Miao have so far been able to practice in their movement through northern Thailand. Its economic benefits, however, are dependent upon their having before them new areas to exploit, and it will be interesting to see whether as these dwindle the marriage system will become more narrow.

Polygyny

A majority of Miao men who survive until middle age will have had more than one wife simultaneously. Sometimes they have three wives and very occasionally more, but two simultaneously is the most common polygynous situation. Because men do not usually take second wives until some years after their first marriage, a majority of families at any given time in a village will have a monogamous form, but, since these families as they expand often come to include second wives, most persons in the course of their lifetimes will have direct experience of a polygynous household, either as children within it or themselves as partners in a polygynous union or as both.

Polygyny therefore is accepted as a legitimate and normal mode of marriage. There is no moral sanction either for or against it. The main value which it serves, and therefore the main inducement to it, is economic. A second wife not only increases the work-force but enables a more effective division of labour in that one wife may look after the house in the village while another attends to duties in the fields. It also tends to enhance a man's social status both by increasing his wealth potential and by making it evident that he already had enough wealth to get a second wife. A further important value which polygyny has is in ensuring family continuity for a man and his children in the event of one wife's death. Thus the practice should be seen in the context both of the Miao economy and the uncertain life span of a people without great medical resources.

Against the advantages of polygyny must be set disadvantages of which the Miao are well aware. These are less for the men than for the women. We have heard men at times complain of the difficulty of living with two women who may be in competition with each other, or sometimes of the even greater difficulty of dealing with them in combination, but generally a polygynous household produces greater rather than less ease for a man.

The situation of wives is often not so happy. Although there is no formal hierarchy, second wives have less prestige than first wives and being usually younger in age and newer members of the household they have less authority. For this reason girls are generally reluctant to become second wives and their fathers reluctant to pass them over to that condition. On the other hand senior wives often feel hurt by the competition of younger women for their husband's affection and attention. Depressed by what she felt was her husband's greater interest in his second wife, the first wife of the headman in Meto told us she would commit suicide if it were not for her love for her children. We gained the impression that if decision on Miao custom were left to the women rather than the men then the society would be monogamous.

Because of the lower intrinsic appeal of second marriages both to the girls and to their families, wealth is more important in securing them. Whereas a family may be content to wait for payment of a bride-price in the case of a first marriage, it is likely to insist on full prior payment in the case of a second marriage. The security and prestige which membership of a rich family will give to a girl, and the advantages of the connections it will provide for other members of her family may outweigh the lower social evaluation of the position of second wife.

Thus polygyny has some of the same social implications as we discussed in the case of extra-local as compared to intra-local marriage. It tends to depend upon wealth and it tends to increase wealth, although we can speak safely only of tendencies because the fortunes of families tend to rise and fall according to a variety of circumstances.

Not all second marriages are based on a cool calculation of utility. Because they have less social standing, and also because the men contracting them are in a stronger social position to press their claims against parental reluctance, the preferences of girls themselves, based on love or perception of advantage, may play a greater part than in first marriages. Their fathers, even though polygynous themselves, will usually counsel them against the unions. But they will not prohibit them, as it is believed that a girl's persistence in a desire to contract a marriage against what appears to be her best interests indicates that the spirits who sent her back to earth meant her to do so.

The event which occasions many second marriages is the pregnancy of the girl. Unmarried Miao may court freely with persons of different clans. The acceptance of polygyny extends this privilege to married men. A married man, however, should not have intercourse with a girl unless he is prepared to marry her if she becomes pregnant, and heavier sanctions in the way of a fine and public disapproval should fall upon him than upon a single man if he fails to do so.

The arrangement of second marriages is less formal than in the case of first marriages, being generally left to direct negotiations between the man contracting the marriage and the family of the woman.

The segmentation of households

As wives for sons are brought into parental homes, simple families with sons who marry will always, for a time at least, change into extended families. For two years after marriage sons are expected to work with their father and not to engage in independent cash-cropping. Members of an extended family are also united by close spiritual bonds and a morality of mutual help which are most fully expressed by their living together. Respect for the leadership status of the father further reinforces the cohesion of the group. Therefore we may say that both marital practice and ideology support the co-residence of the extended family within a single household. It is not an obligatory form of grouping, however, and there are contrary factors which tend to divide it.

If the main efforts of the members are devoted to the production of subsistence crops, a large household may be kept up without much inconvenience, and it may be advantageous. It permits the clearing of larger units of land and allows division of labour, with some adults caring for the children and the home while others work in the fields. It is probably for this reason that the growth of households appears to be greatest during the expanding phase of new settlements.

With increasing size of households difficulties may begin to arise. One of these is simply the problem of containing everybody comfortably within a single dwelling and feeding them from the single cooking place which is the physical and symbolic centre of the household. Another problem is managerial—the difficulty of maintaining a common budget. It is probable too that inter-personal tensions are more likely to occur the more complex the constitution of a household.

The greatest difficulties for extended family households develop from cash-cropping. After the first two years of marriage sons will establish their own poppy fields and begin their separate accumulation of wealth. No longer does the household head have the power to organize the work of all the members, and their differing ambitions in regard to cash-cropping may make it hard for him to get a fair sharing of subsistence activities. Richer and poorer, indolent and industrious, now share the common hearth.

In the early years of settlement, although poppy fields may be planted, enough land is usually cleared to provide the padi needs of a household. As the amount of fertile land dwindles more of it is given over to poppy until most households are able to produce less than half, and some of them none at all, of the padi they require. The household has then lost most of its utility as a common subsistence group.

It is thus in the late years of settlement that the divisive forces in a large household become strongest. This fits well with the Miao pattern of ecological adjustment[8] in the environments in which we have studied them because it is at this time that the need for further migration becomes evident.

Households may divide without migration for the reasons already stated. But migration is the most frequent occasion for division. Not only may it provide a convenient excuse for families feeling strain in a union which they do not wish to appear to disrupt without good cause, it also provides in fact a very good cause. It is both inconvenient and unsafe for large households to migrate as groups. One subsidiary family will usually move away first, knowing that it has behind it a base to which it can return should the venture prove unsuccessful.

The rest of the household may follow later. They will rarely reassemble as one household, but will take up neighbouring cultivations, the division of fields and labour force no longer posing problems

[8] Ruey, who describes a similar family structure among the Magpie Miao, or Hmong Ntzu, of southern Szechuan, gives a different explanation. He concludes, he says tentatively, that the structure has developed under influence from the Han Chinese by whom the people are surrounded, and that neo-local residence may have been the former Miao pattern (Ruey Yih-Fu, 1960, p. 147).

because they begin their farming operations separately. An obligation rests upon the youngest son to stay in the household of his father.

The segmentation may take different forms. Often it is older sons and their families who separate first. Sometimes a father accompanied by his wife and younger children may move, perhaps to an area where he has a married daughter, leaving his older sons in the village. In such a case, if two or more of the sons are married they will not long continue to live together in the same house because it is not customary, in the Miao communities we know, for married sons to participate in a common household without a parent.[9]

A form of segmentation which appears to occur fairly often is for the sons of one wife in a polygynous, or formerly polygynous, household to move away, usually after their mother has died. This is understandable in view of the fact that the household they are leaving could in time come to be headed by a woman who is not their mother. In such a case the sons may form a grouping in one or more households distinct from the groupings formed by the sons of other wives.

The segmentation of an extended family into separate households does not usually mean the complete break-up of the social group because it will persist in whole or in part as a local lineage. Brothers will tend to follow brothers and fathers to follow sons. The reunion, in the form now of household groupings, may never be complete, and it may go through a number of different alignments in various places of settlement, but in whatever areas they settle families will seek to have the company of other families of their lineage.

It may not always prove possible. A migrating family can hope to attract other related families to join it only if it can provide them with access to promising land. In most large settlement areas today one may find a few families without lineage connections with other families in the neighbourhood. They are almost always late arrivals who have found the best land already occupied.

The factor which brings them to the area in such unfavourable circumstances is usually their pre-existing poverty. They may have had to seek land in desperation at the exhaustion of their land in their old area; or when their previous group migrated they may have been the last to leave because they did not have food stocks or silver to support them in a pioneering enterprise. Their poverty will tend to perpetuate itself. Their lack of lineage connections where they now are will mean less chance to profit from new migrations, and their relative poverty

[9] This does not accord with the statement of Ruey: 'Not infrequently, however, brothers continue to live together after the death of their parents, or a young married couple may go to live with an older brother of the husband . . .' At Meto, there were no cases of this, and although it may occur amongst the Thailand Miao, it is certainly not frequent (Ruey, 1960, p. 145).

will give them less status in the community and therefore poorer opportunity to improve their connections through favourable marriages. Thus some families may remain poor even for generations.

Such families are not common but their existence does point up the importance of lineage and close clan connections in providing entry to communities and prosperity once there.

THE VILLAGE

A map of Miao areas in Thailand would show settlements varying from two to three households to a hundred or more. The distribution would not be uniform. In some areas there may be a single large village; in others all the houses may be dispersed in a number of small clusters; or, most commonly, there may be a main village with a few small clusters in other parts of the territory.

An analogy could be with a flock of birds of a socially inclined mountain species, each bird representing a household. Sometimes a whole flock settles together. Sometimes it is scattered in smaller groups. Sometimes the main part of the flock is in one place but there are a few smaller groups picking on the outskirts. Solitary birds are rarely seen. Those which do forage on the outskirts of the flock will often rejoin it to stay with it or just to share its companionship for a while. Sooner or later, when food is exhausted in the area, the whole flock flies off to seek new mountainsides, passing over the territories of alien species in between. They may not all keep together. Some fly away to join other flocks from which perhaps their mates have come.

The analogy is not far-fetched. Yaitong, the headman of Meto village, used a simpler, ruder version of it when he told us that the Miao in regard to land were like vultures which fly in search of dead animals. When they find them they stop to eat. When they finish eating they fly in search of others. Savina, too, quotes a Miao proverb: 'Fish swim in the water, birds fly in the air, and the Miao live on the mountains'.[10] As with the birds in the analogy, two factors influence the settling patterns of the Miao—the desire to get the best pickings they can from the countryside and their love of the company of their kind.

Savina, speaking of the Miao of Laos, suggests that they have a preference for small settlements:

There are indeed Miao villages containing fifteen, twenty, or even thirty houses, but they are rare and much less numerous than those containing only five, six, or even two or three houses. In short, the Miao do not seem to like

[10] Savina, 1930, p. 172.

big settlements. They prefer to live in little groups making up hamlets rather than real villages.[11]

Bernatzik, too, on the basis of his observations in Thailand, states that 'the villages of the Meau consist of only a few houses'.[12]

Savina, however does not tell us how close the hamlets were to one another, or what relationships their distribution bore to the total population of an area, to the length of settlement in it, or to its fertility. Bernatzik apparently encountered recent pioneers into Thailand who were not yet in sufficient numbers to have developed more extensive settlements.

Certainly today in Thailand there are many settlements of thirty or more houses and quite a few of a hundred or more, although it is true that there is often some dispersion of sections within the total settlements, which might therefore be better called 'village complexes' rather than villages. The situation as we interpreted it is that, in the absence of economic incentives to the contrary, the Miao prefer large settlements because of the satisfaction and security they give, but their type of farming disperses them to a greater and less degree and for shorter or longer periods.

During the pioneering of a new area the number of households will at first be small, and different groups of migrants may settle in various parts of the territory. If the fertility and size of the area allow it, some of the settlement centres will grow through further immigration, and then the attraction of their greater size may draw in other groups from the other parts of the territory. Thus a large village, or village complex, is formed which at its peak may embrace all the residents in an area.

As time goes on, however, a new dispersion may occur. When a village is first formed, the farms are usually close to it, but when the nearby land is exhausted the farms get further away. The difficulty of a village distant from the fields is mitigated by the fact that every household has a shelter of some kind on its farm. Usually it is only a small hut, but in some cases it may grow to a secondary house with a barn attached. In many cases only some members of the household will stay in the farmhouse at any time, leaving at least one or two persons in the village house. In other cases, the whole family will close their village house and live for lengthy periods on their farm. The situation will depend a little on the age composition of the household, old people tending to spend more time in the village.

Even when it is not used a great deal as a residence a village house may retain some value. The Miao keep many pigs and fowls because in this way they can use the large quantities of maize which they grow

[11] Ibid., p. 182.   [12] Bernatzik, 1947, p. 102.

on their poppy fields. The animals are taken with them to the farm-house for much of the time, but they should be kept away when crops are young. The village house provides a base for them at such times, and is also a convenient base for other economic activities such as cloth-making. On the other hand there is the disadvantage of the long walks to and from the fields. It requires therefore more than economic reasons to explain why the people are reluctant to give up their village houses.

The village is the centre of community life. A house there provides identification, prestige, companionship, and security. It acts as a magnet holding households attached to it even when their farms lie far beyond its outskirts. But it can do so only as long as enough people stay there to make it worth while as a social centre. In time some families grow weary of the constant journeying. The secondary houses become their main and only houses. Others migrate elsewhere. The dwindling village loses its attraction and is abandoned. If parts of the territory are still capable of further exploitation groups of houses there may form the nuclei of new smaller settlements. Otherwise the households which no longer have a village centre in their neighbour-hood will seek to migrate to where they can be reunited in larger communities.

The clan composition of villages

Most Miao villages or village complexes in Thailand comprise sections of several clans because this is the composition which provides the most satisfactory social life. Describing the Cowrie Shell Miao in China, Mickey says that each village usually has only one surname[13] —that is to say, one clan. We never encountered this situation in Thailand and it probably occurs only in fairly densely populated areas where there are other villages with different clans not far away.

The situation in Thailand can be accounted for by the migratory pattern which is still generally followed. If people move into a new area distant from other Miao, then they will want an association of at least two clans and if possible of several. Often the move is deliberately planned to produce this situation, but sometimes it just develops owing to the fact that relationships which induce or facilitate migration are not just clan ties but marriage connections which imply differences of clan.

If the village area is very large, as in the case of Meto, all or the major-ity of a particular clan may live in a cluster of houses separated from the others by any distance from a hundred yards to a few miles. A ten-dency to clan cohesion becomes manifest with growing population. Given long stability of residence in an area, the clans may come to occupy

[13] Mickey, 1947, p. 9.

separate villages, as they did in the case of the group studied by Mickey, but they will probably remain linked as parts of a wider social complex.

The importance of the village

The local community—be it a single large village, a cluster of villages, or a main village with smaller satellites—offers economic, social religious, and political advantages. Its main economic importance is that it is usually a trading centre. Opium buyers will come there, and a large village usually has one or several stores run by Chinese or Thai traders.

Socially, the village is the venue of a large part of the excitement in Miao lives, in small daily events or on special periodic occasions. Those who have a house there can obtain a much better share of it and a bigger village is more exciting than a small one.

For the young, courting, to which we have already referred, is a great pastime which a large village offers in good measure. On the fine evenings, especially when work in the fields is light, it is a common sight to see boys dilly-dallying in a house carrying blankets under their arms before moving out in courting parties. On the edges of the village the boys will seek to pet the girls, and in most cases, the night is spent in the art of concession and retreat—coaxing, yielding, and resisting in the semi-public shade. There was some difference as to the age at which boys should begin courting. All informants agreed that they should not be too young, and then one man, trying to be more specific, said they should be at least seven years old. Although not at quite such an early age, practice does begin before adolescence. Courting is by far the most popular game of the young. It cannot be played alone. It cannot be played with one's clansfolk. The village provides the best milieu and the most exciting variety.

The village is also the theatre for more organized festivities ranging from household ceremonies to greater occasions involving large parts or the whole of the village community. Even the smaller ceremonies which offer only limited participation provide spectacle, and for everybody the sense of important things happening.

By far the largest and most popular festivities are those of the great New Year Festival. This begins on the first day of the waxing moon in the twelfth month, provided the padi harvest has been completed. If it has not been completed, the spirits must be asked to allow a postponement until the following moon. Thus the Festival is partly a harvest festival and partly a festival to make the new year begin with a beneficent aspect. Everyone comes back to the village for it. So too do the souls of the crops. On the morning it begins, a member of each household visits its fields to call them. He brings back a sheaf of padi from the field stack and some maize from the granary in the field hut. The soul of the opium is called but none is collected as in most fields the poppy heads are not yet ripe for tapping.

A large part of the enjoyment comes from the Festival games. There is top-playing for the men, skipping, and stick- and sword-dancing, often to the accompaniment of pan pipes.[14] But of all the festival games none other matches in colour, gaiety, and interest the ball game which is played by the young persons of both sexes and played only at the Festival.

The Miao ball game is essentially a courting game played to the general delight of the village. It is a simple game, its attractions being the spectacle of bright, intricate costumes and the adventures of love which it mediates. Boys and girls, in opposing lines anywhere from twenty to fifty feet apart, throw soft black cloth balls to one another. On the first day of the Festival, partnerships are random and constantly changing. By the second day boys and girls are becoming selective, tentatively matching themselves in challenges of love in which, to conquer, the boy must prove his superior skill.

The contest is gentle. The ball must be thrown so that it can be caught with both hands. If it can be reached with only one hand and the catcher misses, no penalty is incurred. But if it is a legitimate throw and the catcher misses, then a forfeit can be called for by the thrower. It will be some article of adornment—a sash, a silver belt, or another dispensable part of the festival costume. At night, when the games are over, the boy may go to the girl's home and from the wall outside the part of the house where he knows she will be call her softly. Or he may play a jew's harp, the tunes of which can be varied to convey messages. He calls upon her to come out to redeem her forfeits.

Every unmarried girl tries to have a new kilt ready for wearing for the first time at the New Year Festival. Nearly all the moments that can be spared from duties in the house or fields throughout the year go into its elaborate silken embroidery and into the making of her jacket with its decorated collar,[15] her turban, and her other accoutrements. She

---

[14] Bernatzik, 1947, p. 64, says that the original meaning of the top-playing has been lost and contrasts this ignorance with the situation among the Lahu tribe where it is believed that the playing of the game gives the spirits special pleasure. The Miao in Meto, however, declared that this was a reason for all the festival games.

Other writers report similar beliefs of the Miao elsewhere. e.g., Savina writes: 'All these games which take place at the new year are called Dha Cha, dances of renewal, by the Miao' (Savina, 1930, p. 224). Broumton, writing in 1881 of a visit to tribes in Kweichow, says that they have a tradition that if the festival is not celebrated they will have a bad year (Broumton, 'A Visit to the Miao-Tsze Tribes of South China', *Proceedings of the Royal Geographical Society*, No. 3, 1881, p. 226).

[15] The full beauty of the costume is not to be seen by every eye. The collar is decorated only on the inner side.

must have silver neck rings to go with the costume—the more she has the more she shines—silver ear-rings, silver bracelets, and, if possible, silver finger rings as well. The unmarried boys should also have new costumes and everyone present at the Festival should wear at least one silver ring on their neck. For babies there are decorated hats, different for a boy and a girl.

The village is important not only at festival times and as an adventure ground for love but also as a field of social relationships of many kinds. Inevitably the clans intermarry, creating a network of affinal ties crossing clan lines. These and other ties of friendship broaden social life, for the adults and for the children, providing support in trouble, mediation in disputes, and greater honour in death. Interweaving with one another and with the clan ties, the networks contribute to the over-all cohesion of the village.

At the simplest level the very fact that on certain important occasions all the households carry out the same actions at the same time provides some acknowledgement of village identification. For instance, the first morning of the New Year Festival is the time when every household honours the house spirit, killing a pig as a sacrifice and a basis for the feasting to follow, and invoking prosperity for the household members, their animals, their implements, their weapons, their money, their silver, their padi, and their opium. At a wider level of group co-operation there are the ceremonies during the Festival at which members of each local clan or sub-clan assemble to give offerings of alcohol and food and to make obeisance to their elders; or those at which some clans pay honour to others with which they have particularly valuable relationships.

There may be other ceremonies which more explicitly symbolise village unity. Often there is a local mountain spirit which is regarded as the guardian of the village. At Meto it was believed to inhabit a tree of near-perfect shape close to the peak of Umlong. On the second day of the New Year Festival a ceremony was carried out to secure its good will in the coming year. Each household supplied paper money to burn at the foot of the tree. Emissaries of the clans climbed to the tree, and at an altar affixed to it offered chickens and maize alcohol.

Although representatives of all the clans in Meto participated in the ceremony, it was first instituted and thereafter conducted by the Jang clan, which was the only one in Meto which knew the details and made a practice of carrying it out in the villages with which it was associated. It is not therefore a universal aspect of village religious activity. Nevertheless, it is clearly a widespread and probably long established feature of the culture of many Miao groups. Schotter, writing of groups in Kweichow, remarks that every village worships some tree or stone, which is particularly effective when situated on a hill higher than the houses which it can thus watch, which is its duty.[16] Vannicelli gives the following description, derived from a report in the *Chinese Recorder* of 1931, of a ceremony carried out by the Hua ('Flowery') Miao in the same Province. Apart from details such as buckwheat instead of padi and the month in which it is held, the ceremony parallels closely that which we witnessed in Meto in 1964:

The sacred tree is situated on a hill and is regarded as the protector of the village. To cut its bark or break a branch is sacrilege. A ceremony of public worship is performed to it by a priest at the second moon, before the work in the fields commences. Fertility is sought for the fields and for the cattle. Although this is a public ceremony, women cannot take part, but children can. Buckwheat and a rooster are needed for the sacrifice. The priest builds a little altar of branches near the tree and, kneeling before it, divines whether the tree will accept the sacrifice. If the omen is propitious, the priest proceeds to kill the bird, cutting its throat and holding it so that its blood runs onto the trunk of the tree above the altar. During the ceremony the worshippers stand in front or at the side of the tree, but they are not allowed to stand behind it. The rooster and buckwheat are then boiled. After being cooked, three pieces of flesh, a part of the claw and part of the wing, together with four small portions of buckwheat are placed at the side of the altar, while the priest recites the following prayer: 'O tree! O hill! We pray you to guard our village. Protect us from the tiger, from the wolf, from the leopard, from thieves, from destructive rains, from hail and from illness.'[17]

The village as a political unit

The identification of members with a village and the concept of collective interest which the shared activities and common ceremonies promote is important for its successful operation as a political unit. The village was probably traditionally a political unit, but in Thailand, as in most other modern situations of the Miao, its position in this respect has been affected by the national administration, which may give official status to a selected headman. How well he succeeds will depend upon how closely his qualities accord with those which the people consider desirable in a leader.

Leadership operates in two spheres—mundane affairs and those concerning the supernatural. For convenience we may call the two types of leadership 'secular' and 'religious', and initially discuss them separately although in practice the two types are not always separable and the most powerful leader is the person who combines both roles.

[16] A. Schotter, 'Notes ethnographiques sur les tribus de Kouy-Tschou (Chine)', *Anthropos*, Vol. 6, 1911, pp. 324–5.

[17] Luigi Vannicelli, 'Il culto religioso presso i miao', *Festschrift anlasslich des 25-jahrigen Bestandes des Institutes fur Volkerkunde der Universitat Wien, 1929–1954*, Verlag Ferdinand Berger, Vienna, 1956, section 3.

The secular leader should first of all be a man highly regarded by his own clan for his judgement and selected by consensus as the most suitable person for the office. He may not be the most senior man in the clan because the Miao prefer to have active men as their leaders and older men appear to relinquish office willingly, favouring the man in the next generation of their clan who appears to have the best talents for the position. Secondly, he should belong to the predominant clan in the village. Most villages do have one clan numerically stronger than others, a situation which is usually determined by the circumstances of the migration.

From various causes the actualities of leadership may diverge from the ideal. This may occur especially when the leader is appointed by the Government agency and given a charter which will keep him in office despite changes in village political circumstances. For instance, in Meto a complex situation developed. At the time of the first settlement a man called Jusu, the leading member of the Jang clan, was appointed. He too, being also a leading shaman, located and honoured the mountain spirit and so got spiritual support for his leadership. At this time the Jang and Tang clans were about equally represented among the settlers. Later Tang numbers grew to predominance. Jusu fell out of favour with the sub-district head, a Thai official from a lowland village, and also lost popularity with the villagers because opium addiction made him unreliable. The sub-district head appointed Yaitong of the Tang clan in his place.

The capacity of Yaitong to lead the village was reduced by the behaviour of Jusu who, dissatisfied, moved away to a hamlet consisting mainly of his Jang clansmen on the outskirts of the village territory. Being now out of the area under the influence of the mountain spirit, he felt no need to honour it at the subsequent New Year Festival. Yaitong could not do so as he was not a priest of the right category in any case and he lacked the special relationship to the spirit which Jusu had as its discoverer and medium. He and the village generally felt uncomfortable on the territory of a spirit now possibly alienated from them. Declining crop yields and sickness in the households were attributed to this cause, and the following year the village dispersed.

So long as he holds office a headman always receives at least some respect. This may be given a ceremonial expression at the time of the New Year Festival, as at Meto in 1964 when groups representing all clans in the area visited Yaitong's house separately during the three days of the festival to express their regard and bow down before him. They also bowed down before the certificate of his official appointment which he had placed on the spirit altar in his house as a mark of respect for the Thai District Officer (Nai Amphur) who had presented it to him.

The respect allows the headman to act as a village arbiter and to some extent as a judge. A clan may be able to deal with disputes between its own members or offences against the law which involve only them. Even so, it may be useful to have present when they discuss the issues a prestigious outsider who can be impartial. The headman rarely has a greater role than this in purely clan cases.

Most disputes in a village, however, concern more than one clan. The commonest offences against Miao law are paternity outside marriage and adultery, and the commonest disputes are those resulting from failure to fulfil marriage obligations, such as non-payment of bride-price, desertion, alleged improper care of children, and so on. Paternity cases always concern two clans and the other types of cases also usually do so. These are the cases, therefore, in which the headman's role is most important. His office is superimposed on the clan structure to allow the territorial group to function as a political community.

The headman has no hereditary title and he knows that the writ of a Government when it is granted to him, although it may be pleasing, cannot make him a king. He is aware that in Miao eyes his tenure of office is dependent upon the good will of the people. He has a self-interest in preserving as much autonomy as possible for individual men because he is conscious that future migrations may place him in communities where he is not headman. Therefore, he is never authoritarian. Although he has the final power of decision, the part he is expected to play in cases is as a promoter of consensus and as its mouthpiece. He sits as a member of an informal panel of jurymen comprising usually the interested parties, or senior men of their households or local clan representing them, other leading men of the village, and anyone else at all who may care to come, although generally only men attend.

The headman does have another more difficult role. This is to represent his village in dealing with outside authorities. Frequently these authorities treat him as a person with more power than he has, regarding the village as monolithic. In both directions of the communication process this may cause misunderstanding or complete disruption of relationships. In many cases a headman cannot answer for his whole community without consulting with them. Therefore he may quickly come to be regarded as indecisive or even stupid, and this may happen all the more easily the more accomplished he is as a leader in his own sphere. On the other hand, he may be required to execute unpopular orders. Lacking the authority to do so, he may alienate the support upon which his leadership depends. The response of the Miao to these potentially untenable situations is to insulate themselves as completely as possible from outside interference and to flee to further away into the hills when it begins to impinge too heavily upon them.

Disputes in which the headman is required to adjudicate are quite rare, perhaps only a few each year. Aspects of Miao belief and practice stress harmony within the community. For instance, at the time of the New Year Festival houses convey invitations to other houses to visit them for food and alcoholic drink. Special cakes made by beating glutinous rice, mixing it with sugar, wrapping portions in leaves, and baking them are presented to friendly neighbours and relatives. During the three days of the Festival no debts may be asked for or paid.

The village as a religious community

The village is more than a potential union and more than a social circle giving richness and variety to lives. It provides security, first for the group as a whole against the real and imagined dangers of the world around, and secondly for individual members against the supernatural world. Just as nearly every village has a headman who assists in human disputes and is a mediator in contacts with the outside world, so too in nearly every village there is at least one shaman who assists in troubles with the spirits and acts as a medium in contact with the supernatural world.

The main work of the shamans is in connection with sickness, in either its cure or prevention. Sickness is not always directly attributed to the action of spirits. It may be recognized to have a natural cause, especially in the case of accidents, and can be treated on this basis by medicines and the removal of the immediate cause. But even in such 'natural' cases there remains the question 'Why did it happen?', or 'Why did it happen to this person rather than another?' Supernatural selection of the victim is implied. In cases where no immediate cause is apparent, events in the supernatural world are assumed to be directly responsible. The shaman has eyes to see into this world, or ritual means of finding out what goes on there; he can make contact with its spiritual inhabitants and influence what happens in it.

The supernatural world—the arena of the shaman's operations—is all that part of the total world and those aspects of the known world which are unseeable by ordinary human eyes. Its population is various and its territories diverse. The Miao believe that a person has several souls. Often the number is said to be seven. One or more may become separated from the body, trapped or wandering. This is especially likely to happen in the case of children, whose souls get lost at the junction of tracks, confused how to get back home. Faced by the consequent weakness or sickness of the child in the village, the parents may call upon the services of a shaman, who will diagnose the cause and will usually prescribe that a bridge, wooden in the natural world but of silver and gold in its supernatural aspect, be built at the junction. The child is taken to the far side where it can meet its soul again. Then, at the call of the shaman, it is led by a passer-by across the bridge, its soul, attracted by the splendour, coming with it. On the outskirts of many Miao villages, the remnants of such bridges, sometimes with straw canopies over them, can be seen.

In the majority of cases of sickness soul separation is believed to be a factor. Usually there is a cause for it in some omission—in the case of children mentioned above, it may be a lapse of tenderness or care on the part of the parents—or in some wrongful act or neglect of duty. But it may be due to accident, such as carrying out an action at an inauspicious time or crossing a snare for souls. Heads of households who are priests know the formulas for calling souls back. They may also be able to diagnose the cause of the loss by guessing, and testing the accuracy of the guesses by casting divination horns. But they have no power to see into the supernatural world or to communicate directly with it. Therefore in difficult cases a shaman must be called in.

In the supernatural world, even in that part of it which encompasses the village world, there are spirits of many different kinds which may interfere with the living and are often the agents of soul separation. A shaman can communicate with them pacifying them bargaining with them, or driving them away according to their nature and strength.

Another territory of the supernatural is the land where the souls of the dead, which in time become the souls of the ready-to-be-born, dwell. The spirits in this land determine the length of life a person will have on earth. It is believed that each person is given a licence to live so long. His life can be expected to end when the licence runs out, but it seems that infringement of the conditions of the licence, or perhaps misadventure, may end it sooner.

Even when the licence has run its full course, there may still be hope, as a person may obtain an extension. His chances of doing so are better if he has a shaman to act as his advocate. The shamans themselves are believed to be persons living on extended time. Almost invariably they have discovered their supernatural powers after a prolonged, severe illness. They are believed to have ended their natural lives, been to the spirit world, and been given permission to return awhile to the living as intermediaries between the two worlds, to each of which they in part belong.

There is another belief commonly held that all living persons have counterparts in the spirit world on whose fate their living fate may partly depend. These counterpart souls, as we may call them, are the servants of the spirits. In some cases they are believed to be their domestic animals. The shamans may be able to influence what happens to them in order to protect the living. For instance, in Meto a child was thought to be failing in health. A shamanistic ceremony was carried out and the shaman declared that the counterpart soul of the boy was a pig in the other world which the spirits required to slaughter for a festival. He ordered a pig to be sacrificed so that the life of the boy could be spared.[18]

From this brief account of some of the religious beliefs of the Miao it can be seen that the shaman is a very important person to them. He is their chief hope in crises, their only powerful doctor, and their guide in many actions where there is danger or doubt as to the outcome. It is no wonder, therefore, that households prefer to live where there are shamans. The shamans, on their part, prefer to live where there are clients.

Relatively few persons become shamans. They must have the right mentality for it, have undergone an ordeal by illness, and possess the memory, acting ability, and energy to carry out the ritual, which involves continuous rapid shaking and chanting, interspersed with acrobatic jumps, for several hours. Shamans even of average capacity are fairly rare.

The availability of shamans is one of the main reasons why Miao live in villages. If possible, they like to have several available because of the variety and greater range of spiritual resources which they provide. The presence of a particularly powerful shaman enhances the attractiveness of a village. His departure means the loss of a most valued service and also a loss of reputation for the community. If all shamans leave a village then it will probably not long endure.

Shamans do not belong to any particular clan and may be either men or women, although by far the greater number are men. Frequently they are more than doctors utilizing supernatural aid to diagnosis and cure. They are also leaders in village affairs. The reasons for this are partly secular. Being almost always older persons, they have the experience which age brings in a relatively stable cultural system. Often they are of more than average intelligence and wisdom. They have the public attention which allows these qualities to be recognized. In addition, they have access to knowledge of supernatural forces which the Miao regard as likely to affect any of their activities at any time.

A village headman who is not a shaman may be handicapped if there is also a highly regarded shaman in the village. If the shaman is of the same lineage or even of the same clan, the headman's prestige may not suffer because the two may co-operate. But if they are of different clans, then an uneasy situation may arise which may make the village a less contented place and hasten its disintegration when declining economic

---

[18] There is also a pantheon of superior gods, but the shaman has little or no relationship with them and they exercise only a very general influence over the affairs of men.

conditions lead the people to contemplate more attractive alternatives.

The most favoured village leaders, therefore, are persons who are also shamans. This means that leadership is rooted in the ideology of the Miao—in their total world view, including their concepts of the supernatural. The result is to reinforce their ethnic consciousness because the leadership symbolizes and may actively support values and beliefs distinctive to them. Failure to appreciate this fact accounts for many of the difficulties experienced by agencies seeking to change the Miao way of life. They assume a purely economic motivation and a leadership based upon secular performance, and therefore do not appreciate the wider implications of their programmes. The resistance of the people is frequently compounded by the agents' displaying, through their uniforms, their loyalties, or their religious practices, a different ideology, thus arousing opposition not explained by the narrow situations with which they are intending to deal.

Conclusion

The village is the largest local grouping of the Miao. Membership of a village is always present as an intention if not a reality. All households realize it periodically, if not permanently or semi-permanently, on a greater or lesser scale. But the Miao are a pioneering people who can tolerate small-group or even family loneliness in a wide countryside. Therefore they will forgo membership of a village if it cannot give them the satisfaction they expect from it.

The benefits which a village provides are several. It offers first of all security in numbers, and for this reason alone households may tend to congregate in large groups if the environment for some reason is regarded as potentially hostile. For instance, the pioneers at Meto moved into an area where their presence aroused opposition from the surrounding Karen tribesmen and depended upon the doubtful tolerance of Thai local officials. Therefore there was great advantage in establishing a strong presence. Secondly, village living is more physically comfortable because a large house can be maintained in guarded surroundings distinct from scattered field huts. Thirdly, it provides opportunity for the utilization of wealth to produce a richer social life. In fact, the form to which most wealth is converted—silver neck rings made to a traditional pattern—is such that it requires other Miao to appreciate it. Thus silver is a social magnet drawing the people together.

For these reasons persons fortunate enough to settle in areas of fertile land, instead of trying to preserve it all for themselves, will encourage newcomers. By its growth, however, a large village produces its own disintegration. Owing to intense farming agricultural yields decline. Once the people can no longer maintain a surplus of wealth over subsistence needs a village loses most of its pleasure because it will have no prestige as a unit, the festivals will decline in splendour, and the people will not have much silver to display to one another's eyes. From this cause alone, if the land in the neighbourhood of a village is showing signs of losing its capacity to produce a surplus, thoughts will turn to abandoning it. Stimulus to the thoughts will be added by the fact that the increasing length of journeys to their fields may outweigh in their discomfort the comfort of the houses in the villages. Finally sheer necessity may press the people. Their primary need is to maintain subsistence. When they can no longer find it in the territory of a village then they must seek it elsewhere.

Therefore, although there are some villages which appear to have been stable for decades, most Miao in north Thailand are involved in a more or less continuous process of congregation and dispersion. In the case of Meto, we shall attempt to show how this process is made almost inevitable by the nature of their economy in the environment in which they live.

PART TWO

METO VILLAGE AND ITS AGRICULTURAL ECONOMY

CHAPTER FIVE

METO VILLAGE AND ITS INHABITANTS

The Blue Miao of Meto, who are the subjects of this study, occupied an elevated strip of country between the peaks of Umlong and Meto in the Province of Chiengmai at a location approximately 18° 15′ north latitude and 18° 15′ east latitude. In 1966 the main settlement was on a spur of Umlong mountain itself, so that outsiders would generally refer to this main village, together with nearby smaller settlements, as Ban Miao Umlong, or the Miao village of Umlong. The Miao residents referred to it as Hang Mae Umlong. The principal planting area, however, was closer to the Meto mountain. Even in 1965 there was one small village known as Boreh in this neighbourhood, and by the end of 1966 all the Miao remaining in the district had moved there. It is convenient, therefore, to refer to the whole group of people as the Meto Miao and to the various settlements as the Meto complex.

Typically of Miao settlements in Laos and northern Thailand, and indeed in much of southern China, the Meto people occupied a relatively small area of hilltop land entirely surrounded by the territory of different tribes. The pioneers had looked for land suitable for opium poppies, which imposed the condition that none of it must be below 3,000 feet above sea level. They found an area, part of which had never been occupied, and the remainder of which was temporarily unoccupied. They allowed it to fill up with relatives, friends, and other Miao tribesmen attracted by the prospect of bountiful crops. They exploited it to the maximum of their technology, their available energy, its natural fertility, and the labour they could secure from neighbouring peoples.

The main village at Umlong was at a height of 3,700 feet above sea level and about 2,500 feet above the level of the nearest valley floors. The lowest temperature we recorded in 1964–5 was 42 °F (5·5 °C.) on 31 December 1964, at 11 p.m. During December and January, night temperatures are frequently around this figure and daytime shade temperatures in the low sixties. At the height of the hot season in March they may be as much as twenty degrees Fahrenheit (6·6 °C.) higher and, during the monsoon season, ten to fifteen degrees higher. These figures mean that the climate is markedly colder than that of the Chiengmai plain where the Thai people live. To a visitor from a temperate climate it is extremely pleasant, especially during the bright, cool, sunny days of December and January. It probably is so to everyone, as indicated by the fact that the King of Thailand has had a palace built at approximately the same height on the mountain immediately behind Chiengmai. To the Miao conditioned to the greater coolness, settlement in the plains would require a big change in adaptation.

No fields were visible from the main village, and to reach the nearest one involved a climb of several hundred feet and about half an hour's walk. One may speculate why this large settlement was located on a steep ridge running down into a valley so inconveniently situated in relation to the planting area. The Miao generally prefer to build on a slope because, their houses having earth floors, good drainage is required in the wet season. But neither the aspect of the slope nor the direction of the house being important to them, plenty of suitable slopes could be found in the field area. Water supplies would be a more critical factor. Because the Miao settle near the tops of the hills, a water supply adequate for the dry season is often difficult to find. The Umlong site, being at the source of a large stream, provided enough water for a large village.

Another reason for choosing the Umlong site was that the early settlers cultivated land to the west as well as to the east of the village, which was therefore fairly central. It did not remain central for the majority of the population for very long, however, and therefore one suspects other reasons for the persistence and growth of the settlement on the increasingly inconvenient location. Such a reason could have been the wish to the people not to have visitors easily associate them with extensive opium fields, which were less embarrassing if kept out of sight and protected by a precipitous path from an already weary official. Since 1957 opium has been an illegal crop. Earlier than that the crop was supposed to be sold to a Government monopoly which paid far less than the unofficial price. At times various officials have demanded a proportion of the crop as payment for their good will, and this proportion—usually a very low one in Thailand—has been assessed according to what was thought to be the total production.

The selection of inconspicuous sites for settlements appears to be a long-established tendency of the Miao. In his *History of the Miao* Savina states that their villages are usually placed in a hidden position.[1] In some situations, however, it is impossible to conceal them and in other cases the advantages, if any, of doing so are outweighed by the convenience of more prominent sites. By 1966 any battle to preserve the anonymity or to conceal the extent of the poppy fields was lost. Too many visitors had come into the area. Perhaps because there was no longer anything to gain by remaining where they were, the households

[1] Savina, 1930, p. 182.

which had stayed at Umlong resettled themselves in the centre of the planting area.

THE VILLAGE POPULATION

In 1965 the total number of Miao people in the Meto region was 570, comprising 262 males and 308 females.[2] Four clans were represented in the area. The Tang clan was predominant, the others in order of numbers being Wang, Jang, and Yang. In 1965 Tang numbers were increased by the migration to Meto of a group of 42 persons belonging to a different sub-clan who came from Chiengrai Province. Even without this addition, which lasted only a year, the Tang had twice as many persons as the next largest clan and comprised 52 per cent of the total Miao population of the Meto region.

In addition to the Miao, there also resided at Umlong a number of Chinese traders originating from Yunnan Province. It appears that traditionally the Yunnanese have associated with the Miao in the role of contacts with the outside commerical world, supplying trade goods in exchange for local products. As the Miao have migrated southwards from China, the Yunnanese have accompanied them whenever possible in a generally mutually beneficial symbiotic relationship. In Meto there were seven Yunnanese trading establishments in the main village. This high number reflected the current success of the opium harvests. Not all the activity of the Chinese directly concerned opium. Some of the trading was for money which the Miao people acquired by selling their opium to other larger traders who sent buyers periodically into the settlement.

There is no set order in the way houses are built in a village nor is a particular direction significant. Houses no longer required by their owners may be sold or given away, and abandoned house sites may be built on by anyone else. In regard to all land, whether for farming or home sites, ownership is validated in Miao eyes by use—either actual use or declared intended use in the near future. It is a concept consistent with their migratory way of life and one which they have an interest in upholding because they often seek to move into territory previously occupied by other people.

The fact that the predominant factor in residential group formation, maintenance, and dispersion is clan membership, is shown by the

[2] The ratio in favour of females was also noted in the village of Pasamliem which I studied in 1958. It was characteristic of all clans in Meto in 1965, the ratios of males to females being: Tang 0·81; Wang 0·97; Jang 0·73; Yang 0·73. It is not, however, shown in the figures in the Thailand Government Survey of 1965 which gave estimated totals for the Miao of 27,043 males and 25,988 females. Also, Mickey's report on the Cowrie Shell Miao of China shows a slightly greater number of males (Mickey, 1947, p. 16).

settlement pattern in Meto. In 1965 there were 71 Miao dwelling houses in the Meto area. The majority of them were in groups which we have marked on the Settlement Map as Villages A, B, C, D, E, F, and the Village of Boreh. There were three separate dwelling houses in different parts of the countryside. In regard to Villages A, B, C, and D, the separation between them was largely due to the constraints of the terrain, so that they can be considered as one large settlement which we shall refer to as the A-B-C-D complex, or as 'the main village'. Within it, A consisted of 21 houses stretched down a spur of Umlong mountain; B with 5 houses and C with 6 houses were separated only by a small valley; D with 12 houses was further away across a deeper valley but visible from other parts of the complex. Village E with 13 houses was over the far side of the hill beyond D, and Village F with 4 houses around a further curve of the same hill. The village of Boreh with 7 houses was about four miles walking distance from Village F.

CLAN DISTRIBUTION IN THE METO COMPLEX

Diagram 3 lists the names of the leading person in each household and shows the households' clan membership. In the main village area, A–B–C–D, the Tang clan was clearly predominant. In Village A there were only four houses which were non-Tang. Three of these—Nos. 13, 20, and 21—were Jang. This is primarily explained by the circumstances of the original migration when a Jang man, Jusu, who subsequently moved his house to Boreh village, accompanied Tang men as one of the pioneers of the area. Since that time, a further link with Tang had developed in the case of House 20 through the marriage of its head with a Tang woman. The remaining non-Tang household, No. 14, was Wang. The link here was to the Jang group through the fact that the head was related to the wife in House 13.

In Village B there was only one non-Tang household, No. 22. The head of this household, Sertoa, was an old man who in fact died in 1965. His deceased elder son was married to a Tang woman and his younger son was unmarried. Therefore, he settled with the Tang because his daughter-in-law, the only woman in the economically productive generation, could have the support of close relatives.

Village C, comprising the migrants from Chiengrai Province, was entirely Tang. In Village D, five of the twelve houses were non-Tang, four of them being Wang and one Yang. The head of the Yang household and the heads of three of the Wang households had wives who were Tang. The remaining Wang household was there because of close kinship links with the other Wang households. Thus in the A–B–C–D complex thirty-four of the forty-four houses, or 77·3 per cent were

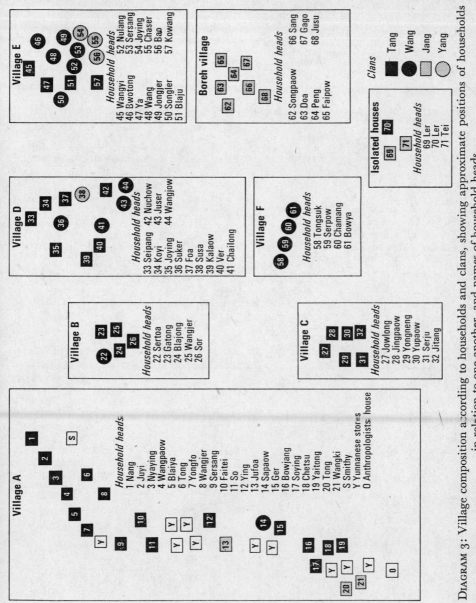

Village E

45	46
47	48	49	54
50	51	52	53	55
57	56

Household heads

45 Wangyi   52 Nulang
46 Bwotong   53 Sersang
47 Ya   54 Joying
48 Wang   55 Chaser
49 Jongler   56 Bao
50 Songler   57 Kowang
51 Blaju

Boreh village

63 65
62 64 67
66 68

Household heads

62 Songpaow   66 Sang
63 Doa   67 Gago
64 Peng   68 Jusu
65 Faipow

Clans

■ Tang
● Wang
▣ Jang
○ Yang

Isolated houses

69 70
71

Household heads

69 Ler
70 Ler
71 Tei

Village D

33 34
35 36 37 38 42 44
39 40 41 43

Household heads

33 Seipang   42 Nuchow
34 Koyi   43 Juser
35 Joying   44 Wangjow
36 Suker
37 Foa
38 Susa
39 Kalaow
40 Ver
41 Chailong

Village F

58 59 60 61

Household heads

58 Tongsuk
59 Serpow
60 Chamang
61 Bowya

Village B

22 23 25
24 26

Household heads

22 Sertoa
23 Gatong
24 Blajong
25 Wangjer
26 Sor

Village C

27 28
29 30
31 32

Household heads

27 Jowlong
28 Jingpaow
29 Yongneng
30 Yupaow
31 Serju
32 Jitang

Village A

Household heads

1 Nang
2 Juyi
3 Nyaying
4 Wangpaow
5 Blaiya
6 Tong
7 Yongfo
8 Wangjer
9 Sersang
10 Faitei
11 So
12 Ying
13 Jufoa
14 Sapaow
15 Ger
16 Bowjang
17 Soying
18 Chetsu
19 Yaitong
20 Tong
21 Wangki
S Smithy
Y Yunnanese stores
0 Anthropologists' house

DIAGRAM 3: Village composition according to households and clans, showing approximate positions of households in relation to one another, and names of household heads

TABLE 8

Village composition by clans

VILLAGES	TANG		WANG	
	Houses	*Persons*	*Houses*	*Persons*
A	17	174 (M 77, F 97)	1	10 (M 4, F 6)
B	4	24 (M 12, F 12)	1	9 (M 4, F 5)
		(CHIENGRAI TANG)		
C	6	42 (M 23, F 19)	—	—
D	7	51 (M 24, F 27)	4	35 (M 16, F 19)
A–B–C–D	34	291 (M 136, F 155)	6	54 (M 24, F 30)
E	4	26 (M 11, F 15)	6	66 (M 36, F 30)
F	—	—	4	25 (M 12, F 13)
BOREH	—	—	—	—
ISOLATED	1	2 (M 1, F 1)	—	—
Totals—all villages and isolated houses	39	319 (M 148, F 171)	16	145 (M 72, F 73)

VILLAGES	JANG		YANG	
	Houses	*Persons*	*Houses*	*Persons*
A	3	23 (M 9, F 14)	—	—
B	—	—	—	—
C	—	—	—	—
D	—	—	1	8 (M 2, F 6)
A–B–C–D	3	23 (M 9, F 14)	1	8 (M 2, F 6)
E	—	—	3	19 (M 9, F 10)
F	—	—	—	—
BOREH	7	46 (M 18, F 28)	—	—
ISOLATED	2	10 (M 4, F 6)	—	—
Totals—all villages and isolated houses	12	79 (M 31, F 48)	4	27 (M 11, F 16)

VILLAGES	TOTALS	
	Houses	*Persons*
A	21	207 (M 90, F 117)
B	5	33 (M 16, F 17)
C	6	42 (M 23, F 19)
D	12	94 (M 42, F 52)
A–B–C–D	44	376 (M 171, F 205)
E	13	111 (M 56, F 55)
F	4	25 (M 12, F 13)
BOREH	7	46 (M 18, F 28)
ISOLATED	3	14 (M 4, F 10)
Totals—all villages and isolated houses	71	570 (M 285, F 308)

Tang. Of the remaining ten, six had direct affinal connections with the Tang clan.

In the case of Villages E and F, the Wang clan was predominant. This was obviously so in the case of Village F, where all the households were Wang. It is less immediately apparent in the case of Village E where only six household heads were Wang, and seven were non-Wang, of whom four were Tang and three were Yang. But wives in all three Yang houses and in two of the Tang houses, Nos. 47 and 57, were Wang. We have no record of the clan origin of the wife in House No. 45 but she, too, was probably Wang. In the remaining non-Wang household, No. 51, the wife was Jang. The presence of this household in the village was due to consanguineal connections of its head with the other Tang households there. Thus in the E–F complex ten of the seventeen households, or 58·8 per cent, were Wang. Five, and possibly six, of the remaining seven had direct affinal connections with the Wang members. The Wang clan, therefore, clearly predominated in this complex.

In the case of the village of Boreh, all the households were Jang. A majority of the wives came from clans such as Tow, Song, Jow, and Her, which were not represented in the Meto complex. This village tended to be a group apart, much as a more distant Miao village would be, and belonged to the Meto complex territorially rather than socially.

From the above analysis we can see the general pattern which settlement in large villages or village complexes tends to assume. The operation of the principle of clan-membership determining neighbourhood is modified as the settlement increases in size by intermarriage between clans leading to associations based upon ties of affinity. Occasionally, a few additional households may get attached for less common reasons, such as distant kinship connections, friendship, or convenience. Separate migrations may converge sections of different clans in the same area.

The modifications, however, are contingent upon circumstances which are not constant and frequently not long-lasting. Economically, politically, and ideologically, clan members have greater common interests with one another than with outsiders. Therefore, the tendency to reassert clan ties by co-residence is strong. This often becomes manifest when a village splits up to pioneer new areas. Then a man living in association with his wife's relatives may decide to move to an area where his fellow clansmen will be. It is true that sometimes the reverse happens. A man hearing of good land in an area where he has an affinal connection may decide to go there. But, out of the total blend of economic and social motivation, the clan principle emerges as the predominant factor in determining the residential scene.

SUB-CLAN AND LINEAGE IN THE METO COMPLEX

The thirty-nine Tang houses in the Meto complex belonged to five sub-clans, which we shall designate A, B, C, D, and E. As was explained in Chapter Three sub-clans are not fixed units in Miao social structure and these five divisions had meaning only in the local context where they were recognized as groupings of clansmen who were more closely related to one another than to persons in the other groups. They were usually referred to by the names of leading persons within them. According to context it might be the oldest man or the richest man or the man most prominent in village affairs.

Outsiders generally have no knowledge at all of the genealogical structure of a sub-clan grouping. Within the sub-clan members may know a real or truncated genealogy extending back five generations from the most junior persons. There is no deliberate teaching of genealogies to the young, however, and many sub-clansmen may just regard themselves as 'distantly related'.

The following is a list of the five sub-clans titled according to the manner in which they are most frequently designated and the households belonging to them:

SUB-CLAN	DESIGNATION	HOUSES
A	SAIYI (name of the common ancestor)	1, 2, 3, 4, 5, 6, 7, 9, 10, 15, 16, 17, 18, 33, 34, 35, 37, 39, 42
B	BLAJONG (name of the most important living person in it)	23, 24, 25, 26
C	CHIENGRAI (they were recent migrants from Chiengrai Province)	27, 28, 29, 30, 31
D	WANGJER (name of the most important living person in it)	8, 11, 12
E	BLAJU (name of the most important living person in it)	45, 47, 51, 57

The distribution of houses clearly reveals a preference of members of a sub-clan to reside near one another. Sub-clan A resided only in Villages A and D, comprising the great majority of Tang houses in Village A and all the Tang houses in Village D. It was the predominant group in both villages. Sub-clan B comprised all the Tang houses in Village B, was not represented in other villages, and had the village completely to itself except for one Wang household with which it had a marriage link. Sub-clan C comprised all the houses in Village C and was not represented elsewhere. Sub-clan D, a small group, comprised the remaining three houses in Village A. Sub-clan E comprised the four Tang houses in Village E, and was not represented elsewhere.

Thus local sub-clans show a distinct tendency to residential cohesion. It is in no way compulsory, as is revealed by the distribution of Wang and Jang houses, and at other stages in their history the Tang house-holds were more scattered. But like the birds referred to earlier, sub-clan members will flock together when conditions of forage encourage no competing desires.

The largest of the Tang sub-clans—Sub-clan A—has been chosen for detailed study in order to show the lineage structure within sub-clans and the nature of the social processes in which they may be involved. The genealogical links within this sub-clan are illustrated in Diagram 4. In subsequent chapters too examples will be taken particularly from this sub-clan in order that a picture of the total workings of a Miao local kin-group may emerge. In addition to the fact that it was the most numerous sub-clan in the Meto area, other reasons for choosing it for detailed analysis were that some of its earlier history was known to me, that it did have an over-all genealogical unity—being in its Meto manifestation one large lineage—and that it included the village head-man.

Diagram 4 illustrates the changes which a sub-clan may undergo owing to the vicissitudes of migration. I first encountered this sub-clan at the village of Pasamliem in the Chiengdao District during my stay there in 1957–8. In that village the local sub-clan did not have the unitary genealogical structure shown later at Meto, because the group shown as descended from Songler did not have a named ancestor in common with the Saiyi group. The Songler group were said merely to be 'distant relatives'. The link via Songler was given to me, uncertainly, later at Meto.

A legend of the Saiyi group says that two brothers left China—about 400 years ago according to a Pasamlien statement—leaving one brother there. One Meto version gave the names of the brothers who migrated as Saiyi and Songlau. It is clear that links at this topmost generation are used—if they are used at all—merely to symbolize a general relationship based on group history.

The closer the relationship between its members the more likely a group is to be preserved during migrations. This is exemplified by the fact that the lineage of Wangser was re-established intact at Meto, but groups connected lineally to it at the next higher generation underwent realignment. The group descended from Serger—actually a younger brother of Wangser—did not migrate to Meto from Pasamliem when that village was abandoned but went in a different direction towards Chiengdao. On the other hand two groups related on the same generation

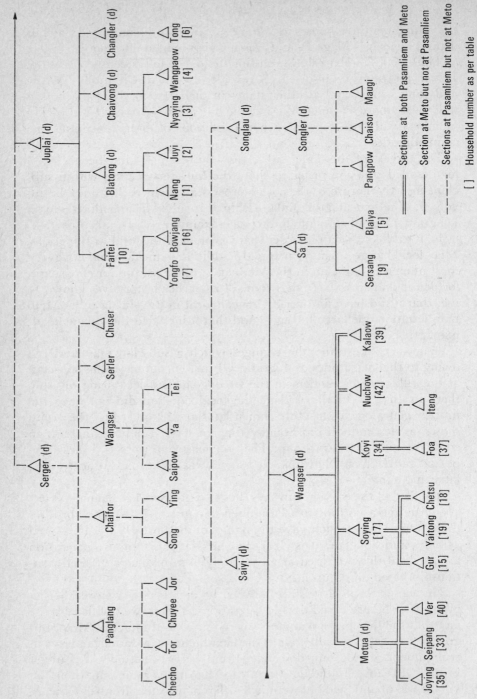

DIAGRAM 4: Genealogical linkage of the 21 households in the main sub-clan (A) of the Tang Clan at Meto, showing also differences in the congregations at Meto and Pasamliem

level—those descended from Juplai, an older brother of Wangser, and from Sa, a younger brother—rejoined it after having been separated from it in other locations. From discussions occurring in Meto during 1965 about possible future moves, it appeared likely that the Juplai and Sa groups would again separate. In some other place later on they might well reunite again but the chances of this happening would become less as each of the groups developed new generations within itself and the older connections, which had operated to bring them together at Meto, became correspondingly more remote. However, no firm prediction can be made on the basis of degree of genealogical linkage because this is only one of two important factors determining congregation. The other is economic attraction. If it is strong enough, common clanship is sufficient excuse for groups to take up residence with one another, and they may do so on the basis of even more tenuous links.

Lineage relationships

A comparison of the situations at Pasamliem and Meto also illustrates the changes which lineages within the sub-clan undergo. In 1958 at Pasamliem, although Wangser was already dead, the lineage originated from him was still a closely co-operating group. Its members lived in neighbouring houses and there was a great deal of intermixing between them. Association between the men of the senior generation was enlivened by the fact that they held, and shared, the village leadership. Kalaow was the official headman but, being junior, he was inclined to consult with his elder brothers. Koyi was the leading shaman. Soying was the head of the largest household.

The lineage, however, was already beginning to lose cohesion through the loss of one generation and the growth of another. The tie between brothers is frequently very strong in Miao society but it is less strong than that between a son and father. An important link had been lost with the death of Wangser. In the middle of 1958 Koyi moved away to join a married daughter in a village in the Mae Chaem district, and although the brothers subsequently also settled there for a short period, the economic co-operation was never re-established with the same intensity.

Koyi separated from his brothers because of new family ties which he had brought into being. The same development was occurring in the case of the other brothers, especially Soying. In 1958 his household in Pasamliem was very large, comprising 26 persons. It included four married sons, the eldest of whom—Ger—had two wives and all of whom had children of their own.

In 1965 the lineage of Wangser now re-established at Meto presented a different picture. The single household of Soying had now split into four separate households. Village leadership had passed away from his own generation, his son Yaitong now occupying the place of official headman which his brother Kalaow had held at Pasamliem. From being a household head Soying was now head of a lineage of his own. In 1958 he was the senior person in a group of 26 persons. He was now the senior person in a group of 46. This remarkable growth of numbers in the short space of seven years was accounted for by the fact that his eldest son who had already two wives had taken a third, his second son had taken a second wife, and his third and fourth sons had each taken two additional wives. Most of them had been quite prolific with children.

The group being so large the interests of its members naturally tended to be located primarily within it. Soying's own relationship with his brothers was perhaps still sentimentally close, but age limited its expression and it was less relevant for the families who maintained friendly relations but not the extent of daily intercourse or economic co-operation which marked the Pasamliem days. A new brotherly bond—that between Ger and Yaitong—had replaced in importance that between Soying and Kalaow of previous years.

New lineages had grown within the old. In economic life—and indeed in most aspects of social life—these are the lineages which are most important, that is to say, the lineages composed of the descendants of persons who are still living.

HOUSEHOLD COMPOSITION

Table 9 provides a detailed analysis of the composition of all the households in Meto, with the exception of those in Village C, which was occupied only for a year by the migrants from Chiengrai. Sixty-five households are in the list.

Certain features of Miao household structure clearly emerge:

a. More than 50 per cent of the households contained eight persons —the modal size—or more, nearly 11 per cent had fourteen or more, and there were two households with twenty members.

b. Seventy per cent of households contained no more than two generations, despite their fairly large size.

c. The structure of the majority of households was simple. 41·5 per cent were nuclear families, that is to say, one married couple and children; and 23·1 per cent were of the type which we are calling polygynously simple, that is to say, where there is only one husband but more than one wife.

d. Sixty per cent of the households were monogamous.

TABLE 9

Household composition in the Meto villages

HOUSE NO.	HOUSEHOLD HEAD	TOTAL PERSONS	GENERATION STRUCTURE			FAMILY TYPE
VILLAGE A						
1	NANG naŋ	10	M 4	0 [2]	: wife; (deceased wife)	Polygynous extended, 2 generation depth
			F 6	−1 [8]	: 3 sons, 3 daughters by present wife; daughter by deceased wife; wife of eldest son	
2	JUYI ɹuyi:	8	M 4	+1 [1]	: mother	Polygynous extended, 3 generation depth
			F 4	0 [2]	: (deceased 1st wife); 2nd wife	
				−1 [5]	: 2 daughters by 1st wife; 3 sons by 2nd wife	
3	NYAYING ɲayiŋ	4	M 1	0 [3]	: 2 wives	Polygynous simple, 2 generation depth
			F 3	−1 [1]	: daughter of 1st wife	
4	WANGPAOW waŋpao	20	M 7	+1 [1]	: mother	Extended, 3 generation depth
			F 13	0 [9]	: 3 younger brothers, 1 sister, wife and one wife of each brother	
				−1 [10]	: 2 sons and 3 daughters; 3 daughters of oldest brother; son and daughter of 2nd brother	
5	BLAIYA bla¹ya	9	M 2	0 [2]	: wife	Extended, 3 generation depth
			F 7	−1 [3]	: son; wife of son; wife of deceased older son	
				−2 [4]	: 3 daughters of son; daughter of deceased older son	
6	TONG tɔŋ	4	M 2	+1 [1]	: mother	Nuclear, 2 generation depth
			F 2	0 [3]	: elder brother, younger sister	
7	YONGFO yɔŋfɔ:	14	M 9	0 [3]	: 2 wives	Polygynous extended, 3 generation depth
			F 5	−1 [10]	: 2 sons of 1st wife; 5 sons and 1 daughter of 2nd wife; wives of eldest sons of each wife	
				−2 [1]	: son of eldest son of 2nd wife	
8	WANGJER waŋɹə	9	M 4	0 [2]	: wife	Extended (with attached colateral relative), 2 generation depth
			F 5	−1 [7]	: 2 sons, 3 daughters; son of deceased brother; wife of eldest son	

TABLE 9—*cont.*

HOUSE NO.	HOUSEHOLD HEAD	TOTAL PERSONS		GENERATION STRUCTURE	FAMILY TYPE
9	SERSANG søsaŋ	9 {M 5 F 4	0 [2] −1 [2] −2 [5]	: wife : son and son's wife : 3 sons, 2 daughters of son	Extended, 3 generation depth
10	FAITEI faite[1]	14 {M 8 F 6	0 [2] −1 [5] −2 [7]	: wife : 2 sons: 2 wives of 1st son, wife of 2nd son : 1 daughter and 3 sons of 1st wife of eldest son; son and daughter of 2nd wife of eldest son; son of 2nd son	Extended polygynously, 3 generation depth
11	SO Sɒ	7 {M 4 F 3	0 [4] −1 [3]	: 2 wives, brother : son and daughter of 1st wife, son of 2nd wife	Polygynous simple (with attached colateral), 2 generation depth
12	YING yiŋ	10 {M 3 F 7	0 [3] −1 [7]	: 2 wives : 2 daughters by 1st wife, 3 daughters and 2 sons by 2nd wife	Polygynous simple 2 generation depth
13	JUFOA jufɔa	7 {M 3 F 4	0 [2] −1 [5]	: wife (deceased wife) : daughter by deceased wife, 2 daughters and 2 sons by 2nd wife	Polygynous simple, 2 generation depth
14	SAPAOW sapao	10 {M 4 F 6	0 [1] −1 [2] −2 [7]	: (deceased wife) : son and son's wife : 5 daughters and 2 sons of son	Extended, 3 generation depth
15	GER gœ	10 {M 6 F 4	0 [3] −1 [7]	: 2 wives : 4 sons and 2 daughters of 1st wife; son of 2nd wife	Polygynous simple, 2 generation depth
16	BOWJANG boʝaŋ	10 {M 4 F 6	0 [3] −1 [7]	: 2 wives, (2 deceased wives) : 3 daughters and 1 son of 1st surviving wife, 2 sons of 1st deceased wife, daughter of 2nd deceased wife	Polygynous simple 2 generation depth
17	SOYING sɔyiŋ	14 {M 7 F 7	0 [2] −1 [7]	: wife, (deceased wife) : 1 son by deceased 1st wife, 2 daughters and 2 sons by 2nd wife; 2 wives (+ 1 deceased wife) of son by 1st wife	Polygynous extended polygynously, 3 generation depth

HOUSE NO.	HOUSEHOLD HEAD	TOTAL PERSONS				GENERATION STRUCTURE	FAMILY TYPE
				−2	[5]	: daughter by deceased wife of son, 3 sons and 1 daughter of son by 1st surviving wife	
18	CHETSU cɛtsu	8	M 3	0	[4]	: 3 wives	Polygynous simple, 2 generation depth
			F 5	−1	[4]	: daughter by 1st wife; 2 sons by 2nd wife; daughter by 3rd wife	
19	YAITONG yaitɔŋ	14	M 4	0	[3]	: 2 wives	Polygynous extended, 2 generation depth
			F 10	−1	[11]	: 3 sons and 5 daughters by 1st wife, 2 daughters by 2nd wife; wife of eldest son	
20	TONG tɔŋ	9	M 3	+1	[1]	: mother	Extended, 3 generation depth
			F 6	0	[7]	: 1 younger brother, 3 sisters; wife; wife of brother	
				−1	[1]	: 1 son	
21	WANGKI waŋki	7	M 3	0	[2]	: wife	Nuclear 2 generation depth
			F 4	−1	[5]	: 3 daughters, 2 sons	
VILLAGE B 22	SERTOA søtɔa	9	M 4	0	[2]	: wife, (deceased wife)	Polygynous extended, 3 generation depth
			F 5	−1	[2]	: son, wife of deceased son	
				−2	[5]	: 2 sons, 3 daughters of deceased son	
23	GATONG gatɔŋ	6	M 2	0	[2]	: wife	Nuclear 2 generation depth
			F 4	−1	[4]	: 3 daughters, 1 son	
24	BLAJONG blajɔŋ	6	M 2	0	[2]	: wife	Nuclear, 2 generation depth
			F 4	−1	[4]	: 3 daughters, 1 son	
25	WANGJER waŋjə	6	M 4	0	[2]	: wife	Extended, 3 generation depth
			F 2	−1	[3]	: 2 sons, wife of eldest son	
				−2	[1]	: son of eldest son	
26	SOR sɔ	6	M 4	+1	[1]	: mother	Extended, 2 generation depth
			F 2	0	[5]	: 3 younger brothers; wife of oldest of the brothers.	

No detailed family data were collected for Houses 27–32 inclusive, the houses in Village C comprising the migratory group of Tang clansmen from Chiengrai Province who remained only 1 year in Meto.

| **VILLAGE D** 33 | SEIPANG se'paŋ | 7 | M 4 | 0 | [2] | : wife | Nuclear, 2 generation depth |
| | | | F 3 | −1 | [5] | : 3 sons, 2 daughters | |

TABLE 9—*cont.*

HOUSE NO.	HOUSEHOLD HEAD	TOTAL PERSONS				GENERATION STRUCTURE	FAMILY TYPE
34	KOYI kɔyiː	13	M F	7 6	0 −1 −2	[2] : wife [7] : 3 sons, 2 daughters; wife of 1st son and wife of 2nd son [4] : 3 sons of 1st son, daughter of 2nd son	Extended, 3 generation depth
35	JOYING jɔyɪŋ	6	M F	3 3	0 −1	[3] : 2 wives [3] : 2 sons and 1 daughter of 1st wife	Polygynous simple, 2 generation depth
36	SUKER sukø	5	M F	3 2	0 −1	[2] : 1 wife, (1 deceased wife) [3] : 1 son by deceased wife; son and daughter by surviving wife	Polygynous simple, 2 generation depth
37	FOA fɔa	6	M F	2 4	0 −1	[2] : wife [4] : 3 daughters, 1 son	Nuclear, 2 generation depth
38	SUSA susa	8	M F	2 6	0 −1	[2] : wife [6] : 5 daughters, 1 son	Nuclear, 2 generation depth
39	KALAOW kɔlao	6	M F	3 3	0 −1 −2	[2] : wife, (3 deceased wives) [3] : son; 2 wives of son [1] : son of 2nd wife of son	Polygynous extended polygynously, 3 generation depth
40	VER βœ	5	M F	3 2	0 −1	[2] : wife [3] : 1 daughter, 2 sons	Nuclear, 2 generation depth
41	CHAILONG cailɔŋ	8	M F	4 4	0 −1 −2	[2] : wife [5] : 2 sons, 2 daughters; wife of eldest son [1] : son of eldest son	Extended, 3 generation depth
42	NUCHOW nucoʷ	8	M F	2 6	0 −1 −2	[2] : wife [3] : son, 2 wives of son [3] : 2 daughters of son by 1st wife, 1 daughter of son by 2nd wife	Extended polygynously 3 generation depth
43	JUSER jusœ	11	M F	5 6	+1 0 −1	[1] : mother [6] : 2 younger brothers, 1 wife of himself and 1 wife of each of his brothers [4] : 2 daughters, son of 1st brother, son of 2nd brother	Extended, 3 generation depth
44	WANGJOW waŋjoʷ	11	M F	4 7	0 −1	[4] : 3 wives [7] : 3 daughters and 1 son of 1st wife, 2 sons and 1 daughter of 2nd wife	Polygynous simple, 2 generation depth

TABLE 9—*cont.*

HOUSE NO.	HOUSEHOLD HEAD	TOTAL PERSONS				GENERATION STRUCTURE	FAMILY TYPE
VILLAGE E							
45	WANGYI waŋyi	5	M F	2 3	+1 0	[1] : mother [4] : Younger brother; wife and wife of brother	Extended, 2 generation depth
46	BWOTONG bʷɔtɔŋ	8	M F	4 4	0 −1	[2] : wife [6] : 3 daughters, 3 sons	Nuclear, 2 generation depth
47	YA ya	5	M F	2 3	0 −1	[2] : wife [3] : 2 daughters, 1 son	Nuclear, 2 generation depth
48	WANG waŋ	11	M F	7 4	0 −1	[3] : 2 wives [8] : 3 sons, 2 daughters by 1st wife, 3 sons by 2nd wife	Polygynous simple, 2 generation depth
49	JONGJER jɔŋjə	5	M F	3 2	0 −1	[2] : wife [3] : 2 sons, 1 daughter	Nuclear, 2 generation depth
50	SONGLER sɔŋlœ	20	M F	8 12	0 −1 −2	[2] : wife [9] : 4 sons and 1 daughter; wife of eldest son (+1 deceased wife), 1 wife each for other 3 sons [9] : son and daughter of eldest son by deceased wife, daughter and son of eldest son by surviving wife, 3 daughters of 2nd son, daughter of 3rd son, son of 4th son	Extended polygynously 3 generation depth
51	BLAJU blaɟu	7	M F	2 5	+1 0 −1	[1] : mother [2] : wife [4] : 1 son, 3 daughters	Nuclear, 3 generation depth
52	NULANG nulaŋ	18	M F	12 6	0 −1 −2	[2] : wife [7] : 3 sons; wife of 2nd and wife of 3rd son; 2 wives of deceased 4th son [9] : 1 daughter and 3 sons of 2nd son, 2 sons of 4th son by 1st wife, 3 sons of 4th son by 2nd wife	Extended polygynously 3 generation depth
53	SERSANG søsaŋ	4	M F	2 2	0 −1	[2] : wife [2] : daughter and son	Nuclear, 2 generation depth
54	JOYING ɟɔyiŋ	8	M F	2 6	0 −1	[3] : 2 wives [5] : 4 daughters and 1 son by 1st wife	Polygynous simple, 2 generation depth

TABLE 9—*cont.*

HOUSE NO.	HOUSEHOLD HEAD	TOTAL PERSONS				GENERATION STRUCTURE	FAMILY TYPE
55	CHASER casə	7	M	5	o	[2] : wife	Nuclear,
			F	2	−1	[5] : 4 sons and 1 daughter	2 generation depth
56	BAO baɔ	4	M	2	o	[2] : wife	Nuclear,
			F	2	−1	[2] : 1 daughter and 1 son	2 generation depth
57	KOWANG kowaŋ	9	M	5	o	[2] : wife	Nuclear,
			F	4	−1	[7] : 4 sons, 3 daughters	2 generation depth
VILLAGE F							
58	TONGSUK tɔŋsuk	6	M	2	o	[2] : wife	Nuclear,
			F	4	−1	[4] : 3 daughters and 1 son	2 generation depth
59	SERPOW sɔpoʷ	8	M	4	o	[2] : wife	Nuclear,
			F	4	−1	[6] : 3 sons and 3 daughters	2 generation depth
60	CHAMANG camaŋ	4	M	2	o	[2] : wife	Nuclear,
			F	2	−1	[2] : son and daughter	2 generation depth
61	BOWYA boya	7	M	4	o	[2] : wife	Nuclear,
			F	3	−1	[5] : 3 sons and 2 daughters	2 generation depth
BOREH VILLAGE							
62	SONGPAOW sɔŋpao	12	M	4	o	[3] : 2 wives	Polygynous simple,
			F	8	−1	[9] : 4 daughters and 1 son by 1st wife, 2 sons and 2 daughters by 2nd wife	2 generation depth
63	DOA dɔa	3	M	1	o	[2] : wife	Nuclear,
			F	2	−1	[1] : daughter	2 generation depth
64	ᵽENG peŋ	5	M	2	o	[3] : 2 wives	Polygynous simple,
			F	3	−1	[2] : son and daughter	2 generation depth
65	FAIPAOW faipao	8	M	2	o	[2] : wife	Nuclear,
			F	6	−1	[6] : 5 daughters and 1 son	2 generation depth
66	SANG saŋ	3	M	1	o	[2] : wife	Nuclear,
			F	2	−1	[1] : daughter	2 generation depth
67	GAGO gago	7	M	5	o	[2] : wife	Nuclear,
			F	2	−1	[5] : 4 sons and 1 daughter	2 generation depth
68	JUSU ɟusu	8	M	3	o	[3] : 2 wives	Polygynous simple,
			F	5	−1	[5] : 3 daughters and 2 sons	2 generation depth
ISOLATED HOUSES							
69	LER lœ	4	M	1	o	[2] : wife	Nuclear,
			F	3	−1	[2] : 2 daughters	2 generation depth
70	LER lø	2	M	1	o	[2] : wife	Spousal,[a]
			F	1			1 generation depth
71	TEI te[1]	6	M	3	o	[2] : wife	Nuclear,
			F	3	−1	[4] : 2 daughters and 2 sons	2 generation depth

[a] Classed as nuclear in the summaries

We can see that family patrilineal extension and polygyny are absent in a majority of households. Yet both have been commonly regarded as typical features of Miao social structure. They appear more typical if the situation is viewed in terms not of households but of population distribution. Although only 35·4 per cent of the households contain extended families, they embrace 47·2 per cent of the population. Similarly, although polygyny occurs in only 40 per cent of the households, nearly half the people (48·5 per cent) are living in these households. Many of the simple households will later grow into extended households and many of the men now monogamous will take a second wife. Therefore, during the course of their lifetimes a majority of the Meto Miao appear likely to experience both types of family setting.

Extension of the family through the marriage of their sons is generally desired by both parents, and the men usually aspire to polygyny. Therefore we may describe both characteristics as ideals of the Miao. If no other forces were involved, both would be normal developments, but in fact the extent of the development is limited by economic convenience and ecological circumstances. Let us discuss the role of each of these factors in relation first to family extension and then to polygyny.

As can be seen from the presence in Meto of two groups of twenty persons, a household can grow quite large and still hold together. But domestic arrangements may become increasingly troublesome. The house may get overcrowded and difficulties arise in managing equitably a common budget.

The more stable the settlement the more likely, it seems, are family extensions within the household to occur. This is indicated by the fact that in Village A—the oldest of the settlements in the Meto area— 51·9 per cent of the households contained extended families which embraced 67·6 per cent of the population. Fourteen of the twenty-one households had nine or more persons—above the modal size for the village as a whole. Even in such conditions, however, economic convenience induces division. There need be no great loss of social intimacy as a result of it because neighbouring dwellings can be built so that as a social group the household is merely transformed into a local lineage.

The effect of economic convenience in bringing about division is increased by the presence of a cash economy. It is usual for each of the constituent families in a large household to handle its cash production separately. In the case of Meto, the economy was primarily directed to the production of opium, and the families were expected to contribute proportionately to make up deficiencies in the houshold's general production of subsistence crops. The mixture of private and joint endeavour complicates the problems of management in large households.

For reasons to be discussed in detail later, the opium economy frequently forces migration to new areas. It also facilitates migration by providing families with means to sustain themselves while they pioneer these new areas. The large families develop in stable conditions. Migration almost inevitably divides them.

Rarely does a large household move as a group. There are several reasons why it does not. One is that the prospects in a new area are often uncertain, and security is provided by only a section embarking on the new adventure. Another reason is that the household may not have enough resources to support the whole of it during a period of resettlement. Those who stay may aid those who are leaving, knowing that they will be repaid by assistance later should the migration be successful and they decide to follow. If they do follow they will often build separate houses in the new area.[3]

The situation in regard to polygyny is more complex. We stated earlier that it was a Miao ideal in the sense that most men appear to aspire to it. But how general is it? Table 10 shows that in the Meto area

TABLE 10

Family structure of Meto households

Number of generations in household	Polygynous extended	Polygynous Extended Polygynously	Extended polygynously	Extended	Polygynous simple	Nuclear	Totals
1	—	—	—	—	—	1	1
2	2	—	—	3	15	25	45
3	3	2	4	9	—	1	19
TOTALS	5	2	4	12	15	27	65

as a whole only twenty-two of the sixty-five households had heads who were polygynous. This figure, however, does not reveal the full extent of polygyny. The following subsidiary table extracts the figures for all marriages at each generation level from level 3—the highest generation

[3] It should be noted that this does not always happen. In 1967 members of Household No. 50 migrated to Pa Khia. When we visited this village in October 1970 the entire household was again under one roof. Through the birth of children its numbers had risen from 20 to 26.

at which marriages were recorded—to level 1, the newly marrying generation:[4]

Generation	Total marriages	Polygynous marriages	Percentages of marriages which are polygynous
3	14	4	28·6
2	76	24	31·6
1	7	—	—

In the highest generation the proportion of marriages which were polygynous is almost certainly much higher than shown. This is indicated by the proportion of men at the second ascending generation who were already polygynous. In the main table from which this subsidiary table is derived, the only wives recorded are those who had survived or those deceased wives who were the mothers of persons still in the household. When a polygynous household divides, there is a tendency for the children of a deceased mother to be the first to separate because a major thread of attachment to it has been severed.

When we examine Table 9 in regard to the marriages of persons who were household heads, we find that twenty-two marriages out of a total of sixty-three—that is to say, 34·9 per cent—were polygynous. When we recall that 70 per cent of the households were of only two-generation depth,[5] we appear justified in concluding that a large majority of household heads become polygynous sooner or later.

On the basis of these figures and information collected in more limited contexts, it appear that polygyny is a normal feature of the lives of Meto men who survive to old age. Individual factors may inhibit it, such as an exceptionally strong attachment to one wife, or unusual dependence upon her as in the case of Bwolong in Village E who had become an opium addict and relied almost entirely upon the income produced by his wife and daughters. A strong-willed wife may hinder it because theoretically the consent of first wives should be obtained and family difficulties may arise if they are overruled. Women generally are reluctant to become second wives, and their fathers, even though polygynous themselves, are expected to counsel them against it. Despite all these factors, however, a great majority of men who travel to old age take two or more wives *en route*.

The frequency of polygyny in Meto raises interesting questions regarding Miao society in general and the typicality of the Meto

[4] We have counted, as polygynous marriages, cases where only one wife was alive but another deceased. In some of these cases the polygyny may have been serial but frequently it was contemporaneous for a period.

[5] A two-generation household could be the remaining portion of a larger household after a division. It is rare, however, for this to be the case, and the vast majority of the households referred to above were still in the developmental stage.

community within it. Obviously if in any society marriage is general, the average age for first marriages is no higher for men than for women, and the sexes are equal in numbers, then polygyny cannot be frequent. At Meto there was no significant number of unmarried men. The average age of first marriages for men appeared to be considerably lower than that of their brides and certainly was not significantly higher. The only one of the factors mentioned above which did appear was a sex ratio in favour of females, which occurred in all the clans. In the sixty-five households subjected to detailed study there were 20·9 per cent more females than males.

A proportion of the extra women came as the result of marriages made with persons from outside the village, and we cannot be sure of the exact extent to which this gain was offset by the loss of women through marriage to outsiders. More informative therefore than over-all ratio is that involving only the unmarried in the sixty-five households. The following tables shows separate figures for the married and the un-married.

Married or once married			*Unmarried*		
MALE	FEMALE	TOTAL	MALE	FEMALE	TOTAL
95	126	221	144	163	307

In the unmarried group there were 13·2 per cent more females than males. But in the married group there were 32·6 per cent more.

The conclusion must be that Meto was gaining a disproportionate number of women from outside. There is nothing to suggest that it was enabled to do because there were communities which had a sex ratio of females much higher than that at Meto. The statistics for the whole of Thailand's Miao population to which we referred earlier do not show a surplus of females. Although we cannot assume that these figures are accurate, it is unlikely that there was sufficient imbalance to permit a general occurrence of polygyny as great as that at Meto. Why then did Meto gain women in greater proportion than the average?

We note that polygyny was greatest in Village A, where it was present in 61·9 per cent of the households which embraced 62·8 per cent of the population. This was probably only partly due to the fact that the families in that village had been on the average slightly longer settled in the area and thus had time to develop a deeper generation structure. More important probably was the fact that this was the primary village of the pioneers who acquired the best land and thereby the means to operate more successfully in the marriage market. All wives have to be bought. The price is double for two. Love and the prospect of primacy in her new household may make it agreeable for a first wife to come on mortgage. This is far less likely to happen in the case of a second wife.

Therefore, relatively poor men may find it fairly easy to gain first wives but much harder to get more.

Success in the opium economy is the means to polygyny. In turn, polygyny is the means to success because it not only provides more labour but also the diversification helpful in a mixed economy of subsistence and cash production.

THE SOCIAL STRUCTURE IN ITS ECOLOGICAL SETTING

We have seen that amongst the Miao of Meto, although there are many small households, family extension and polygyny are favoured. The role of both preferences in determining the actual social structure of the community is influenced by the ecological adaptation of the people.

Normally, fathers and sons prefer to remain closely associated. There are several reasons for this. The clan system is structured on the basis of the father–son link which is therefore emphasized in the minds of the people. There is a strong religious interdependence between the two because the father's welfare in the afterworld depends upon how his sons bury him and how they attend to his ghostly needs, and the son's welfare depends upon a benign disposition of the father's spirit towards him. The institution of the extended family accords with the mutual inclination of fathers and sons to maintain close association and therefore we should expect such families to develop in favourable conditions.

Two conditions which would be favourable are a common household budget and stability of residence. In Meto, the extensive development of a cash economy giving sons with families of their own separate incomes introduced a divisive force. The nature of the cash crop induced migration, thereby reducing family size. No doubt there was sometimes interplay between the two conditions, and the migration was not always due simply to economic necessity but offered a way out of a social dilemma—the wish to preserve family harmony and the need to relieve tensions introduced by the cash economy.

The Miao people from whom the Meto community was formed are not stable and their social structure is not static. Physically, they move from place to place within a total range of territory circumscribed by a particular type of climate. In their individual lives they move through various family forms which range from a small monogamous nuclear family to a large extended polygynous household, all circumscribed by the clan system. Their fortunes in society mirror their economy in its ecological setting. Their social processes and their settlement processes are closely interrelated. The dynamism of the one is dependent upon the dynamism of the other. The family pattern of integration, separation, and reintegration on new or old lines enables them to move with confidence. Family precedent provides them with the initiative to seek new land. Family ties lie behind them to secure their bases while they prospect, and, for the more timorous who follow later, they lie ahead.

The polygyny and the ecology are also interrelated. Additional wives are gained by economic success which in turn they facilitate. Because they have greater resources to exploit, some communities are more successful than others. The poorer communities lose and the richer gain, in women especially but in numbers generally, because other relationships as well as marriage are utilized in the search for better opportunity. Thus the population is constantly being redistributed, through the operation of polygyny and other social and economic factors, according to resources.

If the Miao were to become a settled people, we would expect changes in their social structure. Its general form might remain because it is established by tradition, supported by religion, and because the young are educated to it, but there would probably be a different working out of tendencies inherent in it. For instance, households no longer subject to the divisive forces of migration might grow larger through family extensions. Polygyny at the rate shown in Meto could continue only either by an alteration in the age of marriage or, more probably, by richer or older men monopolizing women at the cost of marriages for the poorer or younger. This is speculation. The possibilities are many. But it is almost certain that a settled condition would mean not merely a change in economic patterns but a considerable alteration of social life as well. A new accommodation between the social system and the economy would have to develop, possibly painfully.

The social organization of Meto as outlined in this chapter is an accommodation to its present economy. We have said more. We have said it is an ecological adaptation. Any economy is, of course, an aspect of ecology. But in the case of a relatively static economy of a settled people other ecological factors, such as climate and type of crop, may need little detailed discussion in a study of social affairs. In the case of the Miao this is not so. They are not a settled people. Their economy is based primarily on the product of one species of plant—the opium poppy. The requirements of this plant, in respect of climate, soil type, and tillage, determine the areas they settle and the way they exploit them. As will be shown in the next chapter on land utilization, their mode of poppy cultivation almost inevitably limits the duration of a settlement and forces migration, thus creating some of the characteristics of their society described above.

CHAPTER SIX

THE UTILIZATION OF LAND

IT is difficult to calculate with absolute accuracy the size of the territory within which the Meto people live, because fields cultivated or claimed by the Karen interpenetrate their own. But if we take all the area from which they are not excluded by Karen claims—whether this area be cultivated or wild—it is not more than 12·3 square kilometres. This means a population density of 46·5 persons per square kilometre, or 120 per square mile approximately. This is a minimum estimate because some of the uncultivated land which we have included probably was subject to Karen claims.

The average population density for Thailand as a whole is 34·1 persons per square kilometre. A good deal of the rest of the country is fertile, irrigated river plain. The Meto country is mountainous. Yet the density there is well above the national average. It is very high indeed for a swiddening area anywhere in the world. Clark and Haswell[1] give the following estimates of optimum density from several regions: Sarawak (Iban), 20 persons per square kilometre; Philippines (Hanunno), 39 persons per square kilometre; Sumatra, 15–20 per square kilometre; Northern Rhodesia (Lala), 2 persons per square kilometre. The terrain in the Meto region is much more precipitous than that in the areas quoted and certainly generally less fertile than the Sarawak area which I know. Therefore it appears certain that the population density in Meto is far above the optimum for settled residence using the agricultural methods prevailing.

The actual area under cultivation in 1965 was precisely determined by means of aerial photographs and ground survey as 1,702·48 rai, or 272·4 hectares, or 2·72 square kilometres. This is a density per cultivated area of 210·3 persons per square kilometre. Because of the excessive steepness of some of the other land, the cultivated area would comprise at least 30 per cent and possibly 40 per cent of the total available to the people at any time for cultivation. Therefore the density on cultivatable land lay between 63 and 84 persons per square kilometre.

The high human density on the cultivated land and the high proportion of the total cultivated at the one time are key features of the Meto Miao socio-economic scene. Clearly there was little scope for rotation

[1] C. Clark, and N. R. Kaswell, *The Economics of Subsistence Agriculture*, London, 1964. These figures are also quoted by Hinton, Peter in *Tribesmen and Peasants in North Thailand*, Tribal Research Centre, Chiengmai, 1969, p. 11.

of the land by means of bush fallow. Generally it was a matter of one period of use only. The best-placed families had opportunity to move their cropping area twice. Most could do so only once and some had to make do with a single area.

The length of the period of use was therefore critical if the Miao were to have any stability of residence at all. It could not be for a single year, as is generally necessitated by dry rice, because even in the case of the most fortunate families two years' fallow of the land would not be sufficient for regeneration. Therefore the crop had to be such as would permit continuous use of their land for several years. The opium poppy fitted this need. Because it could be cultivated in the same fields for many years in succession it made possible the high density of population on a limited land area which was found at Meto.

It is true that with another crop such as rice the area of cultivation per family need not have been so large. But this alternative appears ruled out because the reduction in area would not have been enough to permit a population of such density to maintain long enough fallows. The people pioneered the area with the poppy in mind. Only through devotion to it could they maintain themselves in the territory they acquired. The period they could stay there was necessarily limited, but for that period—considering their numbers—the poppy allowed them remarkably spacious gardens.

The fact that in the more fertile areas poppy could be cultivated continuously for up to ten years might seem to have allowed the better-placed families opportunity to rotate land even though they had only two alternative planting areas. With crops such as padi a spell of ten years after use would allow the land plenty of time to regain its fertility. In the case of poppy cultivation, however, the tillage and the lengthened use of the same soil may prolong effective regeneration beyond this period. Moreover, many families do not possess an alternative planting area, and when they are forced to move others may be inclined to follow them.

How spacious the cultivations were can be seen from Map 2. This is a land use map plotted from aerial photographs. The boundaries of individual fields were determined by traversing them on foot with the owners of the fields or reliable informants and tracing them at the time on enlargements of the aerial photographs. The clan membership of the owners is indicated by the various tints shown in the key and the contours of the land.

Ten fields to the west of Village A are not shown on the map. This is because the aircraft apparently missed that run or weather conditions interfered with it. Although we did roughly measure those fields on the ground later, the measurement was much less accurate than that derived from the photographs, and therefore we have not included them in the survey data. This means that the totals shown are rather less than they were in fact, and it also accounts for the lower than expected acreage shown for some of the families to which reference will be made at the appropriate points.

For a few fields which are shown on the map the owners could not be certainly determined. The ground survey was carried out in 1966 when some of the fields had already passed out of cultivation. Some persons had moved away from the territory. The area for which ownership and crop usage could be accurately determined was 1,586·72 rai, or 626·77 acres, or 253·756 hectares.

We shall now consider certain important features of the economy which emerge from the land use survey.

THE MUCH GREATER IMPORTANCE OF POPPY THAN PADI

Only 17 per cent of the land was planted in padi; 83 per cent was growing poppy. More detailed figures are:

Padi 276·452 rai, or 109·198 acres, or 44·209 hectares
Poppy 1,310·330 rai, or 517·580 acres, or 209·546 hectares.

Direct subsistence agriculture, therefore, is only a small part of the Miao economy. The major part is the production of opium as a cash crop.

The economic importance of poppy is not limited solely to the immediate production of cash. It also contributes indirectly both to subsistence and to more cash. It does so because the fields which carry poppy also usually carry maize beforehand. The nature of the crop sequence will be discussed in greater detail in a later chapter, but, briefly, in Meto maize was planted to keep the fields free from weeds during the period from the beginning of the wet season in April until the time for poppy planting in July or August. The resultant high maize yield was used mainly for feeding pigs. Some of the pigs were eaten and some were sold, both the consumption and sale contributing greatly to the maintenance of Miao ceremonial and religious life.

The most important feature of the Meto Miao economy is therefore the opium–maize–pigs complex. Subsistence rice-growing is a secondary feature.

THE LARGE SIZE OF THE LAND HOLDINGS

The amount of land cultivated by individual households is large. Excluding Village C, which we have explained comprised a group of newly-arrived immigrants, the over-all average for the Meto complex was 3·645 hectares, of which 3·026 hectares were under poppy and 0·619 hectares under padi. It is difficult to find comparative figures for other groups in similar conditions. The 1956–67 *Rapport de gestion et d'activité du Service des Eaux, Forêts et Chasses du Laos* quoted by Halpern[2] gives an estimate of one hectare per family for the swiddening areas in Laos.

The extensiveness of the cultivations is related primarily to the type of plant—the poppy. Because of the continuous use of the fields year after year little time, compared to that required by padi cultivators, has to be spent on clearing before planting. In the pioneering phase new land can be added each year without the old going out of production. An additional factor at Meto was the availability of hired labour from surrounding Karen communities. Many families employed at least one Karen at some time during the poppy season and often several were employed, especially during the harvest.

Thus the poppy, although it limited the period of residence for the Miao in each place, provided them during their sojourns with wide domains and a relatively rich economy. In most cases the prosperity was short-lived. The expansion of cultivation was soon limited by shortage of further land. Productivity then declined as the land lost its fertility. Some families did have enough resources to stay for many years in the Meto area and others were able to move into new areas before their wealth declined. But not many were so fortunate. For most of the Miao who made up the Meto community their life on earth was lived to a slow rythmn of poverty and plenty, of moving, settling, and moving again.

THE ADVANTAGE OF PIONEERING

Table 11 shows the size of cultivations classified according to villages and Table 12 shows it classified according to clans. The figures have to be interpreted in the light of a number of different factors. For instance, if the premiss that early settlers gain an advantage in land holding were true, one would expect a higher average for Boreh village and for Village F, because a majority of families in Boreh were amongst the early settlers and Village F is entirely composed of Wang clansmen who show the highest average for clan holdings. However in Boreh Jusu, who headed the largest household, although an original settler, was an opium addict who neglected his fields, and some of the other households were small. Village F comprised only four households. One of these was headed by a person who was an early settler but who spent most of his time in opium trading, being almost the only Miao engaged in this activity on an extensive scale.

[2] Halpern, 1960, p. 45.

TABLE 11

Size of cultivations classified by villages

VILLAGE	CROP	TOTAL AREA OF CULTIVATIONS			AVERAGE AREA PER HOUSEHOLD		
		RAI	ACRES	HECTARES	RAI	ACRES	HECTARE
A	Poppy	545·020	215·270	87·144	25·953	10·251	4·150
	Padi	77·660	30·669	12·408	3·698	1·460	0·591
21 HOUSEHOLDS	TOTAL	622·680	245·939	99·552	29·651	11·712	4·741
	TOTAL (+ unknown) crop)	626·430	247·420	100·151	29·830	11·782	4·770
B	Poppy	51·230	20·233	8·190	10·246	4·047	1·638
	Padi	26·290	10·383	4·201	5·258	2·076	0·840
5 HOUSEHOLDS	TOTAL	77·520	30·616	12·391	15·504	6·124	2·479
C	Poppy	80·140	31·655	12·815	13·356	5·275	2·135
	Padi	24·770	9·784	3·961	4·128	1·630	0·659
6 HOUSEHOLDS	TOTAL	104·910	41·439	16·776	17·485	6·906	2·795
D	Poppy	232·970	92·017	37·250	19·414	7·668	3·104
	Padi	56·362	27·706	11·213	4·696	1·854	0·750
12 HOUSEHOLDS	TOTAL	289·332	119·723	48·463	24·111	9·523	3·855
	TOTAL (+ unknown) crop)	290·712	120·268	48·683	24·226	9·569	3·874
E	Poppy	269·170	106·318	43·039	20·705	8·178	3·310
	Padi	63·060	24·906	10·080	4·850	1·915	0·775
13 HOUSEHOLDS	TOTAL	332·230	131·224	53·119	25·556	10·094	4·086
	TOTAL (+ unknown crop)	335·220	132·405	53·597	25·786	10·185	4·123
F	Poppy	25·110	9·917	4·014	6·277	2·479	1·003
	Padi	13·810	5·454	2·207	3·452	1·363	0·551
4 HOUSEHOLDS	TOTAL	38·920	15·371	6·221	9·730	3·843	1·555
	TOTAL (+ potato field)	40·920	16·161	6·540	10·230	4·040	1·635
BOREH	Poppy	79·750	31·497	12·748	11·392	4·499	1·821
	Padi	7·810	3·084	1·247	1·115	0·440	0·178
7 HOUSEHOLDS	TOTAL	87·560	34·581	13·995	12·508	4·940	2·000
ISOLATED HOUSES	Poppy	26·940	10·640	4·307	8·980	3·547	1·436
	Padi	6·690	2·641	1·068	2·230	0·880	0·356
3 HOUSEHOLDS	TOTAL	33·630	13·281	5·375	11·210	4·427	1·792
TOTALS	Poppy	1,310·330	517·580	209·546	18·455	7·289	2·951
	Padi	276·452	109·198	44·209	3·893	1·537	0·622
71 HOUSEHOLDS	TOTAL	1,586·782	626·778	253·756	22·349	8·827	3·353
	TOTAL (+ unknown crops) and potato field	1,596·902	630·776	255·374	22·491	8·883	3·596

TABLE 12

Size of cultivations classified by clans

CLAN	CROP	TOTAL AREA OF CULTIVATION			AVERAGE AREA PER HOUSEHOLD		
		RAI	ACRES	HECTARES	RAI	ACRES	HECTARES
TANG 32 HOUSEHOLDS	Poppy	620·500	245·097	99·229	19·390	7·659	3·100
	Padi	132·250	52·328	21·148	4·132	1·632	0·660
	TOTAL	752·750	297·336	120·378	23·523	9·291	3·761
	TOTAL (+ unknown crop)	759·490	299·998	121·456	23·734	9·374	3·795
TANG CHIENGRAI 6 HOUSEHOLDS	Poppy	80·140	31·655	12·815	13·356	5·275	2·135
	Padi	24·770	9·784	3·961	4·128	1·630	0·659
	TOTAL	104·910	41·349	16·776	17·485	6·906	2·795
WANG 16 HOUSEHOLDS	Poppy	370·010	146·153	59·171	23·125	9·134	3·697
	Padi	89·950	35·530	14·384	5·621	2·220	0·898
	TOTAL	459·960	181·684	73·556	28·747	11·355	4·597
	TOTAL (+ unknown crop)	463·340	183·019	74·096	28·958	11·438	4·630
JANG 13 HOUSEHOLDS	Poppy	203·120	80·232	32·482	15·624	6·171	2·498
	Padi	19·290	7·619	3·084	1·483	0·585	0·236
	TOTAL	222·410	87·851	35·567	17·108	6·757	2·735
YANG 4 HOUSEHOLDS	Poppy	36·560	14·441	5·846	9·140	3·610	1·461
	Padi	23·980	9·472	3·834	5·995	2·368	0·958
	TOTAL	60·540	23·913	9·681	15·135	5·978	2·420

It is clear from the tables that the predominant clan, the Tang, had the largest total of land and was second only to the Wang in the size of average holding per household. Village A, in which the majority of early Tang settlers were congregated, had the highest average of all the villages.

No Wang clansmen were amongst the very first pioneers. A group of them came, however, only a year later when much land was still available. Two of these men, Songler and Nulang, were industrious and skilled farmers. They were joined shortly afterwards by Juser, another man of the same type. They appear to have had a background of success in the village from which they came and therefore had the resources to allow them to establish extensive poppy fields immediately.

The holdings of these three men—Juser 98·54 rai, or 14·319 hectares; Songler 70·78 rai, or 11·319 hectares; and Nulang 45·86 rai, or 7·333 hectares—swell the Wang average.

Although there are factors which tend to produce an ultimate evening-out of property differences in Miao society, a person who has a superior position in his jumping-off place is likely to carry with him assets in his migration. Some of the assets may be material. Accumulated wealth means less dependence upon subsistence crops, and greater ability to employ labour. Other assets are mental. The successful grower in one place is likely to be successful in another. This is shown, I believe, by the case of Kalaow who, with 63·72 rai or 101·89 hectares of cultivations, was the largest landholder of the Tang clan. Kalaow had been headman of the Pasamliem community. Although he was a regular opium smoker and in late middle age, he was industrious, skilled, and almost certainly wealthy. He was too an unusually careful planner in that he paid as much attention to rice growing as to poppy cultivation and was thus protected against bad years.

A fact which should be taken into account in comparing positions of the villages and clans is the relative fertility of their lands. Village C was comparatively worse off than it appears from the figures because they were given land by their distant Tang fellow-clansmen much of which had already been over-cultivated. Generally the land of the first comers was the choicest land in the area, so that the advantage of many of the Tang clansmen was greater than it would appear from the figures. The superior position of the Tang clan, and of Village A of which they comprised the greater part, is indicated by Table 12, which shows the distribution of holdings according to clans. The Tang had more holdings in the middle to large range than any other clan.

The landholding situation of a group alters over time. The early settlers attract and usually welcome fellow clansmen, other relatives, and sometimes even Miao strangers with the result that the mean size of holdings diminishes. The position of the pioneers themselves improves in the first few years as they bring an increasing amount of land into production, and then is eroded by the increase in community size. The new comers occupy the unused land leaving no reserves for future expansion or new fields to replace the old as they become exhausted. Thus the social processes in Miao society operate as long-term levellers of economic differences.

THE VALUE OF CHILD LABOUR

Table 13 shows the amount of cultivated land per person in relation to household size. If the increase in household size implied generally an increase in the number of children, one might have expected the

TABLE 13

Land holdings in relation to household size

NO. OF PERSONS IN HOUSEHOLD	NO. OF HOUSEHOLDS IN GROUP	AVERAGE SIZE IN HECTARES OF HOLDING PER HEAD
2	1	1·472
3	2	0·426
4	7	0·647
5	6	0·551
6	9	0·479
7	8	0·527
8	9	0·353
9	6	0·419
10	5	0·547
11	3	0·620
12	1	0·205
13	1	0·229
14	4	0·353
18	1	0·407
20	2	0·419

average amount of holding to decline proportionately. This is not the case. There are some variations in the table, as in the case of the 8-person household, but this can be accounted for by the influence of two or three exceptional cases. Generally the size of the holding is maintained and appears, if anything, to be greatest in the middle range of households.

How great are the numbers of young children in the larger households? It is very difficult to assess ages with much degree of accuracy in a society which preserves no chronological records. It would have been unreliable guesswork to attempt it on a community-wide scale in Meto. However, because of earlier records which I had made at Pasamliem, I was able to compare the position of the seven families listed in Table 14.

In these seven households 36·2 per cent of the children were seven years or under. Probably the proportion was slightly greater because some of the children recorded at Pasamliem in 1958 may have died and been replaced by others. It cannot be said that the proportion in the total community was as high but it would probably have been at least 25 per cent.

If there were so many very young children the others must have contributed markedly to the agricultural work. That they could do so to such a considerable degree at an immature age would be due to the

TABLE 14

Increase in family size in seven Meto families

FAMILY HEAD	NO. IN FAMILY IN 1965	INCREASE IN NO. OF CHILDREN SINCE 1958
Ger (House 15)	10	5
Chetsu (House 18)	8	1
Yaitong (House 19)	14	5
Joying (House 35)	6	2
Foa (House 37)	6	4
Kalaow (House 39)	6	1
Nuchow (House 42)	8	3
TOTAL	58	21

nature of poppy cultivation. The heaviest demand for labour is in the harvesting. It is physically light work in which children from the age of seven or so may share. A child from the age of nine years may do as much as a married woman who has infants to tend. Children may play an important part in the economy in other ways too, such as helping with the planting of padi or maize, or looking after infants and so freeing their parents for more exacting agricultural work. But it is the concentration of the society on opium production which accounts for the greatness of their contribution.

That children are so useful in the opium-based economy may enhance the value placed upon them on sentimental and other grounds, and perhaps tend to encourage the growth of large families. It may also influence the reaction of the people to schools if attempts are made to introduce them in the context of the opium economy.

CHAPTER SEVEN

THE ORIGIN OF THE METO SETTLEMENT

A SIMILE for the Meto community, like many other Miao settlements, could be a pool formed by rain in a hollow on a mountain slope. Many rivulets flow into it, some of them formed by remoter convergences. The pool quickly fills, spilling over into many new streams.

To follow up all the rivulets which make the Meto pool is not possible with our limited knowledge. We can, however, trace the course of one which we first encountered in 1958. We can discover a little of how the pool at Pasamliem out of which it spilled was formed, and we can follow its course to Meto showing its tributaries *en route* and how it was joined there by streams from elsewhere.

In 1958 at Pasamliem, Soying (House 17) told me that his ancestors left China 400 years ago.[1] He was born at Mungkong where he lived for a long time. The village there broke up and his family with others moved to a new site close to Chieng Dao mountain. As the land proved poor they remained there only five years before moving to a new place about four miles from Pasamliem. In 1958 the remains of their houses on this site were still visible in a tangle of lank grass. At the time they settled there Pasamliem was occupied by another group of Miao to some of whom they were related by common clanship. After a very few years this group moved away to the District of Mae Chaem, and Soying's group took their place at Pasmaliem, because it was closer to their fields. As Mae Chaem was too far away for those who had left to carry their house planks with them, the new occupiers of Pasamliem were able to utilize these, which accounts for the fact that parts of their own old houses were still standing. When Soying spoke to me at that time he said he regarded his land at Pasamliem as good for many further years of settlement. Yet two years later he moved away, probably because he did not wish to be isolated when others moved.

In 1958 at Pasamliem Soying's brother, Koyi (House 34) was visited by a son named Chao who had gone with the group to the District of Mae Chaem, where they were living in a place called Mae Suk. He told his father that at Mae Suk there was excellent land for growing poppy. Therefore Koyi, accompanied by another son named Pow,

[1] The time of migration from China cannot be regarded as accurate. The story is as related by Soying.

moved away from Pasamliem to join them. I was present at the ceremonies and feasting which preceded their departure in April 1958.

From persons at Meto we learnt of later events. After Koyi had been almost a year at Mae Suk, Yaitong (House 19), the son of Soying, went to visit him. Yaitong saw the poppy fields at Mae Suk and judged them to be very good. His reports on his return to Pasamliem encouraged others to join him on a migration. In March of 1959, Yaitong, his uncle Kalaow (House 39), his older brother Ger (House 15), his two senior parallel cousins Joying (House 35) and Seipang (House 33), and the husband of Joying's sister, a Wang clansman called Tang who was the son of Sertoa (House 22), moved to Mae Suk. Land there proved more difficult to obtain than they had expected. Some was given to them by fellow Tang clansmen but some they were forced to buy from White Miao who were moving away after having already used it for several years.

In this same year the group at Mae Suk was joined by Bowjang (House 16), a distant junior cousin of Soying, who had been living previously in the District of Omkoi and who had left there because of trouble with the police. The opium crops at the end of that year were disappointing. Some opium addicts belonging to Lawa people who were visiting Mae Suk in order to obtain opium told Yaitong and the headman of Mae Suk, Jusu (House 68) of the Jang clan, that there was good poppy land in the hills not far from their village of Bo Luang.

Jusu, Yaitong, Nyaying (House 3), and Bowjang (House 16) went to explore the area. At Meto they found what they considered very good soil for poppy. They went back to Mae Suk to tell friends of their find and then, accompanied by Ger (House 15), Tu who was the youngest son of Soying (House 17), Koyi (House 34), Gago (House 67) who belonged like Jusu to the Jang clan, and two men of the Yang clan, they returned to begin clearing fields. Karen tribesmen from nearby villages who claimed the area demanded that they stop doing so, and feeling too weak in numbers to resist the threats they returned to Mae Suk.

A meeting of all those who had wished to move to Meto was held at Mae Suk. Some chose not to do so but the majority decided to persist, and in 1961 a new expedition set forth. It comprised four Tang clansmen—Yaitong, Ger, Bowjang, and Pao (a son of Koyi)—and six men of the Jang clan—Jusu, Gago, Faipow (House 65), Songpaow (House 62), Peng (House 64), and one other man. Again the Karen forbade them to make clearings, so they appealed to the Kamnan, the Thai sub-district headman located at Bo Sali, to grant them permission.

The Kamnan said he had no authority to do so but that he would take them to the Nai Amphur, the District Officer, at Hot, to whom they could put their case. At first the Nai Amphur told them that if they wished to resettle they should go to the Nikhom, or Land Resettlement Area, at Chieng Dao. They said they did not wish to go there. Whereupon the Nai Amphur granted them permission to settle at Meto.

In 1962 the settlers were joined by a large group of men and their families from Om Koi comprising:

Tang clansmen: Nang (House 1), Juyi (House 2), Nyaying (House 3), Wangpaow (House 4), Blaiya (House 5), Tong (House 6), Yongfo (House 7), Wangjer (House 8), Sersang (House 9), Faitei (House 10), Ying (House 12), Blajong (House 24), Blaju (House 51), and Low Tatoy, the headman of the village in Omkoi who in 1965 was living in a field distant from the main Meto settlement and not recorded in our census.
Yang clansmen: Susa (House 38), Joying (House 54), Chaser (House 55), and Bao (House 56).
Wang clansmen: Sertoa (House 22), Songler (House 50), Nulang (House 52), and Chamang (House 60). In the following year came other Wang clansmen: Suker (House 36), Chailong (House 41), Juser (House 43), and Wangjow (House 44).

In 1962 and 1963 there was a further movement from Mae Suk comprising: *Tang clansmen*: Seipang (House 33), Joying (House 35), and Nuchow (House 42).
Wang clansmen: Wang (House 48), Tongsuk (House 58), and Serpow (House 59).

Later other persons came from villages in the Provinces of Mae Hongsorn and Lampang, and in 1964 came the migration of Tang clanspeople from Chiengrai Province who constituted Village C.

Family connections, either consanguineal or through marriage, with the earlier settlers provided most of the later-comers with their introduction to the village. One such connection might serve initially as a link for a whole group of families themselves interconnected. Residence together would provide other links through intermarriage. The main motivation for all the movement was the attractiveness of the land at Meto.

THE CRITERIA OF LAND SELECTION

What type of land is it that is attractive to Miao farmers? Ideally, and naturally enough, they would prefer a type of soil and climate which would grow every type of crop excellently. They would be highly satisfied if they could find an area which would grow both padi and poppy well and equally well. Such areas, if they exist, are almost impossible to find. Therefore they have to be content always with a compromise.

Tradition and their culture, with its interrelated material and social aspects, attach them to a cash crop. Opium, in lieu of anything else as profitable, must always be on one side of the scale. Therefore the amount of their satisfaction with the compromise depends on how much loss in padi is outweighed by gains in opium.

Compromise is necessary because poppy and padi for best results require different conditions. More study is still required to determine the optimum conditions for both of the plants in the Hill Tribe environment. But we have some knowledge of the two most important factors involved:

Altitude

Padi may do well at medium altitudes—from 2,000 to 3,500 feet. We are not considering lower altitudes because Miao are rarely found cultivating there.

Poppy generally does progressively better from 3,000 to 5,000 feet. The reasons, according to Miao informants, are several. Poppy, they say, likes cold weather. It does best when there are occasional frosts on hillcrests above the fields but these must not reach down to the poppies. Gentle continual rain when the plants are approaching maturity ensures the best crop, and the rain tends to be gentler and more frequent on the higher slopes. It should stop, however, when the petals begin to fall because wet seed heads drain away the latex when they are tapped.

Another favourable effect of altitude is that it discourages the growth of unwanted grasses. On fields cultivated for several years in succession grasses—along with weeds of various kinds—are the major problem faced by the Miao farmer. At Meto, where most of the fields ranged from 3,000 to 3,800 feet, the grasses were quick-growing and tough. They were considered likely to place an upper limit of ten years continuous cultivation on the better poppy fields. At Pasamliem where most of the fields were 1,000 feet higher than at Meto it was believed that the better of them could sustain continuous cultivation for up to twenty years.

At Meto the growth of grass seriously reduced the productivity of padi farming especially on fields—the majority of them—which had been cropped previously and recently either for padi or for opium. Had the Miao been devoted exclusively to padi farming there were various ways in which they could at least have reduced the problem, as by longer periods of fallow or by more assiduous weeding. But because all of them were also poppy farmers they usually lacked the time, or the interest, or the land to apply such methods.

In regard to their poppy fields they were able to reduce the menace of the grasses by cultivating maize which inhibited the growth of weeds from the beginning of the rains in May until the planting of the poppy in August. As the opium harvest continued usually almost to the end of

January the fields were without standing crops only for the three driest and hottest months of the year.

At Pasamliem the higher altitude was less suited to maize and less was grown, most of the fields where it was planted being at lower levels than many of the poppy fields. At the same time it was less necessary because the growth of grass was lighter and more easily weeded out.

Which of the two ecological adaptations was the better was open to some debate. The Miao at Meto recognized that the opium productivity of a field was reduced by its having to carry maize also. But the maize had much more value than merely as a cover crop. It provided food for a much larger number of pigs than at Pasamliem. On the other hand more vegetables, especially potatoes and cabbages, were grown at Pasamliem. But these were not cash-producing. In terms of Miao desires the Meto economy was the richer. It was also the less enduring.[2]

Soil type

At the time of writing, very little scientific study has been carried out to determine the different characteristics of the soils on which the Miao are growing their poppies. From his observations in Tak Province Keen says that good opium crops can be taken only from selected soils where acidity is low.[3] In the United Nations Report of 1967,[4] Phillips classified the major types of soils in the Hill Tribe shifting cultivation areas as:

1. *Reddish-brown lateritic soils.* These have an acidity between pH 5·0 and 5·5, this being raised in the surface soil by wood ash after the field has been cleared by burning prior to planting. Poppy, he says, can be produced on the soils for a maximum of 3–4 years only.

2. *Reddish-brown earths related to the weathering products of limestone.* The pH is neutral or circum-neutral, usually about pH 6·0, but may be as high as pH 7 or more where limestone debris is incorporated. Such soils, he says, are favoured for the growing of poppy.

3. *Reddish-brown latosols on basalt or andesite.* These soils, he says, are less productive that the reddish-brown earths related to the weathering of limestone but may support poppy for up to 3 to 4 years.

4. *Reddish-yellow podzolic soils.* These soils have a pH of 4·5–5·5. Poppy,

[2] This may seem contradicted by the fact that the settlers with whom we were concerned did not stay long at Pasamliem. But they were not the first group to live there. Also other factors were involved, such as the size of the area available and the social reasons certain people had for moving away.

[3] F. G. B. Keen, *Land Development and Settlement of Hill Tribes in the Uplands of Tak Province* Dept. of Public Welfare, Bangkok, 1963, p. 8.

[4] J. F. O. Phillips, W. R. Geddes, and R. J. Merrill, *Report of the United Nations Survey Team on the Economic and Social Needs of the Opium producing Areas in Thailand*, Bangkok, 1967, pp. 18–19. J. F. O. Phillips, the Leader of the Team, was the author of this chapter of the Report.

he says, is cultivated on only the deeper variants of this group, where these are first cleared from forest.

This classification in so far as it relates to degrees of opium productivity should be regarded as tentative, because the field observation on which it was based was, perforce, cursory.

The soils at Meto appeared generally, although not uniformly, to be of the reddish-brown lateritic type. They could produce satisfactory opium crops for at least seven years. I did take a number of soil samples from cultivated fields. The first two, taken from fields which had been growing poppy for six years, had a pH of between 6 and 7. Unfortunately the other samples appear to have been mislaid in the University of Chiengmai and the publication of this monograph can await their rediscovery no longer. In general my observations support the theory that a fairly low acidity favours opium crops but that this is not necessarily related to the presence of limestone.

This qualification is important because I have heard it said by agricultural experts in Thailand that in selecting land for poppy cultivation Miao are guided by the nature of the surface rocks. It could lead to the assumption that extensive opium production will be found only in limestone areas. Another indicator which the Miao are sometimes said to use is the taste of the soil.

Amongst the Meto Miao we did not find either method used. Nor was soil colour regarded as significant. The main indicators of productive quality were the friability of the soil and the presence of various types of plants on uncleared land. Successful planters whom we questioned said that for most crops the best type of soil is one which is friable until the depth of the forearm and then hard. It should not alter after the burning of vegetation on it. If after burning the soil just beneath the surface becomes powdery then it is considered a 'soil without life', which will not support poppy for more than one year.

A soil which is slightly sticky—'you slip on it when it gets wet'—is not very good for poppy. On the other hand, it tends to be 'too good' for padi. The plants will grow tall but not have much grain. It is said that a field made on such soil should be wide to allow it to become warm in the sun. If this is done good padi crops may be got from it.

Plant indicators

In searching for new land the main attention is to plants. Some are regarded as good signs and some as bad.

At Meto we collected sixteen kinds of plants which were regarded as significant. Botanical identification of the samples was made for us by Mr. Tem Smitinand of the Royal Forestry Department, Bangkok. The plants are indicators of both altitude and soil characteristics suitable or unsuitable for different crops. The samples collected, together with bamboo, are listed below, grouped according to the altitude at which they are most common, with the local Miao name being given first:

LOWER-ALTITUDE PLANTS

1. *Tzolah* (*Musa sp.=Musa glauca*). This is a species of wild banana. In the United Nations Report, Professor Phillips supports Dr. Moorman in saying that the presence of wild banana (*Musa rutilans*) is regarded by the Hill Tribes as a good indicator of soil suitable for the production of poppy for up to 10 or more years.[5] This, however, is a very broad generalization. The Meto Miao distinguish between varieties of wild banana. The commonest variety, the large plant used by the Miao for pig food, is regarded as a bad sign for poppy. A characteristic of this type of banana is that it does not grow in clumps. Tzolah belongs to this class. It is said to indicate a rather sticky soil which becomes slippery when wet and too dry when there is no rain. Also it grows mainly at altitudes where it is not cool enough for the best poppy.

Although not highly suited for poppy, the soil on which these large, non-clumping varieties of wild banana are found is regarded as very good for padi. But, as mentioned above, the field should be made large to avoid excessive stalk growth. Tzolah should be distinguished from Zotchah, a smaller clumping variety of banana, listed below, which gives different indications.

2. *Bamboo*. Prolific bamboo in an area is not a good sign for poppy. It is characteristic of lower altitudes where the air is too hot.

MEDIUM TO HIGH ALTITUDE PLANTS

3. *Konglah* (*Amomum* sp.). This is a low plant with a white flower and a two-inch long red fruit close to the ground. If it is numerous on an area it is a most welcome sign because it indicates that the soil is excellent for all crops. It was not common at Meto.

4. *Mortzauplau* (*Microstegium Vagahs* (Nees) A. Camus). A small hairy grass-like plant. It, too, is regarded as an indicator of excellent soil for all crops.

5. *Blambau* (*Boehmeria sedaefolea* Wedd). A shrub. It indicates good soil for padi and also for poppy as it is found at cooler altitudes. The Miao say that in earlier times they used to make paper for the paper money needed at spirit ceremonies from the roots of this plant mixed with bamboo.

[5] Phillips *et al.*, 1967, p. 18.

6. *Blanki* (*Debreggeasia velutina* Gaud). A shrub. This indicates, because of the altitude at which it occurs and the soil it requires, good land for poppy. We failed to note its indications for padi.

7. *Zotchah* (*Musa acuminata* Colla). This is a smaller variety of wild banana. Its leaves are purple-patched, and it grows in clumps. It grows at higher altitudes where the soil is not sticky. Therefore, it is a very good indicator for poppy. It is also fair for padi, but the plants may show an excessive stalk growth at the expense of grain.

8. *Taua* (*Neyraudia reynaudiana* Trin.). A grass with white flowers. If prolific it is a poor indicator for padi and fair for poppy.[6]

The remaining plants which we have placed in this medium- to high-altitude category are all poor indicators for poppy but some indicate soil which will grow padi with moderate success.

9. *Sangmortzau* (*Scleria terrestris* (Linn.) Fass). A grass. It is a fair indicator for padi but a poor one for poppy.

10. *Mortzaua* (*Microstegium ciliatum* (Trin.) A. Camus). A grass. A fair indicator for padi but a poor one for poppy.

11. *Taumpai* (*Themeda c/f arundinacea*). A grass. This indicates a dry soil. If it is prolific, it indicates a bad soil for padi, poppy, and maize.

12. *Tau Chitcheh* (*Thysanolaena maxima* Kuntze). A large grass, the heads of which are bound together by the Miao for making brooms to sweep their houses. If prolific it indicates a hard soil poor for both padi and poppy.

HIGH-ALTITUDE PLANTS

13. *Blonzai* (*Leea sambucina* Willd). A shrub, also found at lower altitudes. It indicates a soil on which poppy may be grown for ten years or more. Padi can also be expected to grow satisfactorily, but not outstandingly well.

14. *Kau Koying* (*Polygonum chinse* L.). A shrub. It indicates very good soil for poppy. Because of high altitude at which it usually grows it does not indicate the best conditions for padi or maize, although both crops will grow where it is found.[7]

---

[6] This is the plant used in the suter sublong ceremony referred to in Chapter Three. It flowers in the ninth month—September by the western calendar. It is said that in former times when ancestors had no other guides to the time to plant poppy they used the flowering of this plant. This could relate to the importance it gained in religious symbolism.

[7] The plant gets its Miao name from the resemblance of its fruit to the residue of opium smoking. Its young leaves, which taste sour, may be used as a vegetable and the fruit too can be eaten.

15. *Foinjo* (*Pterospermum grande* Craib). A tree. This tree grows only at high altitudes in places where there is moisture and coldness. If there are many such trees, they indicate a good area for poppy. The conditions will not be very good for padi.

16. *Jaujo* (*Commelina* sp.). A grass. A poor indicator for both poppy and padi. It grows in high places but the soil where it is found is soft and lifeless, capable of sustaining only one crop of poppy and giving small padi yields.[8]

There are other plant indicators which we were not able to find at Meto. Generally a Miao farmer will not be guided merely by a single indicator but in assessing the potential productivity of an area will take into account all the important features of the vegetation, the aspect of the land, its slope, the characteristics of the soil which he can observe, and the extent of previous use.

Another factor, not related directly to soil or climate, may also influence the decision to farm in a particular place. This is *the availability of hired labour*. Lowtang said that at Pasamliem he and his brothers could produce about 20 jois (32 kg.) of opium each year. At Meto they can produce about 50 jois (80 kg.). The land at Pasamliem was better suited to poppy. The reasons for the higher production at Meto were two. Less effort was put into padi growing and, more importantly, they could hire Karen tribesmen from neighbouring villages.

In a study of Karen communities in another area of Chiengmai Province, Marlowe found that 30 per cent of Karen families had members engaging in wage labour.[9] He describes the Karen as sub-subsistence rice-producers. Many of them seek paid labour in order to buy additional rice for their families. Employment by Miao in the area is one of the avenues open to them. Another motive some of them have for working for the Miao is to obtain opium. The fact that Karen labour is frequently paid for in opium may help to spread addiction and so reinforce the labour supply. But although a number of the Karen workers in a Miao village are usually opium addicts by no means all of them are, and the Miao prefer to have persons who are not addicted, because they get more work from them.

At Meto practically every family employed at least one Karen at various times of the year. A few households had an addict living more or less as a permanent resident. In most cases the labour was casual, being hired for clearing fields—sometimes on a contract basis for the clearing of a set area—and especially for harvesting. Richer families might

---

[8] This plant is used for the treatment of wounds, being beaten and applied as a dressing.

[9] David H. Marlowe, 'Upland–Lowland Relationships: the Case of the S'kaw Karen of Central Upland Western Chieng Mai', in *Tribes and Peasants in North Thailand* (ed. P. Hinton), Tribal Research Centre, Chiengmai, 1969, p. 57.

employ five or six Karen—men, women, and older children—at the height of the opium harvest. The wage was usually 5 baht (US$0.20) per day, or its equivalent in opium. Sometimes they might also be given rice for food while in the village.

At Pasamliem the neighbouring communities were Lahu who were not interested in wage labour. The only available labourers were a very few Thai opium addicts.

Thus to the pioneers of the Meto area the presence of Karen in large numbers in the neighbourhood was not seen simply as a disadvantage. Their opposition to Miao settlement was an obstacle to be overcome. But their labour potential was an asset worth seeking. The Karen, too, probably had an ambivalent attitude. Marlowe writes:

For many Karen, the Meo represent the most disturbing and forceful agents of change ever to enter their environment. Many Karen say that 'you can't be friends with the Meo' as there is no reciprocal marriage or courting behaviour with the members of the two groups. They also view the Meo as wealthy, and consequently able to manipulate the real well-springs of power, the district government, in a way the Karen cannot . . . Concomitant with these emphases on Karen–Meo differences and with the overt, verbal, negative evaluations of the Meo is the attraction which the higher economic status of the Meo exerts on Karen. For a number of Karen, local Meo settlements provide a nearby, regular source of wage labour income throughout the year.[10]

THE ACQUISITION OF LAND

The territory into which the Meto pioneers came was already subject to two types of ownership: the one validated by national law and the other recognized by local custom. *De jure* ownership lay with the Thailand Government which at present does not grant titles to land anywhere in the Kingdom above the altitude of 600 metres, having declared that all such land constitutes forest reserve. The migrating tribal peoples may not understand the exact nature of the Government's claim, nor appreciate the reasons for it, and they may not regard it as just, but they are generally aware of the suzerainty of the Government represented by a hierarchy of officials of diminishing involvement varying from the local sub-district headman (kamnan) and the local Forestry Officer through the sub-district officer to the District officer (Nai Amphur), all of them backed by the power of the police.

The first need of the newcomers, therefore, was to persuade or propitiate the kamnan and the Forestry Officer to allow their settlement, or if these officials were unable to grant permission themselves, to induce them to act as intermediaries in persuading or propitiating the

[10] Marlowe, 1969, pp. 62–4.

higher officials at the District headquarters. We have seen that the Meto pioneers went the full length of the chain and obtained the authority of the District Officer.

De facto ownership of the area was claimed by the Karen on the basis of prior settlement. The accepted degree of substance in their claim, however, varied with the type of land involved. The land could be divided into three categories roughly in accordance with declining altitude: (A) forest land and grassland, (B) old Karen cultivations under long fallow, (C) present Karen cultivations.

The Miao claimed that the Karen had no real right to the Category A land. Although the Karen attempted to dissuade him, claiming this land as their reserve for future expansion, the District Officer gave permission to the Miao to cultivate there. But there was an important divergence between the officially expressed attitude of the District Officer and the undeclared intention of the Miao as to the use to be made of the land. The former specified that only the unforested land could be used, as the clearing of forests for cultivation is prohibited by law. The Miao knew they could make no use of the grassland and hoped they could circumvent the law.

In regard to Category B land, Karen claims were generally recognized but the degree to which they were regarded as having strength varied according to the length of time the land had been unused. The most overgrown land was simply occupied. If no permission had been obtained from possible Karen claimants, then the Karen might be regarded as having residual rights. This is shown by a case we observed in the later years. In March 1967 Nang (House 1) was clearing a field in high secondary jungle for planting first with maize and then with poppy, having decided the soil was too rich for padi which he said would run to stalk. The field had once belonged, he said, to Karen, but since it had been left at least for seven years they were not taking any interest in it. They could have it back if they wished after he had used it for a few years.

If no payment had been made for it the previous owners were regarded as having the right, if it should come up for disposal, of re-acquiring it on terms which recognized their interest in it. This situation was exemplified by a case we observed in 1966. Field No. 166, comprising 16·41 rai, had been acquired by Songler (House 50) in the early days of settlement from Karen who had abandoned it for several years. He made no payment for it. In 1966 he migrated to Pa Khia. He would have preferred to sell the field to Miao from whom he could have got a higher price, but felt obliged to sell it to Karen who wanted it for 400 baht (US$ 20).

For much of the land the Miao settlers acquired from Karen payment was made, and in these cases absolute ownership in tribal eyes passed to the Miao who could sell it to whatever buyers they could find, or otherwise dispose of it. The process of buying from Karen continued throughout our period of study, although at a slower rate than in the early years of settlement. Prices paid depended upon the quality of the field and the need of the Karen to sell. Fields shown on the map as Karen which were afterwards acquired by the Miao were:

Field No. 19 (19·0 rai): bought by Sor (House 12) for 600 baht (US$ 30)

Field No. 63 (6·07 rai): bought by Bowjang (House 16) who received it in payment of a debt owed by Karen.

Fields No. 50 and No. 51 (3·86 rai): bought by Joying (House 35) for 3 kam of opium (=390 baht or US$ 19·50).

Fields No. 117 (3·75 rai) and No 171 (15·03 rai) bought by others for unspecified amounts.

THE CODE OF LAND TENURE

We may summarize the general code governing the ownership of land which appears to apply generally amongst the Miao and their neighbours. We cannot properly call it a law since there was no force capable of ensuring its acceptance. Its effectiveness, especially as it applied between persons of different tribes, depended solely upon a general recognition of its validity. We know of no cases of physical fighting amongst Miao or between them and other tribes over land, and open disputes were extremely rare, perhaps because courts had not yet been introduced to spawn litigation and add acrimony to disagreements.

In regard to previously uncleared land, the person first clearing it gained complete rights of use and disposal. Persons intending to clear new areas might put marks in it. Other persons considering clearing nearby should first ask them the extent of the areas they intend using and respect the boundaries they define.

In regard to cleared land, it may pass to new occupiers by loan, by mortgage, by gift, or by purchase. If it is by loan the transfer is only for the specified period. If it is by mortgage it can be reclaimed by payment of the debt. If it is by gift the transfer is permanent but the donor usually retains the residual right to receive the first offer of the land on the most favourable terms if it is to be relinquished. If it is by sale the seller retains no rights at all.

Rights to land evaporate with its disuse. After seven years or so the Miao will often consider them weak enough to allow occupation of the land even if the previous owners remain in the neighbourhood. When a residential group moves away from an area all its rights to the land are considered abandoned and cannot be reasserted if a new group moves into the area to occupy the land. The general acceptance of this part of the code is the main factor which prevents the migratory mode of life of many of the tribes from leading to dissension amongst them.

It may, however, be modified in the case of closely connected groups when one group, considering moving into an area which has been previously occupied by another, may first inquire whether that other group intends moving back there itself. This happened in the case of a Wang clan group at Meto in 1966. They planned to go to the Pasamliem area to settle in the place where Ger (House 15) had previously had his fields. They asked him first if he wished to reoccupy the place himself. Having given his agreement to the move, Ger would have had to seek their agreement if he did wish later to move into the area to which they had now established their claim. The courtesy the Wang clansmen showed is expected only amongst relatives or friends. Otherwise the unoccupied hills of Thailand are open in tribal eyes to whoever comes first.

The persons who do first come to an area may lay claim to much larger areas than they themselves can use. They cannot necessarily maintain these claims against migrants or nearby settlers from other tribes because this would be against the general principle of the code. But the Miao can generally expect to maintain them with respect to other Miao because it is recognized as an accepted practice, the grounds for which are that they are reserving the land for the coming of kinsmen. It is known that once the kinsmen are accommodated they will release any spare land to any other tribesmen who wish to settle in the area, and indeed they will usually yield un-needed land at any time in response to a request from other Miao because such extensive claims are not strong.

The first settlers at Meto did claim extensive areas into which they attracted first relatives, and then persons of other sub-clans or clans. The way in which rights may be redistributed by a settled group will now be discussed.

THE DISTRIBUTION AND TRANSFER OF LAND RIGHTS

In many shifting cultivation economies land does not increase in capital value after its occupation. No permanent buildings are put upon it; there are no irrigation works or terraces; no manuring except from the initial burning, the effect of which is soon dissipated; and its fertility declines sharply with use. When the crop is padi it is rarely used for more than one season and for the first few years in fallow it is regarded as unusable.

In the Miao opium economy, however, land does acquire value with use. In the second and later years of cultivation the opium yield of a field may decline, although this is by no means always obvious, but any loss in this respect is usually offset many times by the saving in labour of not having to clear new fields. Indeed, the clearing of fields from heavy jungle growth is particularly difficult in such an economy. The opium harvest occupying all the farmer's time runs on into the middle of the dry season. When it ends it may be too late to get a great area of jungle cleared and prepared for the planting of maize which precedes poppy. Therefore, at least until cultivation upon it has proceeded for several years, cleared land has greater value than uncleared land. It is given up less readily and if money is required for it the price will be higher.

In the early days of the Meto settlement, pioneers who claimed rights over large areas of uncleared land gave freely to kinsmen and to other Miao who asked their permission to settle upon it. The chief value of the land at this time was its power to create around them a wider and richer human community. It was also an asset from which they could accumulate good will to be utilized later, if the need arose, to give them entry into other communities of which they might not be the pioneers.

When the land was cleared it became of higher value to its owners and its transfer was subject to much stricter terms. The two main conditions which determined these were the value of the land to its owners and the relationship of the persons to whom it was to be transferred.

Generally, households retained all the land which they found they could conveniently work. But there might sometimes be rearrangements internal to the household. Padi fields were almost always the conjoint property of the household members. Poppy fields frequently were the separate properties of individual adult men in the household. In most cases wives had no separate fields from their husbands and mothers none separate from those of their sons. But in some cases a wife or a mother might be given the right to the opium product of a separate field in the cultivation of which she might or might not be helped by her husband or son.

Cases in which mothers acquired fields were:

Field No. 115 (3·75 rai): in 1966 Juyi gave this field to his mother, who lived in the same house, and helped her to work it.

Field No. 126 (3·05 rai): Wangki gave this field to his mother, and it is not recorded whether or not he helped her to work it.

Cases in which wives acquired fields were:

Field No. 121 (1·89 rai): Yongfo gave this field to his first wife, who wanted some money of her own. She worked it with the help of her son.

Field No. 83 (3·29 rai): Koyi gave this field to his wife, who worked it without his help but with the help of her children.

Normally, the separate bestowal of land on women in a household occurs only when the household is rich in land and labour resources, having either many children of working age or the means to employ Karen labourers.

Rearrangement within the household might occur also through an older brother giving a poppy field to a younger brother, usually to help him get established as a separate producer. This occurred in the case of Field No. 143 (14·38 rai) in which Kako, an older son of Nulang in House 52, gave the field to Ler, his younger brother.

In some cases, fields may be given to brothers who live outside the household. We noted only one case of this where both parties were remaining in the area: Field No. 247 (3·08 rai). which Wangjow in House 44 gave to his younger brother, Juser, in House 43. Very occasionally a gift, usually small, may be made to another relative, as in the case of Field No. 46 (1·80 rai) which Yaitong gave to his mother-in-law, Nanglee. Usually in regard to gifts of land made to persons outside the household, the value of the land and the closeness of the relationship linking donor and recipient interplay as factors determining whether a gift will be made, and to whom it goes.

The value of land to an owner may decline for two reasons. The first reason is that although the land remains productive its owner may be moving away from the area. In such cases close relatives of the same clan are likely to be most in favour. Cases where this occurred were:

Field No. 157 (9·21 rai), which Seipang gave to his younger brother Ver on going away to Chiengdao.

Field No. 232 (5·84 rai), which Koyi gave to his younger brother Kalaow on going away to Chiengdao. Koyi also gave a smaller field, No. 86 to his nephew, Chetsu.

Next in favour may be close relatives in other clans. Cases recorded are:

Field No. 165 (16·10 rai), which Tow gave to his father-in-law on going away to Tak Province.

Field No. 227 (3·71 rai) which Hsor gave to his elder sister, the wife of Yaitong, the village headman, on going away to Tak Province.

If the land is not given to close relatives it may be given to fellow clansmen not closely connected. This happened in the case of Field No. 237 (1·96 rai) which So gave to Hjotu when he moved away to Chiengdao in 1966.

Within the clan payment is rarely, if ever, requested for land. We recorded no cases of it, although sometimes land might be given in discharge of a debt otherwise contracted, as happened in the case of Field No. 19. This field, of 16·27 rai, belonged to So in House 11. When he left to go to Chiengdao in 1966 he borrowed 220 baht from Yaitong of the same house. His father, Ying, in House 12, wanted to use the field and paid Yaitong 110 baht, whereafter the field was divided evenly between them. Field No. 229 (8·70 rai) was given to Hung by Hgartong, a fellow clansman, in payment of a debt.

Fellow clansmen are also expected not to compete with one another in purchases from other clans. Suker (House 36) of the Wang clan had originally bought Field No. 243 (9·07 rai) from Karen for 600 baht. On going away to Tak Province in 1966 he offered it to Nyaying of the Tang clan for 350 baht. Nyaying thought the price too high. Suker then sold it to Ying, also of the Tang clan, for 400 baht. Nyaying was angry with Ying who then, on receiving 200 baht from Nyaying, divided the field with him.

Between persons of different clans, payment for land exchanged is usual and is almost always given when the persons are not close relatives. The following cases occurred in 1966:

Fields No. 25 (3·41 rai) and No. 26 (19·67 rai) were sold by Jufoa of the Jang clan to Bowjang of the Tang clan for 1 joi of opium (=800–1,000 baht).

Field No. 116 (5 rai) was sold by Songpaow of the Jang clan in two halves each for 55 baht—half going to Pang of the Tang clan and half to a Yunnanese trader.

Field No. 28 (12·31 rai) was sold by Ler of the Wang clan to Ler of the Tang clan for a price which was not recorded.

Fields No. 147 (2·07 rai) and No. 146 (7·91 rai of padi land)[11] were sold by Supor of the Wang clan to Faipow of the Jang clan for 2½ kam of opium (=295 baht).

Field No. 135 (4·41 rai of padi land) and No. 134 (11·99 rai) were sold by Kup of the Wang clan to Nyatoa of the Tang clan for 100 baht.

Field No. 242 (5·19 rai) was sold by Chailong of the Wang clan to Wangpaow of the Tang clan for a price which was not recorded.

Field No. 199 (12·88 rai) was sold by Sopeng of the Jang clan to Ver of the Tang clan for 2,000 baht.

Field No. 198 (10·42 rai) was sold by Songpaow of the Jang clan to Juyi of the Tang clan for 3,000 baht.

Most of the above fields were sold because the owners were moving away from the Meto area. As they had to be disposed of on a buyer's market, the prices were subject to a wide variation. But to some extent

[11] Unless otherwise stated all the fields had been used most recently for poppy. 'Padi land' being usually land which had clearly been planted for several years with poppy, was generally less valuable.

they did reflect the relative worth of the fields. The last two fields listed were highly productive.

Just as land may be mortgaged to fellow clansmen so too it may be mortgaged to persons outside the clan. Tei in House 71 of the Jang clan offered Field No. 34 (6·84 rai) as a guarantee for a loan of 200 baht from Yaitong of the Tang clan. When he moved away to Mae Hae without paying the debt, Yaitong took over the field but in 1966 allowed Ler of the Wang clan to plant poppy on it. Sometimes the dealings are more complex. When he was preparing to move away to Mae Suk in 1965, Tow of the Jang clan borrowed money from a Yunnanese trader asking Bowjang of the Tang clan to guarantee the debt for him in return for his receiving ownership of Field No. 24 (6·78 rai). Juyi of the Tang clan obtained the field by paying Bowjang 3 kam of opium (=390 baht), the amount of the debt owing to the Yunnanese trader.

We said that the first reason land lost value to its owners was if they were moving away from the area. The second reason is its declining fertility. In an area such as Meto, which permitted the earlier settlers to clear or obtain new fields when their first ones were losing productivity, they might be willing to part with the old fields before all their value was lost. Generally they would be difficult to sell. They might give them away to fellow clansmen wishing to settle in the area. This happened in the case of the Tang migrants from Chiengrai Province who comprised Village C. The Tang people already in Meto gave them land without charge. Most of it was much-used land, but in some instances it was good land for which the owners had no immediate use. Bowjang had acquired Field No. 63 (6·07 rai) in payment of a debt from Karen. In 1965 he gave it to the Chiengrai settlers for use as a poppy field. When they moved away at the end of 1965 he divided it into three parts. The first part he farmed himself in 1966 for padi. The second part he lent free of charge to Jongjau, the son of Faitei in House 10, for use as a padi field. And on the third part he allowed Chailong, a close relative in the Wang clan, to plant padi. In 1967 he gave the entire field to some new settlers who arrived from the Mae Sot District. They were of the same Tang clan but belonging to a different sub-clan.

LAND OWNERSHIP IN TRIBE AND NATION

In the national context the Miao do not own land. In the tribal context they do own it, as individuals and as families. Their livelihood, their position in the community, and their relative wealth as groups depend upon the recognition of their titles. The disparity between the national and the local views of their situation is an ever-present danger to them, for dispossession could disrupt their whole economic and cultural life. It is an ever-present danger also to national planners who, with the greatest good will, may seek to introduce changes in the Miao way of life without being aware of the bases on which it is organized. Land ownership is a fundamental fact of tribal life. In the case of the Miao it is individual and often transitory. In the case of the other tribes it may be more permanent and take different forms. It needs to be appreciated in all its variety if the attitude of any tribe is to be explained and the relationships between tribes understood.

CHAPTER EIGHT

CROPS AND THEIR CULTIVATION

THE sequence of agricultural and social activities at Meto was governed by the weather. Phillips in the United Nations Report of 1967 divided the northern seasons as follows:

North-east Monsoon: December–February—cool, dry season.
North-east Monsoon (transition): March–April—hot, dry season.
South-west Monsoon: May–October—rainy season.
Retreating Monsoon: October–November—warm, dry season.

As he points out, however, there are considerable variations according to locality and year.[1] Approximately five-sixths of the rain, averaging about 60 inches per year, falls between May and November, and quite often heavy falls occur in the later months of this period. But the hope of the Miao, quite frequently confirmed, is that lighter rain will accompany the cooling temperatures of September and October because this is the weather most favourable to the growth of poppy, and that the latter half of November will be dry to allow the padi harvest.

The Miao year begins in December with the first appearance of the waxing moon. The great New Year Festival should take place then, although if the padi harvest has not been completed by that time it may be postponed, after an explanation to the ancestral spirits of the vagaries of the climate, until the following rising moon.

The year is divided into twelve lunar months of thirty days. There appears to be no system of a regular adjustment through an intercalary period, although it is said that sometimes the eighth month (July) is doubled. This would be the obvious time for an adjustment to be made because it is the middle of the wet season and the state of the growing crops indicates the stage of the year. Otherwise adjustments seem to be made unconsciously. The climate and the activities determined by it provide clear markers of the passage of time. The afternoon clouding of the sky at the end of April warns of the coming rains and it is time then, and not before, to get first the maize and then the padi seeds into the ground. Sophisticated intercalary procedures are more characteristic of literary peoples. Being illiterate, the Miao read their calendar in the heavens and on the land beneath. Any further correction they need is provided by the visits of traders or government officials who speak with certainty of the position in the annual cycle.

[1] Phillips, 1967, pp. 15–16.

Diagram 5 gives the outlines of the Meto socio-economic calendar. The social activities shown are not confined to the months in which they are listed. For instance, weddings, travel, and trading may occur at any time during the year but these are either the preferred periods or the periods of most frequent occurrence. Roughly, the position of an item in a column indicates its position in the month and an arrow shows the duration of the activity.

The calendar which I recorded at Pasamliem was almost identical with this Meto calendar. The calendar recorded by Keen at Tak, further to the south, shows two main differences.[2] The first is that the main opium harvest is shown as occurring in February. The second is that the maize harvest is recorded as taking place in October. This is consistent with the statement that in Tak poppy is not planted to follow maize on the same land. At Meto it is, and therefore an earlier maize harvest is necessary if the poppy is to grow.

Let us now consider in some detail the two main crops.

PADI

Almost all the padi grown at Meto and Pasamliem was of the upland, or dry-rice, type. It was of a semi-glutinous variety. The people were, however, familiar with the wet-rice type from the terraced Karen fields in the valley floors. Their own landscape did not favour irrigation, but there were three terraced fields (Nos. 70, 232, and 233) at Meto in 1965.

Only a very small number of the swidden fields growing dry rice in 1965 had been freshly cleared from primary or secondary jungle. The majority had been used in the preceding year either for padi or for poppy. It is fairly rare for poppy to follow padi on the same field. We recorded no cases of the 1965 padi fields being so converted in 1966. The reason is not because of supposed loss of fertility due to the padi, but because of the difficulty of clearing the weed growth which follows the padi harvest in November. Usually only when a padi field has been abandoned long enough for secondary growth to reach the stage when it can be burnt off can it then be used for poppy. On the other hand, we recorded many cases of poppy fields being converted to padi (Field Nos. 76, 77, 15, 26, 31, 41, 43, 39, 45, 133, 153, 124, 155 and 178).

In the areas where we have studied them the Miao do not fence their fields. This results in some loss of crop to wild animals, but the Miao apparently consider it not great enough to justify the labour of fencing. The risk from domestic animals is one of the reasons why the people frequently have their main residences distant from the fields. At the

[2] Keen, 1963, pp. 5–6.

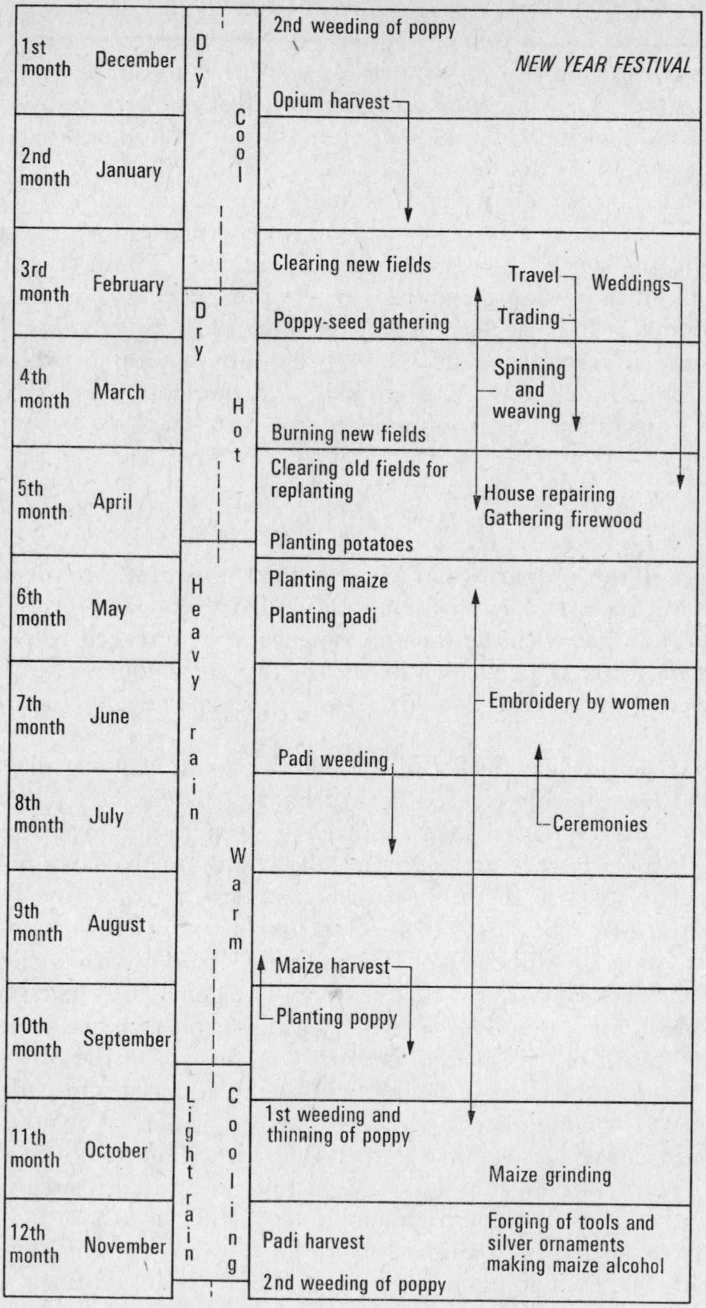

1st month	December	Dry / Cool	2nd weeding of poppy — NEW YEAR FESTIVAL — Opium harvest
2nd month	January		
3rd month	February	Dry / Hot	Clearing new fields — Poppy-seed gathering — Travel — Trading — Weddings — Spinning and weaving
4th month	March		Burning new fields
5th month	April		Clearing old fields for replanting — House repairing / Gathering firewood — Planting potatoes
6th month	May	Heavy rain / Warm	Planting maize / Planting padi
7th month	June		Embroidery by women
8th month	July		Padi weeding — Ceremonies
9th month	August		
10th month	September		Maize harvest — Planting poppy
11th month	October	Light rain / Cooling	1st weeding and thinning of poppy — Maize grinding
12th month	November		Padi harvest — Forging of tools and silver ornaments making maize alcohol — 2nd weeding of poppy

DIAGRAM 5: Socio-economic calendar

farmhouses horses and pigs are usually corralled, especially in the neighbourhood of padi fields.

Describing his observations in Tak Province Keen says: 'The rice is planted by hand in the fields, by the making of small holes with a dibber, iron shod, and planting a dozen or so seeds in each hole, and covering over. A painstaking operation requiring much labour. Cucumber, pumpkin and sweet potato are planted in the same crop association at this time.'[3] This statement describes the Meto practice with one important difference. At Meto the seeds are not covered over. This appears to be a common Miao practice because Halpern reports it also from Laos, stating: 'The grains of rice are left exposed, the Meo claim, to get sufficient water to germinate.'[4] Almost all households plant an area in one of their padi fields, or sometimes in a maize field, with hemp for cloth-making.

The padi is usually weeded only once, a month or so after planting. In the sixth month after planting it is harvested with small sickles and hand-threshed in the field by beating the sheaves on a mat.

MAIZE

Padi is not planted until the first rain has fallen. Maize is planted a week or so earlier as the seed can withstand the dryness of the soil better if the rains do not come quite as early as expected. Holes are made in the ground two or three feet apart by a single stroke of a hoe, four to six seeds are dropped in and the earth pushed back over them by the foot of the planter.

At harvest time, fresh cobs, boiled, are appreciated as food by the people. Once the cobs have become hardened by drying they are not used for human consumption except in an emergency when the grain will be stripped from the cob and pounded into flour. The bulk of the harvest is used for animal food. It is stored in granaries beside the farm huts to be taken back to the village on horses when convenient. Much of it is ground there by use of a millstone to feed to pigs.

At Meto, the area of maize fields was almost commensurate and identical with the area of poppy fields. Normally the two crops were sequential. Sometimes they overlapped. This occurred when the ripening of maize on some fields was late. It was undesirable to delay the planting of poppy and therefore the seed was scattered amongst the still-standing maize which would be harvested before the first weeding of the poppy.

Only one variety of maize appeared to be grown at Meto and it had no commercial value outside the Meto area. In 1966 Sowtong and some other men did consider growing the variety for which there is an

[3] Keen, 1963, p. 5.   [4] Halpern, 1960, p. 7.

increasing market in Thailand, based on trade with Japan, but did not pursue the scheme when it was pointed out to them that they and their neighbours would probably have to change exclusively to this variety if rapid hybridization was to be avoided. They recognized the difficulty in getting the co-operation of all the growers in their family-individual-istic community. And they themselves were reluctant to abandon completely a variety which had proven local value.

Maize, therefore, has no importance as a cash crop or as a direct subsistence crop. It has great importance, however, as part of an economic complex comprising maize–opium–pigs. This complex is the basis of the Meto Miao ecology. Its central feature, making it so profitable, is the opium derived from the poppy.

POPPY

Bernatzik in his work states:

The Miao cultivate three different kinds [of poppy], which are known by the colour of their flowers: Thus white, red, and purple poppies are distinguished. They are sown at the end of June, after the earth has been loosened with a digging stick. Tobacco, spinach, and onions grow at the same time on the poppy fields, and this increases the importance of the poppy fields to the Miao. Six months after the poppies have been sown, opium extraction begins. The almost-ripe poppy heads will be slit with a triple-bladed knife. A whitish sap—opium, in fact—flows out and is carefully collected. After appropriate processing, this becomes the Miao's most precious commodity. The opium crop now consists of the matured poppies, which are highly valued for their oil content as articles of food.[5]

Meto practice does not accord entirely with this statement, but some of the differences may be accounted for by changes which have developed since Bernatzik made his study.

The Meto Miao are familiar with five varieties of the opium poppy which they name as follows:

1. *Na Ying*. This, they say, was the main variety they grew until some time after their settlement at Pasamliem. It is a tall poppy with a white flower and usually only one or two heads to a plant. The heads are large but comparatively low-yielding. It requires five months from planting to maturity. For harvesting in December it needed to be planted in July and could no doubt be planted sometime in late June for a harvest in November after the cessation of the rains.

Because of its early planting it was not a variety which could fit well into the maize–poppy–pigs complex. It is interesting that this complex was not such a marked feature of the Pasamliem economy as at Meto. Bernatzik, too, does not put emphasis on a maize–poppy sequence. He

[5] Bernatzik, 1947, p. 358, translated from the German.

does remark that: '. . . poppy crops can be laid out on old harvested maize fields, so that the fewest demands on land will be made.'[6] He must, however, have been referring either to a divergent practice involving a different variety of poppy or else to maize fields which had been cultivated in a previous year, because it is difficult to believe that maize could have been harvested by June.

2. *Ying Chang.* This variety also appears to have been known to the Meto people for a long time. It was grown in smaller quantities than *Na Ying* for its medicinal rather than cash value. It has a purple flower and purple stem. It may mature in three months. Sometimes it is planted in August but usually in September for a harvest in December. It has a big head but is low-yielding. The opium is believed to be particularly good for stomach ills. The Miao say that because of the reliance they were forced to place upon it, until in recent years they began to obtain other medicines from lowland Thai, it was the main cause of opium addiction amongst them.

3. *Ying Pang Tzai* (the multicoloured poppy). This variety has a variegated red and white flower. They say they first obtained the seed from Thai traders during the regime of Marshall Pibun when they were given licences by the Government to grow opium.[7] For this reason it is sometimes referred to as *Ying Thai*, the 'Thai Poppy'. It takes four months to mature and is usually planted in September for a harvest in late December or more commonly in January. It may have three or four heads per plant and is more productive than the two varieties already mentioned but less so than *Ying Pang Gler*.

4. *Ying Pang Gler* (the white-flowered poppy). This is the most favoured variety and the most recently acquired. It is said that some members of the Jang clan living at Muang Terng in Om Koi District went to Veng Papau with the intention of settling there. They found the region fully occupied by White Miao and decided against trying to settle. From the White Miao they obtained seeds of this variety of poppy which they brought back to plant at Muang Terng. Later Lowtong went to Muang Terng to visit his kinsmen and fellow clansman Lowfai (Tang clan) who had migrated there from Doi Luang prior to Lowtong's move from there to Pasamliem. He brought back the seed to Pasamliem.

According to Lowtong, in very good soil there may be as many as thirty heads to a plant. Sometimes there may be only a single head but the average is seven or eight. They are high-yielding compared to the other varieties. This poppy takes three and a half months to mature

[6] Ibid.
[7] Marshall Pibun was Prime Minister 1938–44 and 1948–57. The period referred to was apparently the earlier one.

and can be planted in late August or September for harvesting in December or January.

5. *Ying Pang La* (the red-flowered poppy). This variety has a dark reddish, almost purple flower and a green stem. It is a productive poppy but not as high-yielding as *Ying Pang Gler*. It averages three to four heads per plant. It takes four months to mature and is usually planted in August for harvesting in December, but sometimes in September for harvesting in January.

Although the white-flowered poppy (*Ying Pang Gler*) is by far the commonest at Meto there is advantage in planting some of the other varieties along with it because the differing maturing rates allow the harvesting to be spread over a longer period, thus gaining a greater return from the limited amount of labour available. The 'red-flowered poppy' (*Ying Pang La*) and the 'multicoloured poppy' (*Ying Pang Tzai*) are frequently seen amongst the white poppies. Sometimes this may not be due to deliberate policy but due to perpetuation of the mixture in the seed gathered from previous plantings. Quite often there are small plots entirely of the purple poppy (*Ying Chang*) which is still grown by some people for medicinal use.

Processes of poppy cultivation

At Meto much more attention, care, and skill were devoted to the poppy fields than to the padi fields. After the surface soil of the field has been tilled the seed is scattered and lightly covered over. When the plants are a few inches high the field is again hoed to loosen the soil around the plants and to thin them out where they are growing too thickly. Young plants removed in the thinning may be cooked as food. They are not an important dietary item, and as far as I know this is the only stage at which the poppy is eaten. We did not find any use of the seed-heads for food, as stated by Bernatzik.

As the plants approach the flowering stage there is further weeding and thinning. In the earlier and later phases of this work both sexes participate as fully as their energy and available time allow, since there is much to be done within limited periods if the crop is to be successful. Because there is need to work with speed and yet to avoid damage to the plants, children do not usually take part.

When the seed-heads have shed their petals it is time for them to be tapped. As Bernatzik says, the tapping instrument is a triple-bladed knife. He does not, however, explain the reasons for this form of instrument and I do not know of any account which indicates its full significance. Strictly speaking, it is not a three-bladed knife. It is three separate blades bound together. They are so bound that they project to different distances with the result that each will cut to a different depth in the skin of the poppy-head, the intention being to tap the sap of the different layers. A skilled poppy tapper knows how deeply to cut and therefore needs no guide on the instrument. But persons may differ in their degrees of skill, especially the children who are required to help out at the height of the opium harvest. Therefore the binding of the instrument is often so arranged as to prevent the blades from severing the skin completely because the sap may then run inwards to the seeds and be lost to the harvester.

Usually a single perpendicular stroke is made with the instrument on opposite sides of the poppy head.[8] The sap begins to exude immediately as a milky liquid congealing sufficiently on contact with the air to prevent its dripping off the head. At least four hours should be allowed for complete exudation and congealing to a consistency at which it may be scraped off. By this time it will usually have become viscous and amber-coloured. Generally, poppies are tapped in the morning and scraped in the afternoon. Sunny days, which are the rule at harvest time, are much to be preferred because the sap flows more freely and solidifies more quickly. Rain may be disastrous because it may liquefy the sap.

The scraping instrument is a flat iron blade three to four inches wide with a short handle. When it has become fully loaded the opium may be taken from it to be wrapped in poppy petals, making small bundles which the harvester carries with him in his clothing or in a bag. Or, if there are several harvesters in a field, there may be a dish moved from place to place into which the loads from the scrapers are deposited.

In Meto poppy-heads were usually tapped only once. But because the flowering is not uniform the fields have to be gone over many times before all plants have been covered, and the total harvest occupies at least a month for almost every household. The planting of several varieties of poppies and different planting dates for different fields may extend the time to two months.

Labour demands of opium cultivation

Because each poppy-head has to be treated individually at least twice—for tapping and for scraping—the harvesting of large areas requires much labour. The size of the fields at Meto taxed the labour of almost all the households to the maximum—and beyond.

The first detailed study of which we are aware of the time taken for opium harvesting operations in a Hill Tribe area in Thailand was

[8] The method, however, is apparently not the one which would give the highest yield. Dr. Kusevic, Director of the United Nations Division of Narcotic Drugs, informed me that because of the way the sap canals run more opium could come from horizontal cuts.

carried out by Mr. Douglas Miles in the course of his socio-economic survey of the Yao community at Phu Luang Gha village in Chiengrai Province. He supplied the following information to the 1967 United Nations Survey Team:[9] 'It takes five minutes per person to incise 100 heads; more than eight minutes to scrape them. There is an average of 1,885 plants in 100 square metres, each plant with an average of four heads.' These figures would yield totals of 30,160 plants and 120,640 poppy heads per rai. The time required for incising them would be 100·5 hours and for scraping them, 161 hours, making a total of 261·5 hours for the harvesting operation. Supposing a worker averaged eight hours per day continuously, it would take him or her more than a month to harvest a single rai.

Although we did not make a similar detailed study, our own subsequent observations at Meto appeared to confirm the accuracy of Mr. Miles's figures regarding the time needed to incise and scrape poppy-heads. How then was it that the Meto Miao could cultivate such large areas? The average total harvesting period for Meto households was less than two months, and for the early part of this period the daily hours were less than eight. If, therefore, the situation were identical with that in Phu Luang Gha, one would expect that the average amount of poppy cultivated per head would be less than two rai. In fact, it was 2·3 rai, and 67 per cent of the households had more than two rai per head. These averages include children of any age as well as adults. Table 15 shows the distribution of households according to size of holdings. The modal size is less than two rai per head but 35 per cent of the households had three rai or more, 16 per cent has four rai or more, and 8 per cent had five rai or more.

One factor which could influence the size of the area which could be harvested would be its degree of productivity. Mr. Miles gave the United Nations Team an estimate of 4 kg of opium per rai for the Phu Luang Gha fields.[10] The average yield in Meto was no more than half this amount. The average number of plants per rai and the average number of heads per plant are certainly much less than the figures he gives. Only the best fields at Meto equal the average at Phu Luang Gha. Partly this may be due to differences in soil type or length of cultivations on the same areas, but generally the Meto Miao appear to plant more widely and tend the individual plants less carefully than the Yao farmers of Phu Luang Gha.

Nevertheless, the average productivity at Meto is not so low that it alone can explain the large size of the poppy fields. Even if the number

[9] Mr. Miles was associated with the Tribal Research Centre in Chiengmai. His study, continued in 1967 and 1968, yielded many other interesting results which no doubt he will publish shortly. Only the figures which he supplied to the United Nations are quoted here.

[10] Phillips et al., 1967, p. 46.

TABLE 15

Area of poppy cultivations per head in households

AREA IN RAI PER PERSON	NO. OF HOUSEHOLDS IN GROUP
0–0·4	2
0·5–0·9	5
1·0–1·4	9
1·5–1·9	11
2·0–2·4	8
2·5–2·9	6
3·0–3·4	9
3·5–3·9	3
4·0–4·4	3
4·5–4·9	2
5·0–5·4	1
5·5–5·9	1
6·0–6·4	1
6·5–6·9	2
TOTAL HOUSEHOLDS	63

NOTE: Village C was not included in this Table and two other households were left out because of uncertainty regarding them.

of poppy-heads per rai is only half that stated by Mr. Miles, the maximum area per head which a household could harvest in the limited time permitted to it utilizing all the labour of men, women, and children it can muster would probably be no more than 2·5 rai.

It is instructive to look at the situation in regard to the largest holdings. Thirteen of the 63 households surveyed had total holdings of poppy fields in excess of 30 rai. All save four of these households had ten or more members, and generally the larger size of the total holding was accounted for by the larger number of people. Thus, Household No. 4 with 20 persons averaged only 1·6 rai per head and Household No. 52 with 18 persons averaged 2·1 rai per head. But there were exceptions as shown in Table 16. How did they do it? Such large holdings were beyond their own manpower resources. They achieved them by employing outside labour—from neighbouring Karen communities.

As stated earlier, a majority of Meto households employ some Karen. Households rich enough to begin the process on a fairly large

TABLE 16

Households with exceptionally large areas of poppy cultivations per head

HOUSEHOLD	TOTAL HOLDINGS	AVERAGE PER HEAD
No. 13 (7 persons)	47·61 rai	6·8 rai
No. 43 (11 persons)	72·84 rai	6·6 rai
No. 39 (6 persons)	36·88 rai	6·1 rai
No. 14 (10 persons)	41·05 rai	4·1 rai
No. 50 (20 persons)	63·78 rai	3·2 rai

scale can maintain their wealth by continuing it. An outstanding case was that of Kalaow in Household No. 39. Although he had a relatively small household he was able to maintain the sixth largest area of poppy fields in the village. To his outside labour resources he added his own outstanding energy.

Primarily the Miao are producers. Conservation is at best a secondary consideration because they do not envisage permanent settlement. When they plant more widely and tend the individual plants less carefully than the Yao they are exploiting their Meto environment. For several reasons Karen labour is most easy to get at opium harvest time. The Karen padi harvest is finished and the people are free. There is the immediate attraction of opium for the addicts amongst them. There is the fresh product of the fields to pay them with. Therefore, the pool of harvesters is much greater than the pool of cultivators for earlier stages of the crop. In these circumstances it proves more productive to have a large crop than a small crop of higher quality.

The Karen are thus an important part of the ecological setting at Meto to which the Miao have adjusted. The form which the adjustment takes is dictated by the devotion of the people to opium production. It determines the size of the fields and the use made of foreign labour. It also governs their own labour patterns, excluding other economic and social enterprises by completely monopolizing the time of their men, women, and children for two months of the year.

OTHER CROPS

The Blue Miao communities in Thailand which we have observed do not cultivate separate vegetable gardens, but a number of different species of vegetables are grown amongst the padi or poppy. The extent to which they are cultivated depends partly upon the degree of concentration on poppy-growing and partly upon the relative suitability of soil and climate. At Pasamliem during a trip to the fields on 18 December 1959, I noted cabbages, peas, pumpkins, potatoes, sweet potatoes, taro, and some yams. Elsewhere I had seen cucumbers, tomato plants with the small type of fruit, and several varieties of spinach. With the exception of the cucumbers, some of the pumpkins, and the spinach, the quality was generally poor. The sowing was haphazard, the plants received no care except for the general weedings given to the whole poppy or padi field, and they were far from prolific.

But they were more numerous than at Meto where the same vegetables were found. There were probably several reasons for this. The greater concentration on opium meant that there were fewer padi fields in which the cucumbers and pumpkins were usually planted. The heavier weed growth after the padi harvest made it difficult to use these fields for growing cabbages and peas. At the same time the richer opium harvest made the vegetables appear less important to the people because they could diversify their diet through trade.

Potatoes were an exception at Meto. In 1965 some farmers planted them as a commercial crop with seed provided by Chinese traders who were to buy the harvest. In 1966 the total area planted had extended to a few rai. The profit in that year was about equal to that which could be gained from the same area of poppy, which induced still more people to plant them. The demand for potatoes, however, was limited largely to the European residents at and visitors to Chiengmai. It reached saturation point and the price collapsed.

If the potatoes had been of better grade they might have reached a wider market or at least competed more successfully for the limited outlet available. But both seed and technique were poor. Some of the potatoes were blighted. They were put into the soil and left to grow in much the same manner as maize, without manuring or mounding.

The Miao are not impressive vegetable gardeners. It is not that they are unaware of the possibility. Most of them have seen gardens in the lowlands, and there were even a few local examples provided by Chinese traders in their area. Nor were they entirely without facilities. Climate and soil were favourable for some crops and they had animal manure available. Against these assets there were disadvantages. They were remote from markets. The great number of pigs kept in the village and allowed generally to run free made vegetable gardening in its neighbourhood impossible without fencing, which was difficult to obtain. But the major factor was undoubtedly the overriding interest in opium production and the overriding demands it made on time.

RELIGION AND AGRICULTURE

The Miao at Meto were practical agriculturists who did not allow the unseen world to inhibit them in their established pursuits. The very small amount of ritual occurring in connection with the agricultural cycle was generally intended to prevent spritual interference with projects already decided upon. The rest of it was to obtain co-operation, either in the way of positive help or in the form of insight into the future. The practices described below were considered desirable rather than obligatory and those who carried them out appeared to be outnumbered by those who failed to do so.

At the time of the New Year Festival chickens should be sacrificed in the household for the souls of the padi, maize, and poppy. At the ceremony we observed in Lowtong's house on 22 December 1965, one chicken was offered for the souls of the padi and maize, which were expected to share it, and one chicken for the soul of the poppy. This ceremony illustrated the practical bent of the Miao in regard to the place of religion in their agriculture. Although it coincided with it, the difference in the relative size of the offerings was not due to the difference in the relative economic importance of the crops. A separate chicken was needed for the poppy because its bones were to be studied to determine the prospects of the crop which had not yet been harvested. The bones of the chicken offered to the padi and maize were not studied because the yields were already known. The interest in the bones was in divination, which would not alter the behaviour to follow.

The games played at the New Year Festival are expected to help the coming agricultural activities by pleasing the spirits. It is not certain whether their pleasure ensures their positive aid or merely placates the potential mischief within them. The reaction may differ according to classes of spirits. They are not accorded a decisive role and the general aim is to keep them benign in whatever role they choose to occupy.

Before persons set out to pioneer a new area, or to join persons who have already settled there, chicken bones may be studied to determine the fortunes of the proposed venture. But it is doubtful if the results really very often govern behaviour. If the omens from the first chicken sacrificed are bad, another may be sacrificed. On one occasion we were with Lowtong when he took omens from three successive chickens. He probably stopped then only because the cost was getting too great. All the omens were bad and the plan being considered was abandoned. But the occasion did not concern a pioneering venture on which he had set his heart. It was a plan into which he had been induced by a Government officer to send his son to a school in another province. No children from Meto had gone to a school before. On this occasion three others did go and no omens were taken by their families beforehand.

The planting areas of a village are not usually selected with any reference to the spirits. When a new cultivation has been decided upon and is about to be cleared, rice and meat—or if no meat is available, salt—may be offered to the spirit of the place with the words: 'Here is some old rice to eat with us. We are going to make a new padi (or poppy) field here. Protect us and our horses.' The owner of the field should then state how many men and how many horses will come to work there. When the fire is lit to burn off the field, the person lighting it speaks aloud to warn the spirits of the forest and the streams to keep clear.

At the time of the first planting of the field a further offering of rice and meat should be given to the spirit of the place and a promise made to it that it will be given a chicken, or even a pig, if the harvest is good. The promise is accompanied by a request to the spirit to keep the crop free of rats, birds, and other harmful things. At the time of the harvest, whether it is plentiful or not, the offering should be placed on an altar in the centre of the field, for otherwise, it is said, the owner may be killed by the spirit for defaulting.

This is the theory of what should be done. No doubt it is sometimes done, but we never witnessed it. However, we saw only a few fields cleared from old jungle and the ceremony may be more frequent in the pioneering phase of a settlement. Most agricultural activities are carried on without overt reference to the spirits. The Miao seek the security of a well-disposed spirit world, but they are rarely deterred by fear. Their attitude to the spirits is assertive. This accords well with their journeyings far and wide into alien places.

Only in regard to novel undertakings are they likely to feel uncertainty and even then the causes may be as much social as spiritual, although the doubts may be given a wholly spiritual rationale. Late in our stay at Meto in 1967 we interested the people in a plan to make a fishpond in a small swamp below the main water-hole, stating that we could obtain fish from a Government station in the lowlands.[11] It was first proposed as a village venture but co-operation between all the households to participate equally in the work could not be obtained. Then Lowtong and his neighbours decided to carry out the work by themselves.

The pond was duly made and stocked with fish which by their fast growth had overcome village scepticism by the time we left. Possibly they aroused jealousy also. Shortly afterwards Lowtong's grandchild died and a little later there were two more child deaths in his group. A shaman was called in to diagnose the cause. He said that the spirit of the swamp was angered that no offering had been given to it before the

---

[11] We did not normally attempt to operate as agents of change. Kkun Nusit, as an employee of the Department of Public Welfare, was interested in measures which might help the economy of the village, but the experiment was made largely for its intrinsic interest, and because of the Miao interest which arose out of its discussion.

pond was made. No fish should be eaten from the pond and the pond itself must be destroyed. The retaining wall was broken open and the fish escaped downstream where they fed Karen.

The planning of the venture was faulty. Greater attention should have been paid to the religious practices of the community and the shaman should have been made a member of the pond-owning group.

CHAPTER NINE

THE PRODUCTIVITY OF THE LAND

As stated in Chapter Six, the total area of land under cultivation at Meto in 1965 was 1,702·4 rai, or 271·75 hectares. Of this area 1,365·6 rai, or 218·5 hectares, was planted in poppy, often preceded by maize, and 290·24 rai, or 46·44 hectares, in padi. Part of the remaining 46·64 rai, or 6·82 hectares, was planted in other crops such as potatoes, and on the rest of it the crops were not accurately determined.

Table 17 gives details of the production of each household in so far as they could be assessed. Data recorded in the table should be considered in the light of comments on various items which follow.

PADI PRODUCTION

The six households in Village C, which stayed only a year in the Meto area, planted very little padi and we were not able to assess their harvests. We were also unable to obtain data in respect to House No. 47, owing to the absence of the household head. The other 64 households, comprising 523 persons, planted a total of 265·5 rai (42·48 hectares), giving a mean of 0·51 rai, or 0·08 hectare, per person. This is equivalent to a production per household of six persons of 3·06 rai, or 0·48 hectares.

According to figures from Government censuses quoted by Chapman,[1] more than half the farming households in Chiengmai Province have holdings of more than 6 rai (0·96 hectares). Hinton gives a mean size for Karen household cultivated padi swiddens of 4·9 rai (0·80 hectare),[2] although most of the Karen in the village he studied also had some wet-rice fields.

In Meto 21 of the 64 households had no padi cultivations in 1964. Eliminating these 21 households, embracing 111 persons, the mean holding for a household of six persons was 3·84 rai, or 0·61 hectare. Therefore even amongst Miao families in Meto which do have padi fields, the average size of their cultivations is small by the standards of surrounding peoples. The fact that one-third of the families had no padi fields at all shows the relatively light attention paid to padi cultivation.

We obtained estimates of production from 34 households embracing 334 persons. The total was 37,491·2 kg, giving a mean yield per person

[1] E. C. Chapman, *An Appraisal of Recent Agricultural Changes in the Northern Villages of Thailand*, Mimeograph, 1967.

[2] P. Hinton, *The Pwo Karen of Northern Thailand—A Preliminary Report to the Department of Public Welfare*, Thailand, 1969, p. 56.

of 112·2 kg. For the nine other households which had padi fields but could give us no statement as to the amount of their harvest we assessed production at 171 kg per rai, making a total for the 64 households (including the 21 which had no padi fields) of 47,409·2 kg. This is a mean production per person of 90·6 kg—an amount certainly less than half the average food needs.

Padi yield per rai and per hectare

For the 34 households (334 persons) from which we obtained harvest estimates the area of land belonging to them which we mapped was 205·5 rai. This gives a mean yield of 182·4 kg per rai, or 1,140 kg per hectare. However, in the case of five of these households (belonging to Village A) part of the production was derived from fields not shown on the map. As mentioned earlier, a very small portion of the Meto territory was missed by the photographing aircraft.[3] Eliminating these five households the total yield falls to 27,819·2 kg and the area to 190·1 rai, giving a mean production of 135·8 kg per rai, or 842·5 kg per hectare.

The first figure of 182·4 kg per rai was probably too high, but the second figure of 135·8 kg per rai is almost certainly too low. There are several possibilities of error. In the first place the five households eliminated were amongst the most industrious farmers in the Meto complex. Secondly, although we visited all the planting areas, we were not in every case accompanied by the owner and therefore identification of ownership and crop pattern could sometimes have been wrong. This could happen because by the time the aerial photographs were obtained and the ground identification utilizing them was made, new and sometimes different crops had already been planted on much of the area. Thirdly, we did not know all the households intimately and therefore the declared yields may have been erroneous. For these reasons we must regard this widest sample as fairly crude.

Greater accuracy can be claimed for figures relating to Village A. We knew all these people well and could trust them, in regard to padi, to give us as accurate estimates as they could of their production. There were 21 households in the village, of which 16 had padi cultivations, and 14 of these were able to give us what they considered to be accurate estimates of their harvests. The average yield for these 14 households was 288·9 kg per rai. Again, however, we are forced to exclude the five households previously referred to. The remaining nine households cultivated 52·9 rai for a declared yield of 9,048 kg, giving an average yield of 171 kg per rai, or 1,069 kg per hectare.

[3] We did attempt a ground survey of these fields later when we realized they did not appear on the aerial photographs but accuracy was impossible because they had all been abandoned and were partly overgrown.

TABLE 17

Padi and opium production and derived cash incomes by villages and households

1 Household Nos.	2 No. in household	3 Padi area	4 Declared padi yield	5 Poppy area	6 Declared opium yield	7 Opium yield at 1·3 kg per rai	8 Value of padi deficit	9 Cash surplus over declared padi need	10 Cash surplus over padi needs (opium yield 1·3 kg per Rai)	11 Cash surplus per head (declared) A/C Column 6)	12 Cash surplus per head (calculated A/C Column 7)
	PERSONS	RAI	KG	RAI	KG	KG	BAHT	BAHT	BAHT	BAHT	BAHT
VILLAGE A											
1	10	3·0	1,160·0	26·1	19·2	33·9	1,152·40	13,247·60	24,272·60	1,324·76	2,427·26
2	8	8·1	928·0	16·2	16·0	21·0	921·92	11,078·08	14,828·08	1,384·76	1,853·51
3 (A, B, C)	4	3·2	547·2*	20·5	6·4	26·6	389·40	4,410·60	19,560·60	1,102·65	4,890·15
4 (A, B, C)	20	2·5	2,320·0	31·6	16·0	41·0	2,304·80	9,695·20	28,445·20	484·76	1,422·26
5 (A, B)	9	3·7	2,320·0	35·4	8·0	46·0	No deficit	6,000·00	34,500·00	666·66	3,833·33
6	4	—	—	13·0	8·0	16·9	860·00	5,140·00	11,815·00	1,285·00	2,953·75
7 (A, B)	14	4·5	928·0	26·8	14·4	34·8	2,211·92	8,588·08	23,888·08	613·43	1,706·29
8	9	6·2	1,060·2*	6·2	11·2	8·0	1,023·22	7,376·78	4,976·78	819·64	552·97
9 (A, B)	9	5·4	580·0	25·2	11·2	32·7	1,436·20	6,963·80	23,088·80	773·75	2,565·42
10 (A, B, C)	14	2·5	1,740·0	32·7	12·8	42·5	1,513·60	8,086·40	30,361·40	577·60	2,168·67
11	7	—	—	21·0	4·8	27·3	1,505·00	2,095·00	18,970·00	299·28	2,710·00
12	10	4·1	928·0	19·1	6·4	24·8	1,351·92	3,448·08	17,248·08	344·80	1,724·80
13	7	4·8	2,552·0	47·6	17·6	61·8	No deficit	13,200·00	46,350·00	1,885·71	6,621·42
14 (A, B)	10	6·8	696·0	41·1	6·4	53·4	1,551·44	3,248·50	38,498·56	324·85	3,849·85
15	10	8·2	1,740·0	30·9	9·6	40·1	653·60	6,546·40	29,421·40	654·64	2,942·14
16	10	—	—	31·9	35·2	41·4	2,150·00	24,250·00	28,900·00	2,425·00	2,890·00
17 (A, B)	14	10·8	1,740·0	19·6	21·6	25·4	1,513·60	14,686·40	17,536·40	1,049·02	1,252·60
18	8	2·0	348·0	26·5	6·4	34·4	1,420·72	3,379·28	24,379·28	422·41	3,047·41
19	14	1·9	174·0	24·8	12·8	32·2	1,513·60	8,086·40	22,636·40	577·60	1,616·88
20	9	—	—	17·0	12·8	22·1	1,935·00	7,665·00	14,640·00	851·66	1,626·66
21	7	—	—	31·8	4·8	41·3	1,505·00	2,095·00	29,470·00	299·82	4,210·00
TOTAL 21	207	77·7	21,327·4	545·0	261·6	707·6	26,973·54	169,226·00	503,726·46	817·53	2,433·46

1 Household Nos.	2 No. in household	3 Padi area	4 Declared padi yield	5 Poppy area	6 Declared opium yield	7 Opium yield at 1·3 kg per rai	8 Value of padi deficit	9 Cash surplus over declared padi need	10 Cash surplus over padi needs (opium yield 1·3 kg per Rai)	11 Cash surplus per head (declared A/C Column 6)	12 Cash surplus per head (calculated A/C Column 7)
	PERSONS	RAI	KG	RAI	KG	KG	BAHT	BAHT	BAHT	BAHT	BAHT
VILLAGE B											
22	9	7·1	1,214·1*	18·8	9·6	24·4	890·87	6,309·13	17,409·13	701·01	1,934·34
23	6	3·0	348·0	11·3	6·4	14·6	990·72	3,809·28	9,959·28	634·88	1,659·88
24	6	9·1	696·0	3·1	6·4	4·0	691·44	4,108·56	2,308·56	684·76	384·76
25 (A, B)	6	3·1	580·0	10·7	8·0	13·9	791·20	5,208·80	9,633·80	868·13	1,605·63
26	6	4·0	928·0	7·3	9·6	9·4	491·92	6,708·18	6,558·08	1,118·01	1,093·01
TOTAL 5	33	26·3	3,766·1	51·2	40·0	66·3	3,856·15	26,143·85	45,868·85	792·23	1,389·96
VILLAGE D											
33	7	—	—	14·2	9·6	18·4	1,505·00	5,695·00	12,295·00	813·57	1,756·42
34 (A, B, C)	13	0·6	812·0	18·0	8·0	23·4	2,096·68	3,903·32	15,453·32	300·25	1,188·71
35	6	9·8	696·0	20·3	11·2	26·3	691·44	7,708·56	19,033·56	1,284·76	3,172·26
36	5	—	—	9·1	8·0	11·8	1,075·00	4,925·00	7,775·00	985·00	1,555·00
37	6	—	—	3·8	1·1*	4·9	1,290·00	—	2,385·00	—	397·50
38	8	3·7	290·0	9·7	9·6	12·6	1,470·60	5,729·40	7,979·40	716·17	997·42
39 (A, B)	6	26·8	1,856·0	36·9	9·6	47·9	No deficit	7,200·00	35,925·00	1,200·00	5,987·50
40	5	—	—	16·4	8·0	21·3	1,075·00	6,425·00	14,900·00	1,285·00	2,980·00
41 (A, B)	8	10·8	1,160·0	7·7	6·4	10·0	722·40	4,077·60	6,777·60	509·70	847·20
42 (A, B)	8	—	—	11·7	4·8	15·2	1,720·00	1,880·00	9,680·00	235·00	1,210·00
43 (A, B, C)	11	15·3	2,320·0	72·8	6·4	94·6	369·80	4,430·20	70,580·20	402·74	6,416·38
44	11	3·1	348·0	12·4	3·2	16·1	2,065·75	339·28	10,009·28	30·38	909·93
TOTAL 12	94	70·1	7,482·0	233·0	85·9	302·5	14,081·64	52,308·36	152,868·36	556·47	1,626·25
VILLAGE E											
45	5	4·4	752·4*	23·1	11·5*	30·0	427·93	8,197·07	22,072·07	1,639·41	4,414·41
46	8	4·8	696·0	22·6	11·3*	29·3	1,121·44	7,353·56	20,853·56	703·32	919·19
48	11	—	—	23·0	4·0	29·9	2,365·00	635·00	20,060·00	57·72	1,823·63
49	5	12·4	290·0	22·2	16·0	28·8	825·60	11,174·40	20,774·40	2,234·88	4,154·88
50 (A, B, C, D)	20	7·0	1,740·0	63·8	42·4	82·9	2,803·60	28,996·40	59,371·40	1,449·82	2,968·57
51	7	4·1	701·1*	20·7	11·2	26·9	902·05	7,497·95	19,272·95	1,071·13	2,753·27
52 (A, B)	18	8·9	232·0	37·0	24·0	48·1	3,670·48	14,329·52	32,404·52	796·08	1,800·25
53	4	—	—	14·5	7·2*	18·8	860·00	4,540·00	13,240·00	1,135·00	3,310·00

55	7	—	—	9·0	12·8	11·7	1,505·00	8,095·00	7,270·00	1,156·42	1,038·57
56	4	—	—	17·9	3·2	23·2	860·00	1,540·00	16,540·00	385·00	4,135·00
57	9	1·2	255·2	15·4	9·6	20·0	1,715·52	5,484·48	13,284·48	609·38	1,476·05
TOTAL 11	98	42·8	4,666·7	269·2	153·2	349·6	17,056·62	97,843·38	245,143·38	998·40	2,501·46
VILLAGE F											
58	6	—	—	—	—	—	1,290·00	—	—	—	—
59	8	7·9	232·0	3·3	4·8	4·2	1,520·48	2,079·52	1,629·52	259·94	203·69
60	4	—	—	10·8	1·6	14·0	860·00	340·00	9,640·00	85·00	2,410·00
61	7	5·9	232·0	11·0	6·4	14·3	1,305·48	3,494·52	9,419·52	499·21	1,345·64
TOTAL 4	25	13·8	464·0	25·1	12·8	32·5	4,975·96	5,914·04	19,399·04	311·26	1,021·00
BOREH VILLAGE											
62	12	—	—	15·4	16·0	20·0	2,580·00	9,420·00	12,420·00	785·00	1,035·00
63	3	—	—	12·3	4·8	15·9	645·00	2,955·00	11,280·00	985·00	3,760·00
64	5	—	—	12·9	9·2	16·7	1,075·00	13,325·00	11,450·00	2,665·00	2,290·00
65	8	6·0	1,026·0*	9·7	9·7*	12·6	837·64	6,437·36	8,612·36	804·67	1,076·54
66	3	—	—	3·7	5·6	4·8	645·00	3,555·00	2,955·00	1,185·00	985·00
67	7	0·6	2,320·0	14·1	9·6	18·3	No deficit	7,200·00	13,725·00	1,028·57	1,960·71
68	8	1·2	1,740·0	11·7	16·0	15·2	1,513·60	10,488·40	9,886·40	1,310·80	1,235·80
TOTAL 7	46	7·8	5,086·0	79·8	80·9	103·5	7,296·24	53,378·76	70,328·76	1,160·40	1,528·88
ISOLATED HOUSES											
69	4	—	—	4·8	3·2	6·2	860·00	1,540·00	3,790·00	385·00	947·50
70	2	3·1	530·1*	15·3	9·1*	19·8	No deficit	6,825·00	14,850·00	3,412·50	7,425·00
71	6	3·6	615·6*	6·8	4·0	8·8	760·58	2,239·42	5,839·42	373·23	973·23
TOTAL 3	12	6·7	1,145·7	26·9	16·3	34·8	1,620·58	10,604·42	24,479·42	883·70	2,039·95
GRAND TOTAL											
63	515	245·2	43,937·9	1,530·2	650·7	1,596·8	75,860·73	415,418·81	1,061,814·27	806·63	2,061·77

NOTES:
(1) Where a Household had land but gave no statement of yields, the yield of padi was estimated at 171 kg per rai and the yield of opium at the average for the village. Amounts so derived in Columns 4 and 6 are indicated by the asterisks.
(2) The value of padi was calculated at 0·86 baht per kg and opium at 750 baht per kg.

In the following season (1966) we made actual measurements of harvests from the fields of six households. The figures are given in Table 18, and show an average yield for the land of the six households

TABLE 18

Padi production of fields of six households

OWNER	AREA IN RAI	TOTAL PRODUCTION	KG PER RAI	KG PER HECTARE
BWOTONG				
(Village E, House 46)	13·97	3,433·6	245·0	1,531·5
JOYING				
(Village D, House 35)	3·67	870·0	237·1	1,481·9
CHETSU				
(Village A, House 18)	6·34	1,484·8	218·4	1,365·0
YAITONG				
(Village A, House 19)	9·86	1,143·6	115·9	724·4
FAITEI				
(Village A, House 10)	15·38	1,508·0	98·0	612·5
JUSU				
(Boreh Village, House 68)	1·88	69·6	37·0	231·5

of 167·1 kg per rai, or 1,044 kg per hectare. However, Jusu was atypical. He was an opium addict who neglected his field. (Bwotong was an addict also but his wife and daughters devoted their time to padi cultivation.) If we eliminate this atypical household the average yield on the land of the other five households was 172·1 kg per rai, or 1,075 per hectare.

It will be noted that this figure from direct measurement compares closely with that derived from the wider sample in Village A—namely 171 kg per rai, or 1,069 kg per hectare.

We suggest, therefore, that 171 kg per rai, or 1069 kg per hectare, is an average yield on fields cultivated to an average standard on land considered suitable for padi. The fact that the average for the Meto complex as a whole was lower is at least partly due to the fact that some of the householders were latecomers to an area where most of the suitable padi land was already being utilized. They were attracted by the opium rather than the padi prospects. The majority of the households in Village A were relatively early settlers.

The figure which we have concluded represents typical Miao production in Meto bears interesting comparison with figures from other groups of people. The average figure for Thailand as a whole calculated over a ten-year period from 1954 to 1964 was 223·6 kg per rai (1,397·5 kg per hectare).[4] Chapman, derving his facts also from official Thailand censuses, gives a much higher figure for Chiengmai Province in the 1962/3 year, namely 428 kg per rai (2,675 kg per hectare).[5]

These national and provincial averages are based almost entirely upon production from wet-rice, irrigated land. Of much closer relevance are comparisons from other swiddening areas. Chapman states that Thai farmers in Nan Province on the swiddens they have as supplements to their wet-rice fields produce 200–50 kg per rai (1,250–1,550 kg per hectare) 'as a maximum'.[6] In a report on Laos Wirtz bases a calculation of the amount of swidden production on the low average figure of 750 kg per hectare.[7]

As a preliminary to the 1967 United Nations survey of the economic and social needs of the Hill Tribes, Dr. Krui Punyasingh of the Thailand Ministry of Agriculture carried out crop-cutting experiments to determine average yields of both padi and opium. From 91 sampling plots among seven different tribal communities he found that the average yield of hill padi was 470·1 kg per rai, which is equivalent to 2,938 kg per hectare.[8] The average yield derived from the experiments is much higher than has been reported by most studies of swidden agriculture. Although there is no doubt that the experiments were carefully conducted, the sampling may not have been sufficiently extensive to yield a fully reliable result. It amounted to not much more than 1 rai (0·16 hectares) per tribe. Nevertheless the figure should be noted as one result obtained by scientific study. It shows the high level of production which can be reached on some Thai mountain fields.

Izikowitz measured the harvests of five Lamet households in Laos. The yields in kg per hectare for each of the five were 1,100/1,180/ 1,480/1,490/1,670, giving an average of 1,335 kg per hectare.[9] Freeman gives a figure of 725 kg per hectare for the Iban of Borneo[10] and my own research indicated a figure of 1,562 kg per hectare for the Land Dayaks of Borneo, although this included some production of wet-rice.[11] Hinton has given a figure of 1,464 kg per hectare for the Karen

[4] Figures derived from the Rice Department, Ministry of Agriculture, quoted in *Thailand Facts and Figures, 1965*, Ministry of National Development, Bangkok, 1965, p. 111.

[5] Chapman, 1967, Table 1.   [6] Ibid., p. 14.

[7] H. A. M. Wirtz, *Rapport interimaire au Gouvernement Royal du Laos sur l'economie agricole du Laos et le developpement des services agricoles*, F.A.O., Rome, 1958. Witrz actually speaks of 0·5 tons of white rice per hectare. We have added 30 per cent for conversion into padi.

[8] Quoted as Annex 4 to Phillips *et al.*, 1967. A full description of the design of the crop-cutting experiments together with references to similar experiments elsewhere in the world is given by Dr. Krui in the Thailand Government *Report on the Socio-Economic Survey of Hill Tribes in Northern Thailand*, Bangkok, 1966.

[9] Karl G. Izikowitz, *Lamet: Hill Peasants in French Indochina*, Etnografiska Museet, Gotenborg, 1951, pp. 287–8.

[10] J. D. Freeman, *Iban Agriculture*, H.M.S.O., London, 1955, p. 98.

[11] W. R. Geddes, *The Land Dayaks of Sarawak*, H.M.S.O., London, 1954, p. 68.

of Thailand and he quotes a figure supplied by Miles for the Yao of Thailand of 1,849 kg per hectare and by Leach for the Kachin of Burma of 1,897 kg per hectare.[12]

Combining these figures into a comparative table and inserting the Meto Miao figure in the sequence we get the results shown in Table 19.

TABLE 19

Miao padi yield compared to yields of other swidden cultivators

GROUP	KG PER HECTARE	KG PER RAI
IBAN (Borneo)	725	116
MIAO (Meto)	1,069	171
LAMET (Laos)	1,335	214
THAI (Nan Province)	1,406	225
KAREN (Thailand)	1,464	234
LAND DAYAK (Borneo)	1,562	250
YAO (Thailand)	1,849	296
KACHIN (Burma)	1,897	303

The comparison is of limited value. In several of the cases the samples were small. There is a wide range of variation even within the small samples which suggests that they might not have been fully representative of the groups as wholes. In Meto it would have been quite possible to pick six households to show a much higher average yield than that given above.

Small samples involve the risk not only of ordinary statistical but also of social causes of error. They may be biased towards the affluent families because association between them and the anthropologist is facilitated by factors on both sides. The anthropologist must seek the favour of the more powerful in the society in order to gain social acceptance; they, for their part, are the persons who can most afford to help him. One can suspect that nearly every small sample includes at least one affluent family. But even when care is exercised to avoid bias towards the affluent, the wide range of environmental conditions and many other factors such as variation in family size, health, and so on make small samples unreliable as the bases for wider conclusions. The variation in Meto is very great.

Nevertheless the comparison is interesting. With the exception of the peculiarly small figure for the Iban, all the yields fall between 1,000 and 2,000 kg per hectare. That the Miao figure is near the bottom of the list is not surprising for the following reasons.

[12] P. Hinton, 1969, p. 59.

By 1965 most of the padi fields at Meto had already been used extensively. There were no truly virgin fields and only a very few which had
been cleared in that year of secondary growth of six or more years'
standing. In many cases the fields had been used for poppy continuously
for several years before being planted in padi. We were not able to
determine exactly how many of the 1965 padi fields were in this
category because of the difficulty of finding out the crop pattern in
earlier years, but we could approach an estimate of it on the basis of
what happened in the following year.

In 1966 fifteen fields which were used for poppy in 1965 were planted
in padi. The total area of these fields was 94·76 rai, or 15·16 hectares,
which represents 32·6 per cent of the area used for padi in 1965. The
1966 percentage of padi land which had just been taken over from
poppy was probably higher than in the previous year as the percentage
tends to increase with the length of a settlement, but it was unlikely to
have been less than 25 per cent in 1965.

The relative productivity in padi of Meto compared to other groups
is also affected by the fact that the primary orientation of the people is
towards poppy. Although some of the land is considered to be better for
one crop rather than the other, a lot of it is equally suited to either.
Poppy usually wins the choice and padi is relegated to inferior land.

In situations such as that of the Meto people declining padi productivity over the years is inevitable. Poppy sets the economic scene and
padi is subservient to it. In the end, however, padi seals the fate of
poppy and the settlement collapses. How does this come about?

Because of the poppy promise of the land Meto, as we saw, quickly
gained a population density which resulted in at least 30 per cent of the
land being under cultivation each year. For the first few years padi
land could be separate from poppy land. But once used for padi, land
cannot be easily cleared again for several years for other crops or for
padi. Therefore if production of padi is to be kept up it must begin to
encroach on poppy land. Resistance to the encroachment results in padi
production falling. For some families—in 1965 one-third of the total—
it ceases entirely. But there is reluctance to abandon it altogether. It
gives assurance of at least some food.

As the poppy fields lose their fertility and the income from them
dwindles, the need for this assurance grows. Padi is planted on more
poppy land. It is about all much of the land is good for now. It thus
suits both the state of the land and the state of the people. But it spells
the end of the poppy and for many people the end of the sustenance
they can gain from that territory. In 1965 much of the population of
Meto was more than half-way to that state. Although total incomes
were generally good, the years of prosperity ahead were clearly seen to

TABLE 20

Numbers and percentages of households according to percentage of padi needs produced

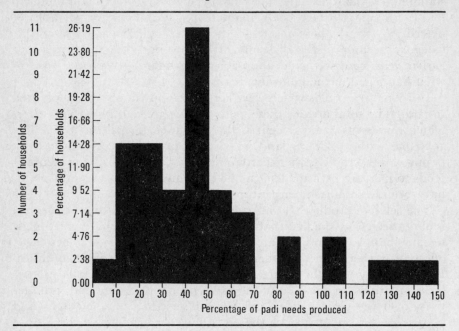

Percentage of padi needs produced

be very few. It was an ominous sign that the daily subsistence of the people now depended on poppy—for many of them exclusively and for nearly everyone partially. Table 20 illustrates the situation.

OPIUM PRODUCTION

The heads of households were asked the amounts of their opium harvests in 1965/6. Statements were obtained from 56 households. Table 21 sets out the results. The total area of poppy cultivation shown on the Map was 1,310·3 rai, or 209·55 hectares. This includes the fields of Village C. If we calculate on the basis of the average yield shown in Table 17—namely 0·53 kg per rai—the opium production of the Meto complex embracing 71 houses and 570 persons, was, in the year 1965/6, 694·46 kg, or almost three-quarters of a metric ton.

We may safely accept this as a minimum figure. But it was almost certainly too low. In other words, we are suggesting that the statements the heads of households gave of their production were inaccurate. There are several possible causes of the inaccuracy. Each no doubt

TABLE 21

Declared opium yields of villages

VILLAGE	Number of houses	Area of poppy land in rai	Total yield in kg	Kg per rai
VILLAGE A	21	545·0	261·6	0·48
VILLAGE B	5	51·2	40·0	0·78
VILLAGE D	11	227·2	84·8	0·37
VILLAGE E	8	208·9	123·2	0·58
VILLAGE F	3	25·1	12·8	0·51
BOREH VILLAGE	6	70·1	71·2	1·02
ISOLATED HOUSES	2	11·6	7·2	0·62
TOTALS	56	1,139·1	600·8	0·53

played a part but, arranging them in the order of their probable importance, they were as follows:

1. The opium was collected piecemeal over a period of approximately a month. Some of it was disposed of immediately it was collected—to pay debts, to pay Karen labourers, to buy things at the store, and some of it perhaps to smoke. Memory would tend to fix on the amount which was in hand at the completion of the harvest. As it is said that approximately half a crop usually goes to pay accumulated debts, this could be a significant factor.

2. The people are reluctant to reveal the extent of their opium income. We said earlier we felt that we could trust them to be honest in their assessments of their padi harvests, but padi is almost never sold whereas opium is almost all transferable wealth. To let the amount of one's holdings be known could disadvantage one in bargaining and involve the risk of importunity either from one's creditors or one's would-be debtors.

3. Understatement has become a habit as a protective device against outsiders seeking a share of the harvest.

4. Whereas padi fields normally belong to the whole household conjointly, poppy fields are usually separately owned by the component families in a household and occasionally separately by different members of the same family. There may be joint work by the members of a household on all the fields but the product belongs to the owner. In many cases, therefore, the heads of the households probably gave only the production of their own fields. This is probably the most important

factor leading to underestimation. The informants may have been honest. They simply did not know all the facts.

What, then, was the probable yield?

Yields of opium per rai and hectare

The first systematic attempt of which we are aware to assess the production of poppy cultivations in the tribal areas of Thailand was made in the course of the socio-economic survey of the tribes carried out by the Thailand Government from October 1961 to March 1962. Anthropological advice and guidance in the survey was provided by Dr. Hans Manndorff, acting as a United Nations expert, and Nai Patya Saihoo of Chulalongkorn University. The Report of the Survey stated that: '$\frac{1}{2}$ rai of intensive cultivation yields about the same amount of opium as 1 rai of less intensive cultivation, which is about 1 kg per year.'[13] This means a range of 1–2 kg per rai.

The crop-cutting experiments directed by Dr. Krui Punyasingh of the Department of Agriculture have already been discussed in regard to padi. Similar but more extensive experiments were carried out by him on poppy during the period January to March 1966. From 190 sampling plots each comprising a 4 × 8 metres rectangle at varying heights from 1,000 to 2,100 metres above sea level he derived a mean yield per rai of 1,294·76 g, with a standard deviation per rai of 588·99 g.[14] This is an approximate yield of 1·3 kg per rai.

None of the sample plots were in Blue Miao territory. Dr. Krui summarized the results for tribal areas in which the sample plots were located as follows:

1. Tribes producing approximately between 0·8 and 1·0 kg per rai were Lahu Laba, Lahu Kwi, Red Lahu and Akha.

2. Tribes producing between 1·1 and 1·3 kg per rai were Lisu and White Meo which is about the average production of opium.

3. Tribes producing between 1·5 to 1·7 kg per rai, which is above average, were Black Lahu, Yao and Haw.[15]

It will be noted that there is agreement between the estimates of the two different surveys, which is the reason why the United Nations Team in 1967 adopted the figure of 1·3 kg per rai as representing the average yield in tribal areas. Later information suggests that tribal yields may be much higher. Miles reports yields of more than 4 kg per rai from Yao fields. One would not expect the yields from Miao fields at Meto to be as high because the Yao in the area Miles studied were extremely

---

[13] *Report on the Socio-Economic Survey of Hill Tribes in Northern Thailand*, Department of Public Welfare, Bangkok, 1966, p. 34. On p. 49 there is a report of an interview with a Meo headman at Huey Luang, Tak Province in which he stated his yield was 0·8 kg per rai.

[14] Phillips *et al.*, 1967, p. 132.   [15] Op. cit., p. 134.

intensive cultivators who tapped the poppy capsules several times, whereas the Meto Miao were content with a single tapping.[16] Meto yields, however, were certainly sometimes much higher than 1·3 kg per rai. In 1967 we roped off a 20 × 20 metres (¼ rai) square in a field which had been planted in poppy for several years successively. The yield from the square was 0·532 kg giving a yield per rai of 2·128 kg.

The figure adopted by the United Nations Team of 1·3 kg per rai is not likely to be an overestimate of the average production at Meto during 1965 when most of the fields still retained good fertility. We have therefore adopted it as our basis for calculating the opium incomes of Meto households. No doubt the yields on some fields were less, owing to neglect, infertile soil, lack of labour for weeding and harvesting, and so on. But on other fields it was probably much greater.

Even if we were to be much more conservative and adopt a figure of only 1 kg per rai, the total production in the 1965/6 season of the Meto complex, embracing 71 households and 570 persons, would have been 1·3 metric tons of opium. This season was probably the peak of production in the area.

The value of the opium

For the detailed study we eliminated the households in Village C (for the reasons already stated) and Households Nos. 47 and 54 because of the unsatisfactory nature of the data. This left a total of 63 households. A few of these households did not give an estimation of their yields. We therefore estimated them at the average rate per rai derived from the declarations of the other households in the villages to which these households belonged. The 'declared yield' discussed below includes these estimates.

The total declared yield of the 63 households was 650·7 kg. Calculating the value of the opium at the minimum price of 750 baht per kg, the total value would be 488,025 baht, or US$ 24,401. The average cash value of the yields for the 63 households, according to the peoples' own declarations, was 7,746 baht, or US$ 387.

Calculating the yields at 1·3 kg per rai, the total for the 63 households would be 1,596·8 kg, giving a total value of 1,197,600 baht, or US$ 59,880. The average value for the households would then be 19,010 baht, or US$ 950.

INCOME LEVELS

The above figures relate only to the gross value of the opium. They take no account of the fact that the majority of the households had to

[16] D. J. Miles, *Report to the Tribal Research Centre*, mimeograph, 1968.

use a portion of their opium to buy padi needed for food. A realistic assessment of incomes must take account of this factor.

We assumed an average padi consumption of 250 kg per person per year—an arbitrary figure which may err on the high side. The deficit between actual production and need was then calculated for each of the households and its value assessed at 0·86 baht per kg, this being the average price at which padi may be bought in Meto. The cost of the padi deficit was then deducted from the gross value of the opium yield to give an income figure for the household. In the few cases where households had produced a padi surplus above need we did not add to the income figure, allowing the people concerned the possibility of eating better. Table 17 sets out in detail the results of the calculations made on this basis.

There are certainly some errors in the data given in the table. Although there was probably almost no error in the classification of land into padi or poppy land, some fields must have been wrongly assigned to various owners. As mentioned earlier, we were not able to take all the owners to the various fields when we visited them, and also a year had elapsed before the detailed survey of the 1965 planting areas was made. The greatest accuracy attaches to the 21 households comprising Village A. Even here there are probably some errors. For instance, one we suspect is a confusion between the fields of Soying (House 17) and Chetsu (House 18). Soying died in 1965 and the division between his household, thereafter headed by his youngest son Tu, and that of his third son Chetsu only became clearly marked later in that year. However, we believe that despite the obvious errors in detail, the over-all picture is fairly accurate.

Incomes per head

The average incomes per head (in baht) according to the peoples' own declarations were:

Village A	817·53;
Village B	792·23;
Village D	556·47;
Village E	998·40;
Village F	311·26;
Boreh Village	1,160·40;
Isolated Houses	883·70.

The average for the 515 persons in all the 63 households was 806·63 baht per person. For a household of six persons this would mean an average income, after padi needs have been supplied, of 4,839·78 baht, or US $ 242. A household of six persons is mentioned to allow comparison with other groups. In fact the average size of the 63 Meto households in the sample was just over eight persons. The income of this average household was, according to the declared figures, 6,453·04 baht, or US $ 322.

The average incomes per head (in baht) according to calculations of opium yield at 1.3 kg per rai were:

Village A	2,433·46;
Village B	1,389·96;
Village D	1,626·25;
Village E	2,501·46;
Village F	1,021·00;
Boreh Village	1,528·88;
Isolated Houses	2,039·95.

The average yield for the 515 persons in the 63 households, according to this mode of calculation, was 2,061·77 baht per person. For a household of six persons this would mean an average income, after padi needs have been met, of 12,370·62 baht, or US $ 613. For the average Meto household of eight persons it means an income of 16,494·16 baht, or US $ 825.

In more detail, according to the declared figures the percentages of houses in various grades of income per head were as set out in Table 22.

TABLE 22

Distribution of households according to income per head (declared yield)

INCOME PER HEAD IN BAHT	PERCENTAGE OF HOUSEHOLDS
Under– 500	29·0
500– 999	35·5
1,000–1,499	25·8
1,500–1,999	3·2
2,000–2,499	3·2
2,500 and over	3·2

According to the calculation of yield at 1·3 kg per rai, the percentages in various grades were as in Table 23.

To grade the households according to incomes per head is not, however, the only meaningful information which can be derived from the statistics. Of great social significance also is the total wealth of households, because this is what gives them their resilience in the face of unusual demands, their strength in marriage arrangements, and

TABLE 23

*Distribution of households according
to income per head (calculated yield)*

INCOME PER HEAD IN BAHT	PERCENTAGES OF HOUSEHOLDS
Under– 500	6·3
500– 999	12·7
1,000–1,499	17·5
1,500–1,999	20·6
2,000–2,499	6·3
2,500–2,999	12·7
3,000–3,499	4·6
3,500–3,999	4·6
4,000–4,499	6·3
4,500–4,999	1·6
5,000 and over	6·3

their power to provide adequately for the migration of some or all of their members.

Incomes of households

According to declared figures of opium yield, the mean and modal incomes of Meto households after padi needs had been supplied were between 6,000 and 7,000 baht. The distribution, based on 61 households (two being excluded because of obvious errors), is set out in Table 24. The richest household was No. 50, headed by Songler, with a

TABLE 24

*Distribution of total household
incomes (declared yield)*

TOTAL INCOME IN BAHT	PERCENTAGE OF HOUSEHOLDS
Under 2,000	9·8
2,000– 3,999	19·7
4,000– 5,999	18·0
6,000– 7,999	24·6
8,000– 9,999	11·5
10,000–11,999	4·9
12,000–13,999	4·9
14,000–15,999	3·3
16,000 and over	3·3

declared income of 28,996·40 baht. It included 20 persons. The next was
No. 16, that headed by Bowjang, which had an income of 24,250 baht.

Calculating on a basis of a yield of 1·3 kg of opium per rai, the
median income of 61 households, after deducting padi needs, was
between 15,000 and 16,000 baht. The distribution is set out in Table 25.

TABLE 25

*Distribution of total household
incomes (calculated yield)*

TOTAL INCOME IN BAHT	PERCENTAGES OF HOUSEHOLDS
Under 5,000	11·3
5,000– 9,999	19·4
10,000–14,999	21·0
15,000–19,999	14·5
20,000–24,999	14·5
25,000–29,999	6·5
30,000–34,999	4·8
35,000–39,999	3·2
40,000 and over	4·8

The richest household on this basis of calculation was No. 43, headed
by Juser with an income of 70,580·20 baht. However, this is one of
the households in the case of which we suspect an error due to wrong
assignment of fields. The next was No. 50, with 59,371 baht. This
household was headed by Songler who was also at the top of the list
on declared yields.

The households varied much in size and family composition. As
mentioned earlier, in a household comprising more than one unitary
family the poppy fields are owned not by the household as a unit but
by the different families within it. As these different families are semi-
independent economic units with their physical separation often not
far off, their wealth superiority over others below them in the scale
may be short-lived. Therefore a grading by families as well as by
households would also be significant for a complete picture of the
economic structure of the community. We attempted such a grading
based on the household compositions shown in Table 8, Chapter Four,
and it resulted in certain households rising in comparative position.
It lacked precision, however, because we did not generally have
information on which fields belonging to a household were the property
of the separate families within it. A crude calculation was made simply
by dividing the total incomes of the households by the number of
families within it.

In Table 17 the number of separate families within a household are shown by letters after the Household No. Households without letters following the No. have a unitary family structure. It should be noted that within the category of 'unitary family structure' are not only simple nuclear families but polygynous families and stem families, the criterion being economic union in cash income as well as subsistence products. The criterion is not always met in the case of stem families. During the early years of his marriage the son may have common poppy fields with his father. Later there may be a separation with each having rights to the products of different fields although they are usually worked in common. This allows for the possibility of the stem family's breaking up and the father's going to live with another son. In the old age of the father a unitary economy may be restored. Sometimes, too, a widowed mother may have a separate poppy field although she is living in the household of a son. For the purposes of the present analysis, however, we did not attempt to separate these different economic units within stem families.

We refer to the form of analysis at present under discussion as the 'split household tabulation'. The 62 households[17] divided into 79 families. The median income according to declared yields was 3,600 baht and according to calculated yields 11,815 baht, the average size of a family being 6·4 persons. According to declared yields, 13·9 per cent of the families had cash incomes above padi needs of more than 8,000 baht and 5 per cent of more than 13,000 baht; according to calculated yields, 16·5 per cent had incomes of more than 20,000 baht and 5·1 per cent of more than 25,000 baht.

Gross incomes from opium

Although income after allowance has been made for padi deficits is the most useful figure for comparative purposes, as some households grow their padi for consumption and others have to buy it, it is interesting also to note gross incomes.

According to declared opium yields, the average household gross incomes (in baht) were as follows:

Village A	9,343;
Village B	6,000;
Village D	5,369;
Village E	10,445;
Village F	3,200;
Boreh Village	8,668;
Isolated Houses	4,075.

[17] Household No. 37 was eliminated because of obvious inaccuracy.

The average for the 62 households in the above groups[18] was 7,871 baht. For the 509 persons in the households the average gross income was 959 baht per head.

According to calculation of yield at 1·3 kg of opium per rai, the average gross incomes (in baht) were as follows:

Village A   25,224;
Village B   9,945;
Village D   13,912;
Village E   23,836;
Village F   8,125;
Boreh Village   11,089;
Isolated Houses   8,700.

This produces an average for the 62 households of 18,350 baht and an average per head of 2,235 baht.

In terms of gross income according to declared figures the leading households in the Meto complex were those shown in Table 26. In

TABLE 26

Gross incomes (declared) of leading households

ORDER	HOUSEHOLD NO. AND OWNER	NO. OF PERSONS IN HOUSEHOLD	OPIUM YIELD IN KG	CASH VALUE
1	50:SONGLER	20	42·4	31,800
2	16:BOWJANG	10	35·2	26,400
3	52:NULANG	18	24·0	18,000
4	17:SUYING	14	21·6	16,200
5	1:NANG	10	19·2	14,400
	64:PENG	5	19·2	14,400
7	13:JUFOA	7	17·6	13,200
8	2:JUYI	8	16·0	12,000
	4:WANGPAOW	20	16·0	12,000
	12:SONGPAOW	12	16·0	12,000
	49:JONGJER	5	16·0	12,000
	68:JUSU	8	16·0	12,000
13	7:YONGFO	14	14·4	10,800
14	10:FAITEI	14	12·8	9,600
	19:YAITONG	14	12·8	9,600
	20:TONG	9	12·8	9,600
	55:CHASER	7	12·8	9,600

[18] Household No. 58 was not included as it grew no poppies in that year.

terms of gross income calculated on the basis of a yield of 1·3 kg per rai, the order changes to that shown in Table 27.

TABLE 27

Gross incomes (calculated) of leading households

ORDER	HOUSEHOLD NO. AND OWNER	NO. OF PERSONS IN HOUSEHOLD	OPIUM YIELD IN KG	CASH VALUE IN BAHT
1	43:JUSER	11	94·6	70,950
2	50:SONGLER	20	82·9	62,175
3	13:JUFOA	7	61·8	46,350
4	14:SAPAOW	10	53·4	40,050
5	52:NULANG	18	48·1	36,075
6	39:KALAOW	6	47·9	35,925
7	5:BLAIYA	9	46·0	34,500
8	10:FAITEI	14	42·5	31,875
9	16:BOWJANG	10	41·5	31,125
10	21:WANGKI	7	41·3	30,975
11	4:WANGPAOW	20	41·0	30,750
12	15:GER	10	40·1	30,075
13	7:YONGFO	14	34·8	26,100
14	18:CHETSU	8	34·4	25,800
15	1:NANG	10	33·9	25,425
16	9:SERSANG	9	32·7	24,525
17	19:YAITONG	14	32·2	24,150

WEALTH DIFFERENCES IN THE COMMUNITY

Are the wide differences in income amongst the households symptomatic of wealth gradations in the community, perhaps even of rudimentary classes?

At first sight it looks unlikely, because the high position on the scale of many of the households is clearly related to their larger size. Eleven of the 17 households on the declared scale and 13 of the 17 on the calculated scale were above average size, the mean in the first case being 11·6 persons and in the second case 11·5 persons per household. Reduced to a per head rating some of the households slip considerably in position, the most notable being that of Wangpaow, which had a per head income on the declared scale of only 600 baht.

The answer is not quite so simple, however. Not all the large households are downgraded to the same extent. We compared the above two rating tables (26 and 27) with tables of rating by net income per head (i.e. income after padi needs have been deducted). Ten of the households in Table 26 also appear among the first 17 in the table of declared net incomes per head (Table 17), and 9 in Table 27 are among the first 17 in the table of calculated net incomes per head (Table 17).

Even where large households do fall much lower on the per head scale, the downgrading may be more apparent than real, for several reasons. Firstly, in the large households there are often a large number of children whose demands on income are at present lower than those of adults, and whose labour will increasingly contribute to the wealth of the household. Secondly, total income is significant because some objects useful to a whole household, both materially and as means of gaining prestige, may be bought at a price which does not increase in proportion to the size of the household. For instance, a radio can serve a whole household; an aluminium roof has to be larger to shelter twenty people than six but not proportionately larger; often the sacrifice of one pig can propitiate the spirits for ten people as well as for five; and even silver neck rings can be used interchangeably by women of a household according to individual occasion for display or passing individual whim. Thirdly, a large total income is an insurance fund for every member of a household against misfortunes which hit more often against single persons than against all.

It is true generally that the larger a household the more likely it is to divide, thereby tending to level wealth distributions. There are other factors, too, which are against, and probably prevent, wealth accumulation above the average on a permanent basis. Most important is the fact that productivity depends upon the labour available to a household. Meto was exceptional in the availability of hired labour from neighbouring Karen, although in other areas there are usually some outsiders who come to work for Miao in return for opium. Variations of skill and industry in poppy cultivation do occur but are limited in extent, scope, and transference from generation to generation.

Necessary migration constantly introduces a new element of chance into the prospects of continued success.

Nevertheless some persistence of wealth distinctions clearly does occur. In Chapter Seven we listed 11 persons who pioneered Meto in 1960. The names of 7 of those persons occur in one or both of the lists of the leading 17 persons in terms of gross income. Of the remaining 4, Tu was a brother of two of these persons and was only in a temporary poorer position as he was continuing to live in the household of his aged father, who died in 1965; Koyi was an old man in 1965 who was planning to move early in 1966 to live with another section of his family in the Chieng Dao district; Gago, although not on the lists, was comparatively rich; only Faipow had a relatively poor income.

In the following year the pioneers were joined by 12 Tang clansmen, 3 Yang clansmen and 4 Wang clansmen. Of the first group 7 of the 12 names appear on the lists of leading persons in terms of gross income, one ranks highly on the list of leading persons in terms of net income per head, and two others are amongst the leaders on the 'split household list'. Of the Yang group two of the three appear on one or more of the lists, as do two of the four Wang clansmen. Considering the probable inaccuracies in the over-all data to which we referred earlier, the extent to which the names of the earlier settlers occur in the lists of people with the best incomes in 1965/6 is striking.

In 1958 I was not able to collect precise data on the incomes of households at Pasamliem. It is noteworthy, however, that the persons from there who appear on the leading lists at Meto were persons whom I adjudged to be amongst the wealthiest at Pasamliem. A particular case is that of Kalaow. He was the headman at Pasamliem. Although considered an old man in 1965/6, a regular opium smoker from the time I first knew him and no longer prominent in village affairs, he appears in sixth place on the list of gross incomes according to calculated figures.

Therefore we conclude that wealth superiorities may persist for at least a generation even through several migrations and changing household composition. As members of a dispersed extended family or sub-lineage tend to support one another, there are enduring categories of rich and poor in Miao society.

The categories tend to endure because income superiority once established confers advantage in future years. It may enable one to employ labour. It makes migration easier, thereby taking strains off families and giving priority in the selection of the best land in new areas. These factors probably account for the richer families at Pasamliem of twelve years ago still being among the richer families at Meto.

The differences in wealth, however, are not such as can lead, at least in the present circumstances, to real economic classes. Firstly, they are too broad. For instance, the 17 leading households in each of the lists above embrace nearly 40 per cent of the total population of the 62 households considered in the census. Secondly, they are not marked enough. Table 28 shows how nearly equal the clans at Meto were in their total production when it was balanced against their numbers. There are well-to-do and less well-to-do families in each of them, but in general, because they all produce the same thing by the same method, the relative superiority any of them can gain is limited. Usually even

TABLE 28

Productivities of clans in padi and opium

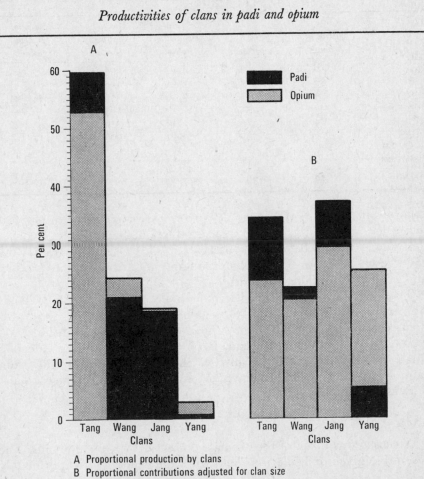

A Proportional production by clans
B Proportional contributions adjusted for clan size

the most fortunate can gain only a moderate margin above subsistence in any one year, and accumulated margins can be dissipated by a few years of poorer fortune, which is the third reason why wealth differences do not lead to true class distinctions—they are not constant enough.

MAIZE PRODUCTION

Information was collected from 47 households on the amount of maize they estimated they had produced in the 1965/6 season. The results were as shown in Table 29. The statistics are probably most

TABLE 29

Maize production by villages

VILLAGE	No. of houses	No. of persons	Total production (gallons)	Production per house (gallons)	Production per head (gallons)
A	18	182	14,480	804	80
B	5	33	2,120	424	64
D	8	65	2,880	360	44
E	4	34	660	165	19
F	4	25	1,320	330	53
BOREH	6	46	5,400	900	117
ISOLATED HOUSES	2	10	800	400	80
TOTALS	47	395	27,660	588 (av.)	70 (av.)

accurate in the case of Village A where the people were questioned more closely about this item of their production. Nevertheless, in order that any error will be on the conservative side, we shall state that the average household in Meto was producing about 600 gallons of corn annually, or 70 gallons per head.[19]

There was wide variation. Seventeen per cent of the households studied produced more than 1,000 gallons apiece, and the most productive household—House No. 1 headed by Nang—produced 2,000 gallons, or 200 gallons per head. No attempt was made to calculate maize production, partly because we had no measured yields from sample areas and partly because maize had significance in the economy only as animal food.

ANIMALS

A census was taken of the animals possessed by 59 households. The results are given in Table 30. The cattle were generally used ultimately

[19] I.e. American gallons (1 American gallon = 3·78541 litres).

TABLE 30

Distribution of domestic animals

		VILLAGES							TOTALS
		A 21 houses	B 5 houses	D 11 houses	E 10 houses	F 4 houses	BOREH 6 houses	Isolated houses 2 houses	
FOWLS	Number	291	54	135	123	40	347	67	1057
	Range	7/25	4/15	3/30	0/34	0/15	12/100	17/50	0/100
	Average	13·86	10·80	12·27	12·30	10	57·83	33·5	17·92
PIGS	Number	127	27	51	78	30	82	17	412
	Range	1/20	2/8	0/10	0/30	4/12	6/22	2/15	0/30
	Average	6·05	5·40	4·65	7·80	7·50	13·67	8·5	6·98
HORSES	Number	36	1	21	11	1	9	3	82
	Range	0/4	0/1	0/3	0/3	0/1	0/5	0/3	0/5
	Average	1·71	0·20	1·91	1·10	0·25	1·50	1·50	1·39
DOGS	Number	32	3	15	23	3	12	5	93
	Range	0/3	0/1	0/3	0/6	0/1	0/6	1/4	0/6
	Average	1·52	0·60	1·36	2·30	0·75	2	2·50	1·58
GOATS	Number	25	—	1	24	—	—	—	50
	Range	0/8	—	0/1	0/12	—	—	—	0/12
	Average	1·19	—	0·09	2·40	—	—	—	0·85
CATTLE	Number	10	—	13	5	4	14	—	46
	Range	0/4	—	0/5	0/5	0/4	0/12	—	0/12
	Average	0·48	—	1·18	0·50	1	2·33	—	0·78

for sacrificial slaughter, either by the household itself or by other Miao to whom they could be sold for this purpose. Occasionally they were sold to outsiders. They were never milked. At Meto in 1965 they could be kept without great difficulty because the padi fields, although not usually fenced, were well away from the village. They would wander in the village environs during the day but were usually stalled and fed at night.

The goats, which were never stalled, grazed on the upper slopes of the main hills above the level of cultivated fields. None were slaughtered while we were in Meto, but they were intended ultimately for food or for sale.

The horses were of the large pony type common in the hills of the region. They served primarily as pack animals and were ridden only occasionally. Usually they were kept in stalls attached to the house, but might be allowed to wander during the day in areas where they would not damage crops. Usually barriers are erected across the main tracks to the fields about half a mile from a village to prevent horses reaching fields. They were always fed each evening, generally on grass or wild bamboo trunks chopped into pieces.

The fowls wandered freely around, and sometimes in, the houses during the day. In the evenings they were either fed separately or competed for the food provided for the pigs. They roosted under the eaves of the houses or on the rafters of the horse stalls. Sometimes a separate shelter was provided for them, and a broody hen might be placed in a basket. The high number of fowls shown for Boreh village was due to the fact that three households—those of Songpaow (House 62), Peng (House 64), and Jusu (House 68)—had 100 each.

The pigs were occasionally penned but generally they wandered freely in the village area scavenging. At night they were fed on boiled maize and maize meal poured into a wooden trough outside the house.

The dogs were kept mainly as pets but were also used for hunting. The Jang clan used dogs as part of the sacrifice at some shamanistic performances but generally they would buy them for this purpose from nearby Karen villages.

The pigs, fowls, cattle, and goats represent additional wealth for households. They add to the food supply, they relieve the necessity to buy animals for ceremonial or festival purposes, and they are saleable.

The horses are especially valuable possessions. By their use as pack animals labour can be saved for greater agricultural productivity. They are expensive, costing between 1,000 and 1,500 baht. Some households cannot afford them and must pay for their hire if they are to use them at all. Therefore horses are a great asset to households in their daily living, a possible source of income, and an investment which can be converted into cash if necessity demands.

CONCLUSION

From the foregoing analysis we can draw a picture of the economic situation of the average household at Meto in 1965. It comprised eight persons; it produced approximately 700 kg of padi, 70 gallons of maize, and opium valued at 13,210 baht; after buying the additional 1,300 kg of padi needed for its food, it had a remaining cash income of 11,000 baht (US $ 550);[20] it possessed a horse, six pigs, a dozen fowls, and one dog.

It must be stressed that this is the statistical average only. In each characteristic the reality of many households diverges from it. For instance, more than half the population live in households above the average size; some produce no padi at all, and in many cases the opium production is much higher than stated above; more than a third of the households had more than one horse and rather more than a quarter had none. One in twelve had cattle and one in ten had goats. Wealth variations between households were marked and in some cases appeared to be enduring.

How do the Miao compare in wealth with other peoples in Thailand?

The World Bank estimated that the Gross Domestic Production per capita for Thailand in 1965 was US $ 140.[21] On p. 189 we calculated that the gross income per capita from opium alone was 2,235 baht, or approximately US $ 112, so that if all other production were added the figure for Meto in 1965/6 would be close to the national average.

The Gross Domestic Production figure includes the production of all the manufacturing industries in the cities. More relevant are regional comparisons. A survey of household expenditures in the northern region of Thailand showed an annual per capita income in the villages (based on expenditure in 1962/3) of 1,076 baht.[22] Even on the declared figures of opium production and making allowance for the value of padi produced, the average for Meto in 1965/6 was higher. On calculated figures it was more than twice as high.

A comparison with Thai farming families producing crops other than opium is similarly favourable to the Miao. A survey carried out in 1965 in six northern provinces (Chiengmai, Chiengrai, Lamphun, Lampang, Phrae, and Nan) gave an average income for households with second crops of 3,103 baht and for households without second crops of 2,781 baht.[23]

Precise figures for neighbouring tribes are not available but it seems certain that outside the opium-producing areas they would be lower than the averages for Thai village households. It is clear, therefore, that in good years the average Meto family could achieve an income through opium production several times higher than that achieved, on the plains or in the hills, by peoples practising other forms of agriculture.

[20] We have assessed the opium figures by taking a mid-point between declared and calculated yields.

[21] International Bank for Reconstruction and Development (I.B.R.D.), *The Current Economic Position and Prospects of Thailand*, Washington, 1966 (mimeograph).

[22] *Household Expenditure Survey*, B.E. 2506, National Statistical Office, Bangkok, p. 24 (quoted in Chapman, 1967, p. 1).   [23] Chapman, 1967, Table 3.

A true assessment of relative wealth, however, must take account of other factors. The first is the wide variation in the situations of households in Meto, which even in 1965/6 resulted in the per capita income of approximately one-third of them falling below the average for northern Thai villagers on declared figures and about 12 per cent on calculated figures. The second factor is the unreliability of the income. Outside the opium-producing areas the level remains more or less constant indefinitely. Within the areas it often declines after a period to almost zero, the length of time taken for this to occur varying between five and twenty years according to the quality of the environment. For many of the families at Meto the decline had already begun prior to 1965 and almost all the others began to be affected by it after that year. Averaged out over a total opium cycle the advantage enjoyed by the Miao over other non-opium producing peoples in the region is much less than the figures above indicate.

Nevertheless the relative prosperity which the Miao may achieve is an important factor attaching them to their way of life. At least in the past when production has declined they have had the prospect of reviving it elsewhere. The promise of the hills will probably continue to allure them even when it can no longer be fulfilled. More than with other peoples in their neighbourhood their aspirations may run ahead of their current conditions.

The difference between aspiration and actual conditions may have great political and economic significance. Faced with a real or imminent decline in wealth the Miao are a restless people—a problem to both politicians and planners, a prey to propaganda, and easy victims of false hopes.

When the Miao visit the plains they may note the prosperity and ignore the poverty. If they are in a state where they are seeking an alternative to economic decline, they may see visions of themselves as rich wet-rice planters or even as workers in the towns, and seek opportunity to become such. The difficulty may come when the gap is revealed between what is in their minds and what is in the minds of those seeking to change their way of life.

PART THREE

WIDER PERSPECTIVES

CHAPTER TEN

OPIUM—THE MAINSTAY OF THE ECONOMY

Of the three main crops, padi is almost entirely consumed in the village. It may be bought, sold, or loaned between households but not to any great extent, partly because most households grow less than their food needs and partly because any redistribution which does occur will usually be through the intermediary of one of the Chinese village stores. Only small amounts, however, are sold to stores.

The maize crop is entirely consumed in the village mainly for animal food. Very little, if any, is sold. On the other hand only a small proportion of the opium is used locally. Most is sold and it is by far the most important element in the cash economy—indeed in the total economy. The role it fills is the product of historical circumstances in the world, in the eastern Asian geographical region, in Thailand, and in the villages of the Meto people.

OPIUM IN CHINA

The original home of the wild opium poppy (*Papaver somniferum*) was probably in the area around the eastern Mediterranean. There are references to it in Greek literature. Homer, in the *Odyssey*, referred to the power of opium to assuage grief. Theophrastus referred to opium in the fourth century B.C., while Dioscorides in the first century A.D. describes opium as it is used in modern times.[1]

According to the *Encyclopaedia Americana* (1963) the opium poppy probably reached China, where it was not native, about the seventh century A.D. through the efforts of Arab traders who advocated its use for medicinal purposes. In Chinese literature, however, there are references to its use earlier than that date. The noted Chinese surgeon, Hua To, of the Three Kingdoms (A.D. 220–64) used decoctions of opium and *Cannabis indica* for his patients to swallow before undergoing major operations.[2]

The extent to which opium was used for other than purely medical purposes in earlier times is uncertain. Wu Lien-Teh associates the beginning of its widespread use as a drug in China with the introduction

---

[1] See references in the *Encyclopaedia Britannica*, 1961.
[2] Wu Lien-Teh, *Plague Fighter, The Autobiography of a Modern Chinese Physician*, Heffer, Cambridge, 1959, p. 471.

in the seventeenth century of tobacco by the Dutch from Java. 'The Chinese mixed opium with tobacco', he says, 'to make the smoking more enjoyable. They later omitted the tobacco, and devised a rather complicated method of preparing opium for smoking, which soon became popular.'[3] He notes, however, that the Arabs in the ninth century sometimes used a decoction of opium as an exhilarating drink, and we might ask whether the fact that the Chinese mixed the opium with the tobacco does not suggest prior experience of smoking it, or at least of consuming it in some form for pleasure.

There is evidence that opium-smoking was known much earlier than the seventeenth century. Thai history records that a King of Ayudhya in the fourteenth century became aware that opium-smoking was sapping the physical strength of his soldiers and enacted a law whereby drug addicts and pedlars could be imprisoned and their property seized.[4]

Nevertheless, the extensive use of opium in China and countries to the south does not appear to have developed until the eighteenth century. The probability that there was no large-scale growing of the poppy in the region before this date is indicated by the profitable trade which foreigners were able to promote. Until 1733 the opium traffic to China was mainly in the hands of the Portuguese. British merchants then became increasingly active and in 1781 the East India Company entered the field. Importations into China multiplied rapidly, increasing fivefold, for instance, between 1821 and 1832.

Chinese opposition to the trade developed early. In 1729 the Emperor Yung Cheng issued an edict forbidding the sale of opium for smoking purposes and the opening of opium dens. Continuously thereafter Chinese leaders showed concern at the spread of the habit. In 1839 the High Commissioner of Kwantung Province, Lin Tsi-Hu, destroyed 1,430 tons of opium at Canton.

China's defeat in the Opium War of 1840–2 blunted its efforts to restrict the trade. Until 1858 opium continued to be classed as contraband, but the connivance of the British Government, and to a less extent other governments, in the trade, and the imposition on the Chinese Government of extraterritorial rights for foreigners,[5] rendered the Government powerless to prevent massive importations of the drug.

In 1858 importation was made legal. To reduce the drain on wealth caused by the foreign trade, opium-growing was encouraged in China itself. A duty of Tls. 30 (US $ 45) per picul (133⅓ lb.) was imposed on

---

[3] Ibid.   [4] Phillips, *et al.*, 1967, p. 61.

[5] The American version of the treaty, however, excluded U.S. citizens from the protection of their Government if they engaged in contraband traffic.

imported opium. This was an added stimulus to internal production. Once Chinese opium began to be grown on a large scale the demand for it grew rapidly, because although the local product was inferior in morphine content to Indian opium, its cheaper price made it accessible to the poorer classes. Large areas in the southern provinces were given over to poppy cultivation.

The deleterious effects upon the society of the great opium consumption led to increasing international and Chinese concern, especially around the turn of the century. Finally in 1908 the Government of the Empress Dowager Tzu-Hsi concluded the Ten Years' Agreement with Great Britain by which China undertook to cease the cultivation of the opium poppy and forbid consumption of the drug on the understanding that the export of Indian opium into China should be reduced *pari passu* and cease altogether in ten years. By this time Chinese opium production had reached vast proportions. The official estimate for 1906 was over 9,000 tons to which another 3,000 tons of Indian opium were added by import.

China pressed her part of the agreement so forcibly that by 1917, according to a statement made in that year by the British representative on the Opium Advisory Committee at Geneva, she had almost freed herself from the cultivation of the poppy. But the same year marked a further turning-point—a turn backwards towards a greater production probably than ever before. The first Republic had carried on vigorously the measures initiated by the Empress Dowager. In some provinces opium-smokers were executed for breaking the new laws. But with the start of civil war in 1917, the military leaders resorted to poppy cultivation in order to raise money for the support of their private armies. Wu Lien-Teh writes, 'During my post-revolution inspections (1912–30) in China, I often saw mile upon mile of land covered with multi-coloured poppy plants in Manchuria, Shansi, Shensi, Jehol, Fukien, Yunnan and Szechuan, from which the various warlords hoped to derive needed revenue for maintaining their troops.'[6] Other observers reported the same situation. Writing of his journeys through Kweichow, Kemp says that nearly all the cultivable land was used for opium and that land formerly used for rice had been turned over to it.[7]

Wu Lien-Teh states that 'it was estimated that as much as 200,000 piculs had been collected previous to 1930'.[8] If he means this amount

[6] Wu Lien-Teh, 1959, p. 471. This book provides the basis for the account given above. Dr. Wu was Physician Extraordinary to President Yuan Shih-Kai and represented China at many international conferences on the opium problem. Aware of my own studies in Thailand, he most generously sent me a copy of his book when it was published in 1959.

[7] E. G. Kemp, The Highways and Byways of Kweichow, *Journal of the Royal Asiatic Society, North China Branch*, Vol. 52, 1921, pp. 157–8.

[8] Wu Lien-Teh, 1959, p. 492.

was collected each year it would indicate an annual production of approximately 12,000 tons.

The historical factors mentioned above probably played a large part in the establishment of opium as a main cash crop of the Miao and other hill tribes in China. In the warmer southern regions the altitude at which they lived was favourable to poppy whereas the same mountainous environment and the difficulties of transport to market centres were disadvantages in the competitive growing of other cash crops. Therefore they probably began to produce opium quite early after its introduction to southern China. The drastic measures introduced by the Empress Dowager, together with the continuing demands from the addict population, must have increased the incentive to grow it in these areas, which were least accessible to surveillance.

Both before and after this time military activity probably stimulated production. A folk story which I have heard in Thailand explains the spread of maize as due to the actions of Chinese armies who planted it on their advances through the mountains in order to ensure food supplies on their retreats. They may also have planted opium poppies, frequently associated with maize, during their longer sojourns in the hills. Certainly the remnants of the Kuomintang army in Thailand in recent years have done so. They have also been a major element in encouraging planting by hill tribes and facilitating their opium trade.

The expansion of poppy cultivation after 1917 probably had the greatest effect on the tribal areas. The armies of warlords sometimes retreated to the hills or used the hills as safe supply bases. In such conditions the production of opium was important for the revenue it supplied. Pressure from Chinese landlords also appears to have played a part. Writing in 1921, Kemp says that the Miao in Kweichow paid rent to Chinese for land and were compelled to plant a certain proportion of it in poppy. Miao Christians were persecuted for refusing to do so.[9] The profitability of the crop and the openness of the market for it during this period would have been powerful inducements to the Miao in favourable locations.

After 1930 the Kuomintang Government made considerable efforts to reduce opium production but was hampered by inefficient administration, the Japanese invasion, and renewed civil war. It appears that a large measure of success was achieved, nevertheless, in Miao areas which were under close Government supervision. In her study of the Cowrie Shell Miao written in 1947, Mickey says: 'At one time the chief crop was opium, but the Chinese Government has tried to stamp out the poppy.'[10]

Far more strenuous efforts against opium followed the establishment

[9] Kemp, 1921, p. 166.   [10] Mickey, 1947, p. 5.

of the Government of the Peoples' Republic in 1949. Consumption and production appear to have been virtually eliminated over a large part of the country. But the remoter tribal areas seem to have posed the Government with the same intractable problem as faced by the Government of Thailand.

In a book published in 1959, Alan Winnington, one of the few Westerners permitted to visit the hill regions in southern China, writes the following passage which typifies many statements made by Thai officials on their own tribal opium situation:

Opium growing has been wiped out in most of China: in all places where the Hans are in the majority and in most national minority areas. It is the policy of the central authorities, while doing everything to discourage it, to leave such matters to the voluntary decision of the national minorities themselves. As a result the poppy can still be found in remote pockets where the transition from primitive, slave and feudal society is still going forward. . . . Abolition of opium other than voluntarily and after secure alternative cash crops exist would make these people feel nervous. Thus to make the poppy illegal in those areas would be an act of political stupidity—merely adding new problems to those already difficult to solve, and presenting allies to those who wish to stem the flow of progress.[11]

Where the Chinese tribal opium goes, if it is still produced, remains something of a mystery. It is a mystery of importance to Thailand, and to the Miao situation there with which we are concerned, because if it does not go to an internal Chinese market it must go south into countries such as Thailand thereby affecting their own capacity to eliminate opium.

There is no proof that great quantities are going south. The suggestion has sometimes been made that China, having learnt from the behaviour of imperialist powers towards her, promotes the distribution of opium to neighbouring countries in order to weaken them or to obtain foreign currency. The matter was discussed at the Eighteenth Session of the United Nations Commission on Narcotic Drugs held in Geneva in 1963. The Chinese representative from Taiwan stated that the Yunnan area must be considered a source of illicit supplies and said that an offender arrested in Tapiei in 1962 had confessed to handling 2 kg of opium which had come from the 'Yunnan border area'.[12] The United States representative stated that a sample of opium seized in Korea in 1958 had been submitted to the United Nations laboratory which reported that the findings 'indicate that this seizure

[11] Alan Winnington, *The Slaves of the Cool Mountains*, Lawrence and Wishart, London, 1959, p. 72.
[12] United Nations Commission on Narcotic Drugs, Report of the Eighteenth Session, Economic and Social Council Official Records: Thirty-sixth Session, Supplement No. 9, New York, 1963 (E/3775; E/CN. 7/455), paragraph 90.

very probably originates from mainland China. It is, however, not possible to be more definite in view of the small number of authenticated samples from the Chinese mainland.'[13]

The Peoples' Republic of China had no representative at the meeting but its reputation was stoutly defended by the representatives of Hungary and the Soviet Union. The Hungarian representative said that 'insinuations about the Peoples' Republic of China were being made with growing frequency; and in the absence of a representative of the Republic, the suggestion that that great country was supplying the illicit traffic in order to finance activities abroad and to purchase strategic materials must be rejected.' He argued that there were no charges of morphine and heroin being exported from China, and this indicated Chinese innocence because if the Government was interested in the drug trade it would be much more advantageous to export these forms because of their high price and small volume. The fact that there were such high profits being made by the clandestine manufacture of drugs in other countries made it evident that China was not supplying them. He concluded, however, by stating that he was 'of the opinion that trafficking and addiction were not problems of any one race as such, but rather the scourge of society in general'.[14]

The representative of the Soviet Union, after deploring what he termed 'one-sided ... unverified and unfounded accusations' against the Peoples' Republic of China, said that 'So far as the actual position in the Peoples' Republic of China was concerned, a decree strictly prohibiting opium and other narcotic drugs had been issued by the State Administrative Council of the Republic as early as February 1950. The decree prohibited the cultivation and smoking of opium throughout the country.'[15]

The Central Narcotics Board of the United Nations has estimated that about 1,000 metric tons of opium are being produced annually somewhere in the South-East Asian area.[16] It is highly likely that a portion of this comes from southern China. It is improbable that in the remote and mountainous border regions production areas are clearly demarcated by national boundaries. But it is also unlikely that the Chinese Government encourages the trade, because the flow of a narcotics product is not easy to channel in one direction, especially from areas of difficult administration, and Chinese society could suffer as well as that of foreigners.

All Chinese central governments over the last century and a half have shown concern at the narcotics problem and made attempts to reduce it. By its public declarations and its actions elsewhere in China,

---

[13] Ibid., paragraph 95.   [14] Ibid., paragraph 96.
[15] Ibid., paragraph 98.   [16] Phillips et al., 1967, p. 68.

the present government has continued this tradition with far greater firmness, and it is probable, therefore, that poppy-growing has been at least reduced even amongst the recalcitrant Miao.

But the consequences of past events continue. Because of historical circumstances in China the Miao developed a cash economy based upon opium, which they brought with them to Thailand. It included not only cultivation techniques but trading processes as well. Production for cash is meaningless without market connections. Therefore traditionally associated with the Miao were Chinese traders who acted as intermediaries between the towns and the tribal producers. As the Miao migrated into Thailand from the Province of Yunnan, Yunnanese traders came with them. These traders, locally called Haw, who live in Miao villages should not be viewed as outside exploiters. They, and frequently their fathers, may have spent all their lifetimes in association with tribesmen. They are part of a human symbiotic complex which has cultural consequences to Miao society going far beyond purely economic relationships. They are to be distinguished from the rich Chinese traders in the towns to whom they are the intermediaries.

OPIUM IN NEIGHBOURING COUNTRIES

The attitude of the Miao in Thailand to opium is influenced not only by what goes on in Thailand but by practices and policies in neighbouring countries. Because of the lack of surveys no precise figure can be given for the extent of Laotian opium production today, but a United Nations estimate in 1967 put it at between 80 and 150 tons annually. 'Virtually no enforcement exists', states the United Nations Report, 'either in Government controlled areas or in the Pathet Lao region where the bulk of opium is produced.'[17]

Generally the Miao in Laos appear in no way different from their fellow tribesmen in Thailand in their keenness to cultivate poppy wherever the environment is favourable to it. The fact that they can usually do so freely increases the resentment of the Miao to Government restriction in Thailand, which they tend to regard as unwarranted interference, although in the past this feeling was counterbalanced by the generally higher regard in which government was held in Thailand for its relative lack of corruption and superior efficiency. Lately the spread of political subversion and Government reaction to it has exacerbated the situation in many Miao communities bordering on Laos.

The Meto Miao are much closer to the Burmese than to the Laotian border. In Burma opium production is still legal in the Shan States

[17] Phillips et al., 1967, p. 64.

east of the Salween river. It is illegal in the Kachin area but much production occurs there also. A United Nations Survey Team which visited Burma in 1964 estimated that the annual production was at least 300 to 400 tons. The average yield was estimated as 2 viss per acre and the average area of poppy fields per household of five members was about 2 acres, or 0·8 hectares.[18] Translated into Thai equivalents this means an average yield of 1·2 kg per rai and an average household productivity of approximately 4 jois or 6·4 kg. These figures are not grossly out of proportion with the Thailand figures, but they are lower and probably represent an under-estimation of Burmese production.

Because of the political strains between the Shans and the Burmese a considerable proportion of the opium produced in the Shan States is smuggled into and probably through Thailand. The armed Chinese military refugees encamped in the hills have been the main agents in this trade, making suppression difficult, but even without their activities a good deal of the opium would probably have filtered through. The reservoir of opium across the border attracts traders. Their operations encourage local production, including that in the Meto area, by providing a ready market outlet for all opium.

OPIUM IN THAILAND

A King of Ayudhya in his wars with Sukothai in the fourteenth century A.D. became aware that opium-smoking was sapping the physical strength of his soldiers, and enacted a law whereby drug addicts and pedlars could be imprisoned and their property seized. Succeeding Kings passed further legislation to suppress opium-smoking. The extent of it greatly increased when Chinese began entering the country in large numbers during the reign of King Rama III (1824–51). In 1839 an endeavour was made to enforce the existing laws against opium-smoking but it failed because the Chinese traders formed secret societies to protect their activities. In 1852 King Rama IV, recognizing that opium-smoking could not be suppressed by force, legalized it but only for Chinese. Sales of opium were taxed and by 1907 the Government had created a monopoly, although undoubtedly illegal sales continued outside it. In 1913 an opium refinery was established and the opium was sold by distributing firms under special licence.

The monopoly was valuable to the Government. In 1950, for instance, it produced a revenue of more than 5,500,000 US dollars. Not only sales but production were officially under Government control. The Opium Act B.E. 2472 (1929) states: 'Article 5. It shall be unlawful to cultivate the opium poppy, or to possess opium seeds, except under a

[18] This information is derived from the Report of the Preliminary Joint Survey Team in 1964 which is unpublished.

licence granted by the Government.' This article, which has been reiterated in subsequent legislation, is still in force.

Despite the revenue benefit, the Thailand Government has become more and more concerned in recent years about the adverse social consequences of the availability of opium, particularly the spread of drug-taking to the Thai people and the increasing use of the powerful opium derivatives, morphine and heroin.

In 1955 the Government issued a proclamation stating that the sale of opium would be outlawed from 1 January 1956. On 9 December 1958 the 37th Proclamation of the Revolutionary Party made the sale and smoking of opium illegal throughout the Kingdom and seven months later the paraphernalia of the opium dens were publicly destroyed in a huge bonfire in Bangkok.

Opium production was dealt with by Section 20 of the Harmful Habit-Forming Drugs Act (No. 3) B.E. 2502 (1959) which states: 'Whoever grows, produces, imports or exports . . . any type of harmful habit-forming drug . . . shall be liable to a term of imprisonment of six months to ten years and a fine equal to ten times the value of such drug but not less than three thousand baht.'

While the United Nations Mission was in Bangkok in 1967, two Chinese heroin producers were executed under a special provision of the Interim Constitution, now no longer operative, empowering the Prime Minister to act in the case of illegal production of narcotics without resort to legal procedure.

The effect of the legislation on the consumption of opium and opium derivatives is difficult to assess. Opium-smoking has been greatly reduced in the towns and in most closely settled lowland areas. But the total consumption of drugs appears to have risen. Heroin users have been estimated to number between 150,000 and 300,000.[19] It has been suggested that the heroin rise is a consequence of the prohibition of opium-smoking, traders and consumers having been forced to turn to a form of drug which is more easy to conceal, but probably the legislation did no more than accentuate a change which was already occurring.

If it did in fact accentuate the change to heroin, the legislation, designed to reduce the incidence of drug-taking, may well have had the immediate effect of increasing it. This effect, however, could be short-term, merely creating earlier a situation which would have arisen anyway if no legislation had been introduced. Although there may be valid arguments to the contrary, the general opinion of national

[19] Phillips *et al.*, 1967, p. 66, states: 'United Nations sources, concurrent with those of the World Health Organisation, suspect that 1·6 per cent of the population is certainly affected by the use of narcotic drugs, with the main incidence falling, after the abolition of opium smoking, on the working age population.'

governments, endorsed by the United Nations, is that prohibition is necessary to control narcotics consumption. The Thailand Government shares this view. The number of addicts is a cause for great national concern. The Government has now adopted laws giving it full powers to enforce prohibition against both users and producers. How it operates these laws on the production side is of great significance for the Hill Tribes.

All the raw opium produced in Thailand is grown by the Hill Tribes in the northern regions. Recognizing that it is a basic element in the economies of several of the tribes, the Government has not enforced prohibition. Instead it has sought substitution. The tribes are to be encouraged to find alternative means of income, especially through other cash crops. This official policy derives from a blend of tolerance, insight into tribal needs, humanitarianism, and political good sense. No time limit has been imposed for the elimination of opium and the only sanction is the indirect one of the withering away of their opium market which it is hoped will result from the sterner measures applied against traders, manufacturers of heroin, and consumers.

In pursuance of this policy the Government invited a United Nations Team to Thailand in 1967 to survey the economic and social needs of the opium-producing tribes. There is no doubt that until this time the Government had underestimated the extent of tribal opium production. As a member of the Team, utilizing data on crop areas and expected yields supplied by Government survey teams in the previous year and co-ordinated by the National Statistical Office, I arrived at an estimate of an annual production of 145 tons. Subsequently this figure was accepted by the Government and the United Nations as probably fairly accurate. My own experience in limited areas tends to confirm it.

The recognition of the considerable extent of tribal production has, in the thinking of both the Narcotics Division of the United Nations and the Thailand Government, added urgency to the need for crop replacement. A second United Nations Team was invited to Thailand in 1970 the main task of which was to prepare a pilot project for the replacement of opium in a selected area.[20] The Team visited Meto and included it in the selected area. It was intended that the project would be jointly financed by the United Nations Special Narcotics Fund and the Thailand Government.

[20] The Team, entitled a Project Preparation Mission, actually had four tasks: (a) the replacement of opium poppy by alternative activities in an area or areas of the Highlands, (b) the treatment, rehabilitation, and social reintegration of narcotic drug addicts, (c) the strengthening of measures against illicit traffic in narcotic drugs, and (d) the expansion of educational programmes to alert the public to the dangers of drugs. It was proposed in accordance with the General Assembly Resolution No. 2434 (XXIII) (Annex I) and was in Thailand from 1 October to 10 December 1970.

Despite the political pressures resulting from current border conditions, the tolerant official policy towards the Hill Tribes is likely to continue because it now has the great advantage of Royal support. In recent years the King of Thailand has taken a close personal interest in the Tribes, devoting time, money, and influence to securing and seeking to improve their welfare.

OPIUM HISTORY IN METO MINDS

From Jusu (House 68), one of the pioneers of Meto and a leading priest, we heard two stories accounting for the origin of opium as a Miao crop.

The first story states that a very long time ago there were a husband and wife who dwelt together for very many years in the countryside. When the husband died the wife could not overcome her grief. One day when she was crying at his graveside she noticed a strange plant. She plucked it and sap flowed out. She smoked it and it relieved her grief.

The other story is that opium came to China from a place called England. Many of the Chinese smoked opium. Other Chinese did not like this so they came to burn the stores in which opium was held. This story is surely an echo of historical events in China. It suggests that well back in Miao ancestral memory is the knowledge that opium and officialdom are a troublesome pair.

The account of his own experience given by Lowtong bears this out. As a child he lived at Doi Luang, a village, now abandoned, half way between the present village of Pa Khia and Chiengdao mountain. Faitei (House 10) was the headman. Twice police came and cut down all the poppies except in two fields which they did not notice. Faitei then went to see the District Officer at Chiengdao District headquarters. In return for a payment of 80 baht (US $4 in 1970) the District Officer gave a paper licence to each household permitting it to grow opium. Each licensed household was expected to supply two jois of opium to the agent who came to collect it. Because of poor crops the amount was changed to one joi. If any households could not supply this amount other households had to make up the total for the village.

The village fell short of the quota. The Government became angry, accusing the people of holding back the opium for their own use. It refused to renew their licences and called them outlaws. But the police did not come to cut down the poppies in the fields.[21]

In his early manhood Lowtong moved to the neighbourhood of Pasamliem and then to Pasamliem itself, where he stayed until the end

[21] It is clear that the people maintained their poppy fields. Therefore the Government belief that they were witholding opium for their own purposes was probably correct.

of 1958. During this period, he says, the villagers were not troubled by officials seeking opium. The fact that they were free from such demands was one of the inducements attracting some Meto residents back to the Pasamliem region at the time of our writing this study.

Lowtong's next place of residence of any long duration was Meto. At Meto, in common with other villagers, he experienced trouble again with officials over opium. Meto territory crosses a dividing line between two districts. In 1962, not long after Lowtong had arrived in Meto, a police party from one of the districts came to demand 10 jois of opium from the village as a whole. The people refused. When the next harvest was approaching a police party, said to be forty strong, came to slash down a portion of the poppies. At the end of the harvest Jusu, who was headman at that time, gave the police four jois. Whether or not a similar payment was made the following year we do not know.

In January 1965, when we ourselves were present in the village, a police party of four with two carriers arrived. They summoned a meeting of all household heads at their camp and requested a total of twelve jois. After discussion they reduced it to four jois. Lowtong, who was now headman, said that the poppies had not been good this year and asked them to accept two jois. The police leader said they would be ashamed to return to their headquarters with less than four. Lowtong said that he was in his first year as headman; if he was forced to collect a lot of opium from households he would not get respect. The police said they could not reduce their demands below four jois and if this amount was not given they would visit the fields the next day. Lowtong begged them not to do so as the presence of armed men in the fields would frighten the women and children. The police leader said he would regret this but he would be forced to carry out his duty. Thereupon the villagers agreed to pay the four jois.[22]

News of the 1965 police visit reached the Governor of Chiengmai, who took action against the officials concerned. There was no more police interference with the opium production, as far as we know, until 1967, when a police party investigating the murder of a Karen tribesman in the area seized the poppy seed in some of the houses not long before planting was due. We were present in the village at this time also. The police officer in charge told us that the action was taken because opium was illegal, but the exact motives were obscure. Complaints were made to senior officials and the people were allowed to recover their seed from police district headquarters.

These stories are told deliberately because a true picture is necessary

[22] We were not present at this discussion. The above account is that given by the villagers. The reason that the police gave us for their visit was that they had come to investigate reports of communist subversion in the area.

if relationships of Miao to local officialdom are to be fully explained. They are not told to criticize the police. Indeed such criticism would be largely unjustified, one-sided, and of little value. If the stories point to any need it is for greater mutual understanding and possible changes in the administrative organization.

For fair judgement the events have to be seen in the perspective of the Thailand situation in general and the local government situation in particular. The most important general feature is the existence in the country of large-scale opium production leading to extensive illegal trade. Considering the number of opportunities and the size of profits to be made the degree of corruption in official circles which results from the trade is less than might be expected and has been reduced in recent years by some strong Government measures against it. But illegal opium and corruption inevitably coexist, just as illegal alcohol and corruption coexisted in America. Lower officials are aware that some higher officials are deeply involved and in certain cases they are subjected to pressure to become their agents. Viewed in this context and also in the light of the temptations facing them the officials who took opium from the villagers were only mildly corrupt.

Seen through the eyes of the local officials the opium tribute may appear as a slight return for services given. The only direct legal tax which the Meto Miao pay is a sum of 10 baht (US $ 0.50) from each household which wishes to distill maize or rice spirit for its own consumption. There was also a 'rice tax' of 5 to 10 baht per household levied, at least in the early years we were in the village, by the Kamnan, which the Miao believed to be legal.

In their almost complete freedom from direct taxes the tribesmen are not in a much superior position to most of the Thai rural population who are also lightly taxed. But tribesmen are not required to render military service and have no other demands made upon them. Although, because of their remoteness, they generally receive fewer services than many Thai, they do get government assistance. In serious trouble cases, such as murders or even marital disputes where these involve conflicts between kin groups, the Miao do not hesitate to involve the Thai authorities. Sometimes this means the Kamnan and more rarely the police climbing the hills to reach the village, an activity which they do not see in the light of pleasurable exercise. The tribesmen are not normally asked to pay anything for this help. But when and where it is known that the tribesmen have collected an opium bonanza, it seems reasonable that a small gift should be made and even a prod to extract it may be appropriate.

The scales of natural justice, taking no account of the law, favour the officials because the tribesmen want something for nothing. At least at the harvest time of the year, the policeman is probably poorer than the tribesman. He can scarcely be called corrupt because his demands are modest. In the distant hills a compromise must be expected between the legality laid down in Bangkok and local circumstances, which include all the disadvantages of service in remote areas. It does not mean that the law is ineffective because fear of the law is a major factor in keeping the demands moderate. Considering all the conditions the behaviour of most officials in Thailand compares favourably with that in most countries and we must repeat that in some areas in which we studied, such as the Chiengdao District, no illegal demands at all were made.

Nevertheless, whatever the abstract merits of the case, the opium demands caused great bitterness. The reasons for this appear to be several. First, it was known that the demands were illegal and people everywhere want their legitimate rights preserved, whether they be better off or poorer than other people. Secondly, the demands at Meto were great enough to sting. Six jois meant an average contribution from each household of about 85 baht (US $ 4.25). Because some households were unable, or unwilling, to pay, the sting was greater for others.

Thirdly, the attitude of the Miao to officials is at best ambivalent. They may use their services if they are available but they fear them. The fear goes back long into the past. The Miao have a history of resistance to governments. Their migrations have been partly caused by their wish to escape from their impositions.

Government is looked upon as dangerous because it has usually meant giving up goods. They do not regard it as just that they should be asked to do so. They feel they have a right to the domains they occupy, and outside government is an unwanted intrusion.

For many Miao in Thailand, such as those at Meto, the situation is changing. They have been in the country now for several generations and they are acquiring a trust in government because of the protection it gives them and the benefits they are beginning to receive. They nearly all want to become full citizens. A number go so far as to say that they would like to be absorbed culturally so that in language and customs they would become indistinguishable from the Thai. Even this attitude, however, springs partly from a sense of insecurity. The Miao know that they are a small people. They suspect that they are despised and are frightened that their interests will be overridden. Their hackles rise defensively on slight provocation. They fear that if they yield a little they will have to yield a lot. Added to their peasant tenacity and their ethnic pride this makes them very stubborn when it comes to giving up their opium.

Is there any remedy for this situation? If the Miao are to be incorporated into the nation and receive its benefits they must expect to contribute something in return. It is in their own interests to so do because their future will always be uncertain and their status low so long as they are seen merely as the recipients of charity. Rights must be earned through reciprocal obligations.

The answer, I believe, lies in a policy taking as its starting-point present Miao attitudes. Socially and economically they have never been part of wider government structures. They have lived in the hills as small independent communities of producers. Their psychology is that of independent traders. If they give something they want something back in return. Therefore, if taxes are introduced, they should be related to specific services rendered or the granting of definite rights. There might be a payment for medical services or fees for land titles, if these should be granted. Whatever tax is required the amount should be clear and fixed, because only in this way can the Miao fear be overcome that it is the thin edge of the wedge.

The opium tribute, which was sometimes collected in the past, was unsatisfactory in several ways. It offended the basic trading concept of the Miao, fundamental to their cash economy and to most of their social relationships outside their family groups, that they should not give something for nothing. They could not readily accept the fact that it was a return for general government services, partly because self-interest blinded them to it but mainly because it was unrelated in time to the services rendered. The collection was capricious and the amount uncertain. The people feared that the more they had the more they would be asked to pay. They were forced to concealment and, if that failed, to escape.

The resentment and fears of exploitation aroused by the opium exactions have undoubtedly been a disturbing influence on Miao movement patterns and on their relationships with the Thai Government. In Meto, according to one informant, they were responsible for the settlement's dwindling from 100 houses in 1962 to about 70 houses in 1964, although excessive pressure on the land must also have played a part.

Stricter Government discipline and growing concern for the welfare of the hill tribes have practically eliminated the exactions in Meto and many other areas. For this reason the issue would be hardly worth the time taken to discuss it were it not for a new factor which has entered the scene.

In their remote border regions the Miao are trapped in the war between Communist and anti-Communist forces. Their fears are fostered. Instances of corruption are now used to foment political rebellion. The rewards of opium are bound to tempt some officials from the path of virtue, and the remoter the area the greater the temptation. By making opium illegal the Government has compounded its problems of political control because illegal opium and corruption go hand-in-hand. The Government acted deliberately in ultimate national and international interest. The Miao are the victims. They can be saved only by Government restraint, difficult in the circumstances because of the real losses suffered and the amount of uninformed criticism which has to be borne, but aided by an increasing understanding of the problem.

For the Miao sympathy is deserved. Within the span of the present adult generation they have first been encouraged to grow opium and then told that they should give it up, although in most cases their livelihood depends upon it.

THE USES OF OPIUM

The opium produced at Meto, as with that produced in all Hill Tribe villages which cultivate poppy, is used for three purposes— consumption within the village, as a medium of exchange for goods or services within the village area, and for external trade. Of the three uses the third is the most important, accounting for probably three-quarters of the total production.

Consumption within the village

Opium is used by the Miao for relieving pain and giving pleasure. Because of the nature of the drug the dividing line between the two easily becomes blurred and a reciprocating pain–pleasure complex creates the addict and binds him almost inextricably in his addiction.

The purely medical use of opium, by persons not already at least partly addicted, is not great. Adults may take to smoking it during a prolonged illness but unless the illness is severe they usually try to avoid doing so because they are aware of the dangers of addiction. This is especially so in the case of young adults.

Bernatzik, who studied the Miao in 1936–7, refers to opium being applied to snake bites and being eaten to ease pain and relieve diarrhoea.[23] He also makes a general reference to the 'nutritional and medicinal value' of the poppy.[24] The only nutritional use which we have seen is the boiling for consumption as a vegetable of some of the young poppy plants thinned out at the time of the first weeding. We never saw any cases of snake bite. We never saw opium applied in the case of other wounds, perhaps because it would make a very expensive

[23] Bernatzik, 1947, p. 236.   [24] Ibid., p. 519.

poultice. We were not aware of its being eaten to relieve diarrhoea, although we were given the following rather frightening recipe:

Prepare a solution comprising two-thirds of raw opium and one third of water. Boil and strain. The liquid may be used for injections to cure stomach-ache. Dry the solids, mix with deer antler, boil, strain, and dry the solids again. These may be eaten as an aphrodisiac.

This was probably a recipe learnt from Chinese traders. It could not have been used very often for stomach-ache because none of the Miao in Meto had hypodermic syringes.

In one or two exceptional cases we have known opium to be eaten by addicts, but it is unlikely to have been a common therapeutic practice because of the considerable risks of over-dosage. Indeed danger and discomfort make opium a rather unappealing medicine. The first smoking, although not unpleasant to everyone, may be upsetting and is quite likely to cause a hangover which would not cheer the novice already suffering. Solace usually comes only with repeated use. Even then smoking is quite likely to have unpleasant after-effects, which is one reason—the other being that it makes the raw opium more pliable—why habituated Miao opium-smokers often mix powdered aspirin tablets with their opium, these being a major trade item in the hills.

We may conclude therefore that, at least at the present time in the more accessible Miao villages, opium is not very important in the treatment of sickness or accident and that its use in this regard is not a major reason for the attachment of the people to poppy cultivation. Smoking is occasionally resorted to as a palliative in the case of long illness and this is a cause of some of the addiction, but few people will turn to it in preference to other methods of treatment if these are available.

The people are well aware of its power as a poison. One sad use which it has, within the medical category, is as a means of suicide. Two tragic cases occurred in Meto in 1970, both concerning young unmarried girls. More common have been cases of married women who have quarrelled with their husbands. Because on marriage they have passed over into the clans of the husbands, death appears to them, or they seek to make it appear, their only recourse.

Suicide attempts, it is said, occur in Meto at the rate of one or two a year always by women and always with the use of opium. In 1969 a married woman died. The Miao belief in reincarnation, possibly as a happier person among a more prosperous race, appears to be a factor in the frequency of suicide. But the majority of attempts are threats only. Sometimes the opium is wrapped in a piece of paper before

swallowing to allow plenty of time for remedial action. In other cases
the announcement of swallowing is made almost immediately. The
Miao distinguish those 'who really want to die' by the fact that they
keep silent. When the symptoms of poisoning become obvious after
about six hours it is usually too late to take effective action. The social
shock which follows a suicide enlivens apprehension of the dangers of
opium. It is not a product which the Miao think of as wholly benign.
They see it as a necessary feature of their lives but also, on several
different scores, as a necessary evil.

Opium-smoking has been said to give energy. Until a few years ago
British timber firms operating in the north used to issue regular rations
of opium to their labourers in the teak forests.[25] A Karen addict
working for the Miao in Meto blamed his addiction on the fact that
when he was carrying opium from Meto for Chinese traders he was
given some for smoking at each stop to enable him to walk further.

The strength which opium gives is in fact largely illusory. Most of
the carriers whom we ourselves employed on occasions to take goods
into Meto were Karen who smoked opium. Invariably the journeys
took longer than when we were able to hire non-smokers. The start
was delayed while their bodies were fuelled with opium smoke, they
had to be replenished half-way along the track, and immediately on
arrival in the village the used energy had to be replaced. But there
were some benefits. The knowledge on the part of the smokers that
they could obtain supplies of opium at Meto, using their carrier fees,
was an incentive to undertake the journey. And drugged feelings may
have led to fewer complaints about the loads.

This indeed is probably the real truth of the matter. The positive
value of opium as a stimulant is at best short-term, especially as it
often leads to neglect of food, but it eases burdens once they are on
one's back. Belief in its energy-giving properties is not a significant
cause of addiction amongst the Miao at Meto because they are all
aware of the debilitating effects of habitual prolonged use.

Religion also is not a significant cause. Bernatzik observed a shaman
smoking opium before beginning a ceremony.[26] In Meto, too, this
always happened, although the smoking was in no sense part of the
ceremony. All the Meto shamans, male and female, were opium-
smokers. A precondition of shamanism is a period of physical or mental
suffering—often a long illness. According to one theory, the person
concerned, having reached the end of his allotted span on earth, dies.
His soul goes to heaven but, instead of staying there until rebirth, is

[25] Information supplied by Mr. Richard Wood, former Manager of the Borneo Company
in Chiengmai.

[26] Bernatzik, 1947, p. 180.

sent back for a further period on earth in its old body. The shamans therefore have spiritual acquaintance with the afterworld which gives them their power as mediums between men and spirits. The long illness may have been the initial cause of their addiction.

Probably opium is an important aid to them in their shamanistic performances, sustaining them in their lengthy shakings and contributing to their trances. As the shamans are powerful figures in moulding Miao opinion their dependence on opium must mean some religious influence in support of its production. But their personal needs are relatively small. They do not preach its use by others. Thus they are not a cause of the massive production and, if rightly treated and their needs supplied, they should not oppose its reduction.

Opium appears to have no direct part in religious ritual. When I visited the wake for the body of a child at Pasamliem in 1958 two men were lying on the floor smoking opium and when each visitor entered he was handed one of the pipes. But this was probably no more than an expression of hospitality. In Meto on similar occasions several years later no invitations to smoke were made. It is true that in the intervening years antipathy to ópium-smoking seemed to have widened.

Why then do Miao become smokers? Sickness plays a small part, as we have seen. Companionship with addicts probably plays a larger part. Opium-smoking is not really a social activity, because each person, with barely a mutter or two of intercommunication, withdraws into his own silent, private dream. But there is sociability in the offering of opium and the bodily proximity; conversely a member of the group who does not share the activity has to bear the pains of social isolation.

Like tobacco and alcohol opium appeals because it promotes euphoria, that is to say, it cheers in one way or another, even if it is merely satisfying a craving it has itself created. It is a pleasure-giver and tranquillizer, and, above all, a comforter. Strong men may take it in the belief, often correct, that they can control it, but it is resorted to more often by the poor, the weak, and those suffering from one cause or another. It is taken to more often, also, by the aged than by the young because they have greater need of solace and less need for activity. For what must be other reasons men take to it much more often than women.

Another explanation has recently been put forward by Dr. Westermeyer based upon a study of opium use in fourteen Miao villages in Laos. He points out that the Miao have two drugs available to them —alcohol and opium. They apparently never become addicted to the former. The difference between them is that whereas alcohol is a cathartic drug implementing behavioural expression of internal states opium is a control drug aiding suppression of disruptive impulses. In Miao society release of inhibition would only serve to ostracize a person. At the same time the society does tend to make demands on the person to be 'daring in adversity and ambitious for wealth'. Under such circumstances 'opium provides not only a soothing but also a safe retreat via its drive-reduction action.' He suggests that it may contribute to an integrated Meo society by allowing certain individuals, 'stressed by the demands of their monolithic culture, to continue to live in and contribute to Meo society.' [27]

The author makes a valuable point in drawing attention to the fact that opium never leads to aggressive behaviour in Miao society and may well contribute to the preservation of social harmony by actually preventing it on the part of maladjusted persons. One need never fear a Miao opium-smoker. The association of drug use with criminality which occurs in other societies is due to the difficulty addicts have in obtaining it, a condition which does not exist among the Miao. But it is difficult to accept Westermeyer's implication that the nature of Miao society actually induces its use, which is less amongst the Miao than amongst the groups to whom it is not so freely available. Also against its possibly adaptive effects on some persons must be set the social dissatisfaction it causes for others associated with them.

The strongest sanctions against it come from the women, especially from young women against men of their own age group. A man who is known to smoke opium will find it very difficult to persuade a girl to marry him. He will also find it difficult because of his lower working capacity and expenditure on opium to accumulate a bride-price which might overcome her objections. Married men who are addicts will find it harder to get second wives because, although the women who become second wives often have less scope for choice, their clansmen will be reluctant to pass them over to burdensome unions. Within established marriages a husband's addiction may cause ill-feeling in his wife and consequent misery to himself.

In Meto we recorded a song composed and sung by a woman whose husband was an addict. It tells of a girl who hates her husband because he smokes opium. She has to go out herself to gather the grasses to feed the horses and do all the work in the fields. She would like to run away but cannot do so because he has paid a bride-price for her. The public singing of this song must have caused her husband great shame. He came to us to ask if we could help him to get cured of his addiction.

Almost all serious addicts in Meto below the age of forty, and some

[27] Joseph Westermeyer, 'Use of Alcohol and Opium by the Meo of Laos' *American Journal of Psychiatry*, 127:8, February 1971, pp. 1019–23.

who are older, would like to be cured of their addiction. They are
aware that it reduces their working capacity, placing a heavier load on
their families, and that it uses up a sizeable portion of the product of
that extra effort. It may spoil the marriage prospects of their sons by
making it impossible to accumulate the bride-prices they would need,
and of their daughters by lowering their family status. For talented
men it ruins their chances of village leadership or of staying in office
because it makes them lazy, physically and mentally, when they should
be active, and lowers their respectability, and hence that of all members
of their group, in the opinion of outsiders including officials. Jusu, for
instance, had to yield the headmanship of Meto to Yaitong, because
the people lost faith in him as an example, a reliable counsellor, and as
a worthy representative of the community. Jusu was bitterly conscious
of his degradation and many times sought cure for his addiction.

The lowering of health and human dignity which addiction may
bring is kept vividly before the eyes of the Miao at Meto by the spectacle
of the Karen addicts who labour in Miao fields for wages ranging from
two to five baht per day usually paid in opium. No Miao would wish
this condition for themselves and none at Meto have reached it. The
Karen provide not only a convenient work-force but a warning.
Neither Jusu nor any other Miao addict of whom we were aware
at Meto was a complete slave to the habit. Their resistance was
higher.

That Miao resistance to opium addiction is higher in general than
that of other tribes is indicated by the results of the sampling survey
carried out by the Government of Thailand in 1965–6 as a preliminary
to the United Nations Survey of 1967. Figures for addiction were
given as follows: Miao, 9·55 per cent of the population; Lahu, 11·17
per cent; Yao, 15·9 per cent.[28] With the exception of the Lisu, for
whom we have no separate estimate, other tribes were not substantial
poppy cultivators, mainly because of unfavourable terrain, and therefore had much more restricted access to opium. The over-all figure for
the tribal population as a whole was calculated to be 3·6–6·1 per cent
for males and 1·2 per cent for females.

Because of our lack of detailed knowledge of the other tribes we can
speak here only of the Miao and compare their resistance with that of
the Karen who came to them as temporary labourers.[29] The Miao had
a much longer familiarity with the drug, extending at least over
several generations. They were richer and their richness gave them

[28] Quoted in Phillips *et al.*, 1967, p. 65.
[29] In fairness to the Karen, no conclusions can be drawn regarding the tribe in general.
The labourers were an exceptional group drawn to the opium fields probably because of
failure or poverty at home. Also not all of them were addicts.

not only more pride but more food, which is an important factor in reducing the debilitating effects of opium.

Although addiction is a social problem, and recognized as such by the people themselves, it is not severe in most Miao communities. There are some indications that the extent varies inversely to the wealth of the communities and their independence. At Meto there were a number of men who smoked only occasionally and others who smoked moderately but seemed to suffer no ill-effects. A person in the latter category was Kalaow in House 39. We first knew him in 1958 at Pasamliem where he was headman. He smoked then as much as he did at the time of the present study—two or three pipes in the evening and occasionally a couple at midday. He retired as a headman when he left Pasamliem but in 1970 he was still, for his age, one of the most vigorous men in Meto, with large cultivations. Serious addiction in Meto appeared to affect no more than 4–5 per cent of the population.

It has been calculated that an addicted smoker consumes about 1·34 kg of raw opium per year.[30] Assuming a 5 per cent addiction rate, this would account for a consumption in Meto of approximately 33 kg. Even if we double this figure to allow for consumption by occasional smokers and add, say, another 40 kg to supply Karen addict labourers, it is still less than one-tenth of the local annual production.[31] Basically the Miao are producers for an external market. Their own consumption is relatively insignificant.

Exchange within the village

Two forms of credit system based upon opium occur in the village, the first one involving villagers only and the second, much more important, linking them with local Chinese storekeepers.

During the wet season when their own opium stocks are exhausted but the new fields have yet to be cultivated men may borrow opium to pay Karen labourers. They are able to do so because richer farmers hold back some of their opium from sale immediately after the harvest knowing that they can dispose of it more profitably later, either by selling it or loaning it at interest. The borrower may be required to pay back 20 to 30 per cent more than the amount borrowed when his next harvest comes in.

For much of the year the Yunnanese Chinese storekeepers extend credit to the villagers against opium to be supplied at harvest time. It is estimated that the average household in Meto must pass over at least half its crop immediately to pay accumulated debts.

[30] Phillips *et al.*, 1967, p. 65.
[31] For Thailand as a whole, however, consumption may well exceed local production.

The role of the Chinese storekeeper

The credit relationship between the local Chinese trader and the Miao villager is a most important feature of the economy which would have to be considered in any plan for economic change. Although arrangements appear to vary, the storekeeper may not charge any direct interest. He gains in three other ways. First, he has his retail profit on his trade goods. Competition usually prevents this being excessive, especially considering his difficulties of transport, and alone it would probably not be sufficient to support the majority of traders. Secondly, he can pay the minimum harvest-time price for opium to his debtors because they must pay him all their debts, or at least pay to their maximum capacity, immediately after the harvest. This price is often as low as 800 baht per joi, or 500 baht per kg. Thirdly, he may sell the opium for 1,200 baht per joi, or 750 baht per kg, to outside traders more or less immediately, or hold it till later in the year so as to obtain a higher price.

Thus the local Chinese trader is firstly a storekeeper, secondly a produce merchant, and thirdly a kind of banker for the villagers. In the last role the difference between the price he pays for the opium and the price at which he sells it takes the place of interest on his loans.

The threefold role of the Chinese storekeeper explains why Miao who sometimes establish stores, in one or two cases with official support, generally do poorly in comparison. They are usually retailers only. They lack the market knowledge or the market connections to become successful produce merchants; and, as the main form of produce is illegal, they may be unwilling or prevented by their charter from dealing in it. They are therefore unable to oblige their customers with credit—that is to say, they fail completely as bankers.

The Chinese storekeepers succeed because they give a better service than any of the alternatives so far tried out in the hills. They have sometimes been spoken of as exploiters but a more discerning view is expressed by the writer of the report of the socio-economic survey of the Hill Tribes carried out by the Department of Public Welfare in 1961–2:

The symbiosis with the Haw traders, and in a somewhat reduced sense with the Thai traders, is another important factor in the social structure of the hill tribes. Nowadays, the traders, shopkeepers and merchants in the hills have to be regarded as factors in the tribal life almost in the same way as are the headman and the spiritual leader. In fact they have become a normal feature in the daily routine. . . . Whether the traders could be utilised in bringing about certain economic changes, like the profitable marketing of new cash crops is still a question. However, if possible, one should work not against the traders but through them.[32]

It seems to me that the system can be criticized seriously on only two grounds—that it is controlled by outsiders to the tribal structure and that it is based on opium. How valid are these criticisms?

Are the Chinese storekeepers really outsiders? They are so in the sense that they are different ethnically and to a large extent culturally. Socially, too, they participate only slightly and informally in the ordinary life of the Miao community, mainly as spectators, commentators, and mediums of gossip. Their children play with Miao children but adolescence draws them apart and they never intermarry. However, the economic field has a wider periphery than that of other social relationships and the Chinese are long-standing elements with it.

That they are not outsiders but elements of a system is shown by the enduring character of their links with the villagers and the sense of obligation which sustains the relationship. A Miao can be given credit because the trader can rely on him to pay. It is true that if he does not pay the trader may pursue him for years even if he migrates. As a defaulter he will find it hard to get credit elsewhere, for the Chinese, linked by common interest, quickly spread the information amongst themselves. We have heard of some cases where physical punishment has been meted out. But none of these sanctions would be strong enough to be effective in a general moral vacuum. The real strength of the relationship lies in the duty which the Miao feel to pay their debts.

This duty is a norm of the society transmitted to the young by example rather than by precept. It is reinforced by religion. There is a belief that if a man's debts are not settled when he dies he may be born again as a pig, a chicken, or a horse, or in some other form in which he can serve his creditors. Therefore on the evening before burial a man asks all present in the house where the body of a deceased person is lying if he has any creditors. If any debts are outstanding his sons are expected to promise to pay them. It is said that they have no absolute obligation to do so, because the debts are not their own, but they do so out of sorrow for their father. The Chinese are included in the scope of the duty because they are an important part of the economic system.[33]

[32] *Report on the Socio-Economic Survey of Hill Tribes in Northern Thailand*, Department of Public Welfare, Ministry of Interior, Bangkok, 1966, English translation p. 28. This Report was prepared under the guidance of Dr. Hans Manndorff.

[33] An example of the Miao conscientiousness in regard to debts is the following case: When he was living in Om Koi, Juyi (House 2) was accused of stealing a horse from a lowlander and fined 8,000 baht. He borrowed some of the money from Nang (House 1), who belonged to a different sub-clan. When Nang migrated to Meto Juyi followed him and built a neighbouring house as evidence to Nang that he would not part from him until he had paid the debt.

The Report quotes above recognizes the symbiosis between the Chinese and the tribesmen. But it regards it as a recent development, stating that the Chinese 'are accepted by the tribesmen as a new factor in their social relations'.[34] In the case of the Miao it does not appear to be new. The Chinese traders have probably been associated with the Miao as long as they have had cash crops.

Unless stimulated from outside, the Miao show no particular desire to exclude the local Chinese from their social universe. The relationship between the two tends to be hierarchical, with the Chinese in the dominant position, but this is sanctioned to some degree by the sentiment, nurtured by centuries of cultural contact and intermittent political control, that the Chinese are the ancient mentors of the Miao. Some myths assign them the position of older brother, and frequently Miao customs are said to have been learnt from them. Any tendency to Miao inferiority and Chinese superiority which this produces is balanced by Miao ethnic pride and their assured independence. Although the relationship with the Chinese is not free from the tensions inevitably associated with dealings between traders and clients, it is generally harmonious and seen to be of mutual advantage.

What, then, of their involvement with opium? In 1965 there were in the main village complex at Meto ten Chinese stores. Near Boreh village there were another three and on the outer edge of Meto territory another two. This is approximately one store to every fifty Miao. The needs of the population at Meto could have been adequately served by at most three or four stores, and in fact only three or four did substantial retail business. Some of the others operated only at the harvest-time for opium. Even allowing for the fact that the stores also served neighbouring Karen settlements, the number seems fantastically high, and was clearly related to the high opium productivity of the area. The question can therefore be asked: Do the local Chinese stimulate the production of opium?

Probably so. Although genuine stores are happy to sell for money as well as opium, the smaller trading posts, which are little more than opium-receiving agencies, seek opium practically exclusively. By offering favourable loan terms they are able to secure Miao clients who may then remain tied to them for year after year. It may be incorrect to say that these ties to agents who are primarily interested in obtaining opium actually stimulate production, because there are other reasons why the people at present want to grow it, but they would tend to make it more difficult to abandon production.

[34] Op. cit., p. 28.

Nevertheless there is little true debt-bondage. Factors on both sides induce caution in the credit relationship. On the trader's side there is his comparative isolation in the tribal community, his usually small capital, the risk of crop failures, and the possibility that the Miao will migrate out of the range of easy contact. On the Miao side there is the wish to avoid bonds limiting their freedom of movement. Debts appear to be rarely so severe that persons could not find the means to discharge them if they had the incentive to do so.

The Chinese in their present numbers and with their present interests in the village are part of an established economic system which is based upon opium. If the productive system changed, their numbers would probably grow less. Some of them get their capital from Chinese in the towns who finance them solely for the opium they can deliver. Loss of the opium supply would put these persons out of business.

Those with the largest stores in the village could probably survive so long as the village itself survived because they depend less on outside capital and more on reciprocal trade with the Miao. In the absence of other marketing systems, they appear to have a necessary role. In return for their modest profit they contribute a business expertise. There is also the humanitarian consideration that they are long-term citizens of the local Miao–Chinese world.

The traders from outside

By no means all the opium produced at Meto passes through the hands of the local Chinese storekeepers. Once or twice a year buyers come from the lowlands, sometimes from as far afield as Nakhon Sawan, the large city in the central plains strategically located at the junction of the Ping and Chao Phya rivers. These buyers are interested only in large quantities of opium and usually will not come to villages unless they have an assurance of collecting at least fifty jois (85 kg). Some of it they may collect from local Chinese agents to whom they give a commission usually of 100 baht (US $ 5.00) per joi; and some directly from Miao. By the time they leave the hills they may have collected a considerable quantity from various villages. Miao may act as carriers to get it off the hills, each man carrying approximately twenty jois (42 kg) and being paid 10 baht per day.

The routes followed by the buyers to their main disposal points are devious. Although we did gain a sketchy knowledge of some of them it would not be fair to our informants to discuss this aspect of the trade further. The whole question is fraught with danger and shrouded in great secrecy.[35] The buyer who visits the hills appears never to be the principal in the operation. He is usually at least the third in a chain from the principal and may not know his identity. From indications we received, it seems that all the principals behind the operations in the Meto district were Chinese merchants in the large towns. Rumours to the contrary sometimes circulate. One buyer was alleged to have claimed that he was a senior officer in the Border Patrol Police. This, however, was almost certainly a masquerade adopted to lend a shadow of authority to his operations.

The Miao will, if they can afford to do so, hold back their opium for sale to the lowland buyers. The price they receive is always higher than that given by a local storekeeper. If they can hold back the opium for sale to the large traders later in the year the price may be as much as 50 per cent higher than local storekeepers' harvest price.

There are two reasons for the price increase in the off-season. Firstly, the opium is in shorter supply. Secondly, it is more concentrated. The Miao do not 'cook' the opium.[36] This is done by the traders some time after purchase. The Miao always sell it in a raw state but within a month or so after harvesting it loses about 15 per cent of its weight through evaporation of part of its water content.

There are also at least two reasons for the higher price given by the large traders. Firstly, by buying directly from the Miao, they are by-passing local agents to whom they would have to give commissions. Secondly, there is a premium on large quantities. The trader takes a risk in getting the opium out of the hills. It also requires considerable organization to conduct the trading trip. Therefore the trader seeks a large load to make both the organization and the risk worthwhile. Also, in the past, large loads meant greater safety. Armed men could be employed to travel with the carriers and interference which could not be bought off might be fought off. Even now, although police

[35] For example, according to information given to us in an informal conversation with a Thai judge in Chiengmai there were in 1965 approximately 200 murders in Chiengmai Province. Only half the cases were brought to trial. Of the other half the vast majority were in his opinion connected with the opium traffic. No murder cases involving the traffic were successfully prosecuted in that year.

[36] The 'cooking' process is as follows: Raw opium is boiled in sufficient water to cover it, then strained to remove impurities. The solution is then brought to a boil over a slow flame. When the water has evaporated, a thick paste remains. This paste is called 'prepared', 'smoking', or 'cooked' opium. According to information supplied by the United Nations Narcotics Division, 1 lb. of raw opium yields ¾ lb. of prepared opium. This, however, must be raw opium which has already dried out considerably. Although Miao, at least in the Meto region, do not cook opium, Yao communities in other districts do so. According to information supplied to the 1967 U.N. Team by Mr. Douglas Miles the cooking process reduces newly harvested opium by half.

The Miao smoke raw opium. Perhaps this is one reason why they do not show a high rate of addiction. It takes so much longer to get each pellet ready for the pipe!

efforts at suppression have become much more rigorous, opium trains are usually accompanied by armed guards to protect them from banditry.

Dealings in opium tend to show a reverse process to that which is usual in trade whereby lesser quantities usually cost more than greater. This is indicated by the prices which were being paid in Meto shortly after the 1966 harvest.

Measurement scales for opium

Although in practice they were intermixed, two scales for measuring opium were commonly used at Meto:

A

Measure	1966 Harvest Price (baht)
1 peh [37]	0·50
1 moo (=2 peh)	1·00
1 salerng (=2 moo)	2·00
1 tap (=4 salerng)	8·00
1 joi (=120 taps)	1,115·00

It will be noted that a calculation based on the price of one peh would result in a price of 960·00 baht per joi.

B

	baht
1 hong	28·00
1 kum (=4 hong)	115·00

The price for a kum consistent with the price for one hong would have been 112·00 baht.

A rather different scale was used at Pasamliem where many of the smaller traders were Thai. All scales, however, make use of the joi, although the term for this weight is not everywhere the same. The two scales are interrelated by the fact that 1 hong is equal to 3·5 taps. A kum is therefore equal to 14 taps and 8·5 kum make one joi. A tap is an Indian silver rupee. Rupees are still in plentiful supply and provide a convenient basic standard for the system.

The actual weights used on scales vary in kind. Rupees are frequently employed, especially for small quantities of opium. They are trusted because of their known silver content and traditional value. Probably

[37] The spelling of these measures has been chosen to record as closely as our ear and non-phonetic script allow with Miao pronunciation. There are other spellings in use. 'Salerng', for instance, is a rendering of the Thai word, sometimes spelt 'salyng', for the 25 satung (¼ baht) coin.

too much faith is put in them. Some which bear the date 1839 and the portrait of William IV are much thinner through wear than those minted in the early years of the twentieth century. Smaller coins may be used for lesser weights such as the Thai 25 satang ($\frac{1}{4}$ baht) coin for the salerng. Five Thai 1 satang coins can be used for the peh and ten for the moo. Other objects of presumed standard weight, such as torch batteries, are sometimes used.

Storekeepers and traders use customary forms of scales and weights for larger quantities. We never saw in use at Meto the attractive bronze weights in animal figurine form corresponding to the joi, multiples of the joi, or divisions of it, although we have heard of their use to a small extent in other hill villages. These weights, commonly called 'opium weights' but apparently used for general purposes, may have passed out of common use because of their value as collectors' items—a value which has led to a great deal of inferior copying for the tourist trade. Most of them appear to have been made in the Kengtung district of Burma and they had currency in Thailand mainly in the regions near the Burmese border. Today weights made of the old fine alloy can fetch more than the value of their weight in opium, and we learnt of several cases where Miao from other villages had brought them for sale to antique shops in Chiengmai.

In metric terms the weight of a joi is 1·6 kg and of a peh approximately 3·3 g. The term used by local traders for a 'joi', and usually by the Meto Miao themselves, is 'haw' (falling tone). This is a Thai word meaning 'package' and is sometimes translated into English as a 'packing of opium'. The word 'joi' is used by Chinese traders who come from south of Chiengmai.

The traders, as we said earlier, put a premium on large quantities. On the figures shown above it amounts to about 2·5 per cent for a kum and over 16 per cent for a joi—that is to say, it multiplies roughly in proportion to the increase in amount. There appears to be no additional increase, however, for amounts above a joi. The profits in the trade itself grow in proportion to the distance the opium travels from the source of supply. This is shown by comparative figures for wholesale prices supplied by the United Nations Narcotics Division to the Project Preparation Mission in 1970:

Wholesale Prices of Opium (per kg)

	North Thailand	Bangkok	Kuala Lumpur	Hong Kong	U.S.A.
U.S. $	50	75	95	265	937[38]
Baht	1,000	1,500	1,900	5,300	18,740

[38] As no figure for opium was given for the U.S.A., the above estimate was arrived at by comparing the prices of white heroin in Bangkok and the U.S.A.

Conclusion

The present Meto economy is patterned around opium. It provides the Miao with much of their livelihood and determines many of their modes of relationship with other peoples. Like the different patterns of other tribes, their pattern has become established over many years and it is difficult to change because their technology, the size and location of their settlement areas, their population density, the timing of their social and economic activities, and many of their material values such as the importance placed on silver, are parts of it.

In the evaluation of the surrounding world the pattern has now lost its legitimacy. This has not entirely taken the Miao by surprise. Throughout the history of their attachment to opium, they have had hints of the ambivalence of outsiders to it. The change is not complete. The ambivalence is still there, as witnessed by the fact that the Miao can still dispose of their crop at much the same price as before. But the disapproval is growing and their way of life is threatened.

Many of them share the ambivalence. To an increasing degree they are aware of the disadvantages of the crop and would welcome an alternative to their dependence on it. They will be very lucky, however, if an exact ecological replacement can be found. It seems almost inevitable that the boundaries of their world and the way they live within it must change.

CHAPTER ELEVEN

DISPERSAL

IN 1965 the main villages of the Meto complex, A, B, C, D, E, contained fifty-seven houses. By mid-1966 not a single house remained. The ridge down which the 21 houses of Village A had ranged spectacularly was now bare and within another year it was to become a poppy field. The basin beneath the high peak of Umlong which had sheltered Villages A, B, C, and D and which had been the scene of the crowded festivals of 1966 and earlier years was deserted. When we revisited it in 1970 it had become just another jungle valley with few signs of its former habitation.

The sight of this valley appeared to offer striking confirmation of the Miao as a migratory people. The impression would not be wholly wrong. But closer investigation would modify it, revealing a complex pattern of movement controlled by several factors and drastically affected by the circumstances of the time.

Although the valley was deserted, the farming territory was not. In 1965 there had been seventy-one houses in the total complex. In mid-1971 the number of Miao houses in the general area was only six less, although they were all located some kilometres north-east of the former main settlement and many of them contained different people. Substantial migration out of the area had occurred. Some of it had been abortive and the people had returned. New people had arrived. How and why did this movement happen? The answers show much about the society of the Miao and their situation in Thailand today.

EMIGRATION AND IMMIGRATION

Because most Miao have the outlook of speculators rather than permanent settlers, a village usually has some fluidity of population nearly all the time. In the early phases of settlement, if land is plentiful, movement will be mainly into the area, although there is likely to be a little outward movement even then for various reasons. As the settlement grows the balance in favour of inward movement lessens until a size is reached at which the population starts to decline. At Meto this point was apparently reached in 1963 and there had already been a diminution in numbers before we took up residence in December 1964, but because of lack of accurate information on the earlier period we can speak only of the process after that date.

Outward movement, even when it has become pronounced, does not preclude inward movement sometimes on a large scale. This was exemplified at Meto by the immigration in 1965 of the six households comprising Village C. For these people their speculation proved a failure and their departure in 1966 represented the first major loss of population during their period of our study.

To explain the movement of population we may separate, for analytical purposes, two sets of factors—economic and social. Let us consider the economic factors first.

Miaoland—that is to say, all those parts of Thailand utilized by the Miao—comprises groups of people in various degrees of prosperity determined by the harvests they are getting from their land. In the early years of their migration into Thailand they could all hope to find optimum conditions in areas of new settlement when returns from old areas grew poor. But today their increase in numbers and severe competition from other tribes also with increasing numbers make it necessary for many of them to settle for less. How much less they will settle for depends upon their degree of poverty in their present locations and upon the extent of opportunities open to them.

The richer and better-connected Miao will seek to move as soon as their returns have fallen significantly below the optimum. By doing so they leave openings which may be filled by poorer and less well-connected people who believe that conditions in these areas will at least be better than where they have been living. This explains why a movement out frequently attracts a lesser movement in, as in the case of the Village C people who replaced Miao who had left prior to 1965. Whether the immigration will fulfil expectations depends partly on the size of the gap left by the departing people. The Village C people were disappointed and did not stay. Their expectations may have been too high; they felt they could find better opportunities elsewhere; but mostly the cause was that they came too soon, joining a clan that had not yet suffered great enough loss of numbers in the area to leave vacant reasonably fertile areas. Other people of other clans have come to Meto since and apparently intend to stay.

If new immigrants do not arrive, a movement out of an area may improve the conditions of those persons who remain, although probably only temporarily, by expanding the resources available to them. Therefore, exodus from an area often proceeds in stages. Both immigration and greater availability of resources may halt the decline in population for varying periods.

The rate of movement out of an area in the final stages, like the initial occasions for it and the varying courses it takes, is greatly affected by social factors. In order of inclusiveness, these are relationships between persons and groups, relationships between groups, and finally the nature of Miao groups in general.

On the inter-personal level kinship connections are of first importance. Each household has a range of ties through both husbands and wives. They are like invisible telephone lines linking the household to areas near and far, and along any one of them may come a message of hope stimulating a movement. Ties between males linked patrilineally are likely to be most often activated because they carry the additional voltage of clanship, but those between women also frequently occasion movement because the strength of the message may offset the weaker power of the line.

Some relationships are of especial strength. They may be ties between brothers, such as that between Yaitong and his elder borther Ger which means that neither will move without the other. Quite often there is a strong attachment between a man and his wife's brother, the mediating link being the wife. By extension this may cause a strong relationship between children and the group of their mother's brother. The inter-personal relationships of members of a household to others outside it thus have both a general range and a number of specific intensities varying in type from person to person.

Factors of the second order—relationships between persons and groups—are mainly political in a broad sense. A man prefers to live with a number of fellow clansmen because of the support they can give him. They will help in dealings with non-clansmen. They will be a much greater help too than non-clansmen in dealings with the supernatural world because the ceremonial for this purpose is slightly different for each clan and therefore only clansmen can combine in a joint effort giving greater power. Groupings of clansmen are also related to leadership. A man can usually become a leader only through the support of fellow clansmen and the extent of his wider influence in the community at large tends to be commensurate with the numerical and wealth strength of his clan base. Conversely, those who wish to be led rather than to lead will tend to gather round a fellow clansman who will assume the role of leader either through choice or persuasion.

The size of groupings of clansmen, however, is limited by the fact that people prefer to live in communities which include other clans, which brings us to factors of the third order—relationships between groups. The advantages of having more than one clan in a neighbourhood are a freer sex life, especially but not exclusively for the unmarried, greater ease of marriage, a more varied ceremonial, and livelier festivities. But such combinations of clans tend to be unstable because competition for political dominance or dissatisfactions over relative status may develop within them.

At the final level is the Miao preference for large groupings however constituted. Asked the reasons for this Jongjow, in House 10, expressed some typical views when he said:

a. In a small village when someone dies there are too few people to make the big funeral which a Miao should have.

b. When people in a small village seek wives for their sons people in other villages don't like to give them their daughters because they believe that the village has too few people, that it must have poor soil or else it would have attracted more people and that it must break up soon. Also they say it will not be enjoyable for them to visit their daughters in a small village which must be very quiet.

c. To stay in a small village is to risk robbers from other tribes.

Another important reason is that powerful shamans are attracted to large villages where they will find clients more plentiful, and therefore the quality of spiritual protection is better in such villages.

We may now look at the operation of all these factors in the history of Meto.

MOVEMENT FROM THE METO VILLAGES

As described in Chapter seven, Meto was pioneered in 1961 by a group comprising four Tang clansmen and six Jang clansmen. Jusu of the Jang clan was the first headman; it was he who located the spirit of the place where Village A was built and paid homage to it according to the ceremonial of his clan.

As the settlement grew in size the Jang clan was outnumbered, most greatly by the Tang but also to a less extent by the Wang clan. Ostensibly on personal grounds but also probably as a response to relative clan strengths, Jusu was displaced as leader by Yaitong of the Tang clan. Jusu was discontented with the new situation. In 1964 he moved to Boreh where his fellow clansmen had settled near their fields and talked of leading them on a migration to an area about two days' walk away where he intended to set up a new village under his own leadership. In 1965 he attempted this move but the land proved unsuitable and he and his followers returned to Boreh.

Yaitong's position as headman was not entirely happy. He gained in status by having it validated officially by the District Officer but he had to bear the surreptitious rivalry of Jusu, an erratic but clever man who was superior to him in spiritual knowledge. His unease was reflected in concern about the fact that the tutelary diety of the place was in special relationship to Jusu. At the 1964 New Year festivities it was Jusu who, though no longer resident in the village, led the ceremony of homage to this spirit. At these same festivities Yaitong in an unusual act bolstered his status by gathering village elders together for a ceremony of homage to the District Officer, *in absentia*, the ritual object being his certificate of leadership.

Yaitong had strong support from Nang and Juyi, wealthy and highly respected Tang clansmen who were the sons of his father's elder brother. At first too he had the comfort of the presence in the village of Bowjang, the rich son of his father's oldest brother. In 1963 Bowjang, whose main fields were now distant from the village, spent most of his time in a house he had built near his fields. At the beginning of 1964 he returned to the village to reside in a new house he had constructed there. However, many of his animals died and then one of his wives. In 1966 he sold his house to Khun Nusit Chindarsi, who dismantled it for transport to Chiengmai as part of the Tribal Research Centre museum, and moved permanently to the neighbourhood of his fields.

In moving closer to his fields Bowjang was adjusting to convenience. In the first years of the Meto settlement there had been some fields to the south-west of Village A so that it was reasonably central. But by 1966 almost all the planting area was to the north-east and much of it about five or six kilometres away. Therefore the comfort of established homes in the village and the trouble which would be involved in moving them was now counterbalanced by the tiresome journeys to and from the fields and the difficulty of keeping them adequately supervised. Some people already were expanding their farm huts to the stature of secondary homes and spending less and less time in the village. Bowjang took the next step and abandoned his residence there completely.

It may have been partly the increasing inconvenience and the incipient disintegration of the village that accounted for Yaitong's growing discontent after Bowjang's departure. But the reason he stated was that his clan had not given first recognition to the village spirit and had no intimate relationship with it; he was uneasy about its disposition towards him and his fellow clansmen and therefore he did not want to stay in the village. He asked Nang and Juyi to move away with him but they said they did not want to go.

The move Yaitong was contemplating was to another district far from Meto. His wife was the sister of Chailong (House 41), who belonged to the Wang clan. Chailong wished to move to join fellow clansmen in Huai Ngu in Tak Province where he believed the land was very good, and he asked Yaitong to go with him. Yaitong, and probably even more so his wife, wished to preserve the association with Chailong, but he also did not wish to part from Nang and Juyi who refused to accompany him. He compromised by persuading Chailong to stay in the Meto area on condition that he himself would move his house from Village A to the neighbourhood of Chailong's house in the planting area which Chailong had now established as his permanent residence. When Yaitong did move there Nang and Juyi followed him.

The move rapidly became general. Chickens were sacrificed and the omens in their bones declared it propitious. For most people it had the practical appeal of convenience without the disruption and uncertainty of a real migration. Soying, the aged father of Yaitong, said the constant journeying to the fields from Village A made him very tired. A few people were reluctant to leave the old village but they feared being left alone. By the end of 1966 the old ABCDE complex was entirely replaced by a large new settlement marked on the Map facing p. 130 as Ban Miao Meto (1966) and several small clusters of houses within two kilometres of it.

The change in settlement site was typical of Miao communities after a period of residence in an area varying in duration according mainly to soil fertility. It was the first of the two types of movement to which we referred earlier:

1. *Short-range movements*, which are relocations of the settlement site to adjust to extension of the planting area to distant parts of the territory after the first fields in close proximity to the original settlement become exhausted. In this type of movement the community usually retains much of its integrity—that is to say, it is a mass movement of many of the households.

2. *Long-range migrations*, which occur when the territory is unable to provide a livelihood for the families resident within it. This type of movement, when it becomes general, usually results in the dispersal of the community to a number of different territories.

Some movement of the second type is usually coincidental with movement of the first type. Not all the families in the original settlement are able to be accommodated at a desirable level of productivity in the now reduced village territory. Therefore some will seek better opportunity elsewhere. If the total territory is relatively large, however, exodus from it will often not occur on a mass scale until after the primary shift of residence.

The short-range movements are symptomatic of ecological decline. They are frequently the preludes of movements of the second type which, given the existing ecology of the Miao, they can delay but not indefinitely avoid. This appeared likely to be the situation at Meto.

In December 1966 Soying (House 17), the father of Yaitong, died. Relatives assembled for the funeral, and amongst them was another brother of Yaitong's wife who came from a village called Pa Khia in Chieng Dao District. He asked several people in Meto to move to this village. In addition to the prospects of better land which were presented to them, Pa Khia was attractive to many of the Tang clansmen because close relatives—amongst them all the living descendants of Serger shown on Diagram 5—had moved there from Pasamliem when that village broke up in 1959. Thus old intimacies could be re-established.

The emissary from Pa Khia paid particular attention to Koyi (House 34), who was both a vulnerable subject for persuasion and a valuable asset to any village. Because he was an opium addict he had not succeeded in establishing extensive fields in Meto and his crops were relatively poor. But he was a leading shaman.

The emissary promised Koyi that if he moved to Pa Khia he would supply him with rice until his own fields were established. Koyi decided to go. When his decision was known, four other Tang households elected to accompany him—those of his son Foa (House 37), of his nephew Seipang (House 33) and those of two members of sub-clan B, Gatong (House 23) and Wangjer (House 25). Three Wang households also decided to move to Pa Khia—those of Sertoa (House 22),[1] Wang (House 48), and Songler (House 50). Gatong was married to a daughter of Sertoa, Songler already had a son living in Pa Khia and Wang also had relatives there. In general Tang and Wang clansmen were intermarried extensively in Pa Khia.

This movement of eight households to Pa Khia is the largest movement to any one area which has yet occurred from Meto. It is interesting in that it is to some extent a movement back to an area of former settlement because the territory of Pa Khia includes part of that which belonged to Pasamliem, some of which was being cultivated again in 1970.

More families might have gone to Pa Khia had not a warning sign appeared. Songler, the last man to go, decided to take his eighteen pigs with him instead of selling them as is normally done when the migration is to a far-away place. He had to walk them fifteen kilometres or so to the road where they could be put on a bus. Five died on the way. This was regarded as a bad omen against further movement at that time. If the land at Pa Khia lived up to the hopes of the migrants more persons would probably have followed later.

About the same time as the movement to Pa Khia was occurring Chailong (House 41) decided that he would move to Huai Ngu. He was accompanied or followed by four other Wang clan households—those of Suker (House 36), Juser (House 43), Wangjow (House 44), and Sersang (House 53). Although no Tang clansmen went to Huai

[1] Sertoa himself died in Meto in mid-1965 before the movement took place.

Ngu on this occasion, the links between present Tang residents of Meto and this village are likely to remain strong and may lead to a later movement if expectations of the recent migrants are fulfilled. Nang, Tong, and Blaju, important men of the Tang clan, all have daughters married there.

Two Wang clan households—those of Serpow (House 59) and Chamang (House 60)—returned to Mae Suk, in Mae Chaem District. One Wang household (House 61) and one Yang household (House 38) went to Mae Sa Noi in Mae Rim District. Also the second wife of the son of Faitei (Tang, House 10) paid back her bride-price and took her four children to this village whence she had come. Tongsuk of the Wang clan (House 58) went with his family to the Karen village of Huai Kung near the road to Mae Sariang where he intended to engage in trading.

Two Jang clan households (Houses 62 and 64) moved to Huai Kamban in Mae Chaem District. Two others (Houses 13 and 71) moved to Mae Lanoi in Mae Hong Son Province in 1967 but House 13 returned to Meto in 1968 and House 71 in 1969.

One Tang household—that of Kowang (House 57) moved to Ban Palang in Hot District because a brother's son lived there and he believed it was a good area for padi.

Thus by 1970 twenty-seven of the seventy-one households at Meto in 1965 had moved out of the area. Six of these were the Tang households comprising Village C which moved back to Chiengrai Province in 1966. We may leave these households out of further consideration as their stay in Meto, being confined to a single year, could not be termed a true settlement. Of the sixty-five households apart from those from Chiengrai which had been in the settlement in 1965 twenty-one had moved away by 1970, the clan composition of the migrants being six Tang households, twelve Wang households, two Jang households and one Yang household.

Economic and social factors may interplay both to induce migration and restrict its extent. We have already mentioned the main economic inducement to movement—the appeal of more and better land. The main social factors in movement are two: the pull of inter-personal ties, which means that if one person in a strong relationship moves the other will tend to go with him; and the bond of clanship which, if there are no contrary strong inter-personal ties, induces people to join in a movement which would otherwise leave them relatively isolated.

The social factors may carry a movement on past the point at which the economic factor would be a sufficient motivation. This probably accounts for the large migration of Wang clansmen. Once a majority had decided to move others preferred to follow them. Only four of the sixteen Wang households remained at Meto in 1970, and all of them had strong kinship ties to the Tang households which were still there. These Tang households now had a much stronger relative strength in the settlement.

As circumstances alter through migration the economic factor mentioned above may operate as a restraint upon it. The departure of some of the households allows those which remain to obtain more land. Frequently this occurs by deliberate arrangement, which is to the advantage also of those leaving by adding to their resources of good will or cash. Land may be given away to clansmen or close relatives without any payment. Thus Koyi, when he left, gave Field No. 86 to Chetsu (House 18), his nephew of the same clan. Seipang (House 33) gave Field No. 157 to his younger brother Ver (House 40). Tow, the son of Juser (House 43) of the Wang clan gave Field No. 165 to his father-in-law Foa (House 37) of the Tang clan. To persons of other clans who are not closely related land may be sold, sometimes to the highest of several of bidders. Thus Suker (House 36) of the Wang clan offered Field No. 243 to Nyaying (House 3) of the Tang clan who said he would pay him 350 baht for it. Suker then sold the field to Ying (House 12) also of the Tang clan for 400 baht.

The same social factors, too, referred to above as encouraging migration may discourage it in other circumstances. It is notable that none of the households comprising Village A in 1965 had yet moved out of the Meto territory by 1970. This was partly because these households were generally the better placed economically. But it was also because certain people central to the complex of kinship interrelationships linking members of this village were impelled by personal circumstances to remain. Ger (House 15), the elder brother of Yaitong, the headman, had become chronically ill with advanced tuberculosis and it was felt that he could not survive a move. Yaitong, who was closely attached to him, would not separate from him, and his other brothers, Chetsu and Tu (the youngest son of Soying), were unwilling to part from Yaitong to whom they looked for leadership.

The improved relative position of the Tang clan in the territory as the result of the migration which had taken place enhanced the political status of its members in general and of Yaitong in particular. The four Wang households which remained were all closely linked to the Tang households by affinal ties.

The events in Meto confirm the statement made earlier that owing to the differential operation of the economic and social factors migration from an area of large population tends to be not continuous but spasmodic. Once begun, however, the process is likely to continue until a critical minimum size is reached. To stay longer then may be to face economic and social catastrophe.

MOVEMENT INTO THE METO AREA

The migration from Meto was followed by a lesser movement into the area. Six Tang households have arrived. One (New House 6) came from Mae Lamea, in Mae Hong Son Province, in 1967. In 1968 one household (New House 7) came from a village in Om Koi District of Chiengmai Province and two from La Song Yang in Mae Hong Son Province. They were all distantly related to, or had had some previous co-residence with, Meto Tang households. The two other households which came had close relationships to existing households. The head of New House 1 was a brother of Ya (House 47). The mother in New House 14 was a widow of a Tang man whom Juyi (House 2) had brought to Meto with her children as a second wife. She quarrelled with him and her eldest son, Saw, established a separate household in which she lived with the four children of her first marriage and one son by Juyi. In 1970 a household (New House 3) arrived from Doi Kam, near Hot District headquarters. It was of the Klee clan not previously represented at Meto, but was closely related to Tang clan members resident there by the fact that the mother of the household head was a sister of Soying, Yaitong's father.

There have been six new Jang clan households. Four arrived in 1968 from Mae Prig in Mae Hong Son Province, and two from Mae Lanoi in the same province in 1970. They all had some previous relationships with Jang households resident in Meto.

The other household to arrive was a Wang clan household from Mae Jog in Mae Chaem District of Chiengmai Province. We have no record of exact relationship but believe it was related to one of the four Wang households remaining in the Meto area.

RELATIVE CLAN STRENGTHS

The appeal of an area to a clan may be affected by its strength relative to the clans in the area. This is not usually because of overt political competition between clans but because of the nature of the Miao political process in general. Leaders are appointed and decisions taken in a popular assembly in which, in matters of any uncertainty, the clans tend to be the elements. Members of lesser clans may feel themselves overruled and are often the first to leave in search of other congregations where they will be better represented.

Even a numerically dominant clan may find itself uncomfortable if its numbers are not sufficiently superior to provide a clear community leadership. Near-equal clans may create an ambivalence of leadership which no one enjoys but is liked least by those who are the nominal leaders. There may also be difficulties in the religious sphere because each clan conducts its relationship with the spirits slightly differently and therefore the community may lack a single strong voice and a consistent order. The result can be a near stalemate in both secular and supernatural affairs.

Situations of this kind tend to develop in Miao settlement patterns because of the operation of potentially contrary tendencies—the willingness of the people to welcome relatives, or even acquaintances, of other clans, and the wish of each clan to aggregate its own numbers. In the early stages of settlement no great difficulties may arise. Although one clan may predominate, members of other clans may be content to live with it because they are linked to it by close inter-personal ties which make for consensus. Even if, as at Meto, the migrants are of several different clans, there may still at first be no problems: the total numbers are small; the territory is large; the need for combination against external forces strong; and the occasions for argument infrequent.

If the territory remains large, tension between clans can be avoided or relieved by each forming its own separate nucleus in the settlement area. It is when the territory becomes congested or dwindles in size through exhaustion of resources that real difficulties of multi-clan accommodation are likely to develop. Such a situation may stimulate movement out of the area as a means of social readjustment.

The movement at Meto since 1965 has improved the position of the Tang clan. In 1965 the relative numbers of households were: Tang 33; Wang 16; Jang 12; Yang 4. This meant that there were only 33 Tang to 32 non-Tang households, a situation which, as we saw earlier, caused unease to Lowtong as headman and probably influenced him to encourage the six Tang clan households from Chiengrai to settle there, a migration which, however, proved abortive.

The emigration from Meto after 1965 left the clan strengths in households as follows: Tang 27; Wang 4; Jang 10; Yang 3. This was an overall superiority of 27 Tang to 17 non-Tang.

Subsequent immigration has lessened the relative strength slightly, the current numbers being: Tang 33; Wang 5; Jang 16; Yang 3. It has also increased the strength of the Jang residents led by Jusu, who was earlier Lowtong's most important rival, but this matters less now as all the Jang are living with Jusu in the separate village of Boreh.

Thus one stimulus to migration by the remaining Tang clansmen has been removed. If economic conditions permitted they could expect to enjoy superior status in the Meto domain for some time to come. The critical question is—will economic conditions permit it?

THE PRESSURE ON MIAO LAND

The most striking feature of the Meto situation since 1965 has been the maintenance of population density in an area of declining agricultural productivity.

In 1966 the almost universal opinion was that the land was reaching exhaustion. Everywhere the talk was of migration to fields more fertile. Scouts went out and their reports as well as those of visitors were eagerly discussed. Expectations were moderate. The Miao were too experienced to believe in a paradisical land where padi and poppy would bloom in equal profusion. It was recognized that a balance would have to be struck between the merits of an area for one crop against its disadvantages for the other. But most people believed they could find areas better suited than Meto had become and which could sustain them for as long into the future as they thought it necessary to calculate. Thus in December of 1966 after a visit to Huai Ngu in Tak Province Chailong encouraged his friends to migrate there on the grounds that land was available which was very good for padi although not so good for poppy and where they would be able to farm successfully for at least ten years.

But reports coming back from the first migrants appear to have dampened enthusiasm to follow them. In most settled areas only poor land or isolated pockets of fertile land distant from main settlements were still unoccupied. Unsettled areas have so far proved impossible to find. In some cases migrants returned to Meto. Thus So (House 11) moved to the village of Pah Puh Chom, inside the Chiengdao Land Settlement Area, in 1966, but came back to Meto in 1968. Jufoa (House 13) and Ler (House 71) went to Mae Lanoi in 1967 but returned in 1968.

Emigration ceased. Although some persons had particular reasons for remaining at Meto, many stayed just for want of any better place to go, and instead of the area continuing to empty in consonance with its declining fertility it began to fill up again with new immigrants forced away from even poorer places.

Without information over a longer period and from more areas it is difficult to be certain of the conclusion, but it appears that the Miao are facing a new situation. Although, as we said earlier, migration from an area often does not proceed at a constant rate, what is happening at Meto seems to be more than a normal dip in a population wave and the influx more than a normal eddy in an outgoing tide. The flow of Miao migration which has brought them from southern China and northern Indo-China in the space of 100 years or less has reached its southern limits in the final ranges overlooking the populous Thai plain. The consequences of this are made more serious by three other factors.

The first is that they are now meeting an upward pressure from the increasing Thai population. Traditionally wet-rice growers, poorer Thai farmers in the northern provinces are finding it necessary to supplement their irrigated crops with dry-rice planting in the lower hills. Chapman has shown that 32 per cent of all Thai farmers in the north have foothill swiddens, and in Nan Province the proportion is 81 per cent.[2] The Thai have not generally reached an altitude where they directly affect the Miao but pressure comes upon them through the intermediary of other tribes which populate the intermediate slopes.

The second factor is the increasing competition for land from different hill dwellers. Not only the Miao but other immigrant tribes, particularly the Lahu, the Lisu, and the Yao, have converged in the final hills. In the Meto region the much longer-established Karen, faced apparently with a rising population, are resisting more strongly encroachment on their territory.

The third and probably most critical factor is the rise in the Miao population itself through natural increase. For Meto at least this is revealed in the following population analysis.

THE CONTEMPORARY POPULATION

Of the 71 households in the Meto complex in 1965, 27 had emigrated by 1970. Table 31 shows the 1965 composition and subsequent changes of the 44 which remained. Because some of them had subdivided, the 44 households of 1965 had increased to 51 by 1970. Fourteen new households had arrived from elsewhere, making 65 in all. The changes in the household composition of the complex are shown in Table 32. The analyses in this and following tables are made in terms of the 1965 groupings of households, but it should be noted that, with the exception of Boreh, these groupings are no longer preserved. There is now one large settlement and several nearby small hamlets.

The average number of persons per household changed comparatively little, although it was lower for the new immigrants. In 1965 the average number per household for the 21 households in Village A was 9·86. For the 26 households to which this village had expanded in 1970 it was 9·9. The over-all average for the 71 households in 1965

[2] E. C. Chapman, *An Appraisal of Recent Agricultural Changes in the Northern Valleys of Thailand*, paper presented to the Sixth Academic Conference of the Agricultural Economics Society of Thailand, Bangkok, 1967 (mimeograph).

TABLE 31

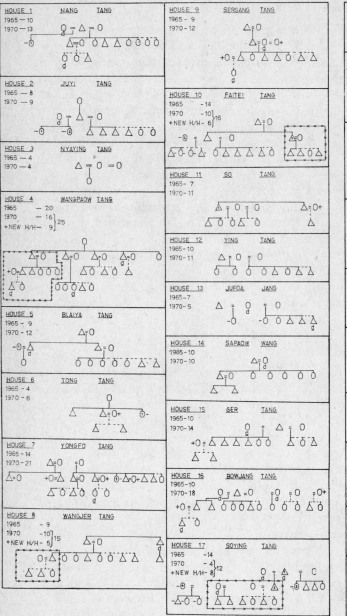

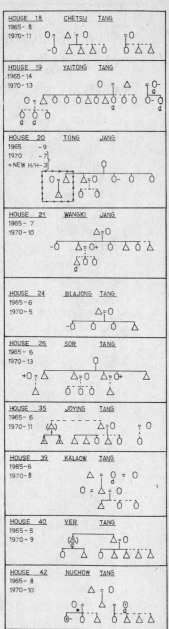

Composition of Meto households in 1965 and 1970

HOUSE 45 WANGYI TANG 1965–5 1970–5

HOUSE 46 BWOTONG WANG 1965–8 1970–6

HOUSE 47 YA TANG 1965–5 1970–7

HOUSE 49 JONGJER WANG 1965–5 1970–4

HOUSE 51 BLAJU TANG 1965–7 1970–9

HOUSE 52 NULANG WANG 1965 –18 1970 –9 +NEW H/H–9

HOUSE 54 JOYING YANG 1965–8 1970–11

HOUSE 55 CHASER YANG 1965–7 1970–10

HOUSE 56 BAO YANG 1965–4 1970–5

HOUSE 63 DOA JANG 1965–3 1970–4

HOUSE 65 FAIPOW JANG 1965–8 1970–8

HOUSE 66 SANG JANG 1965–3 1970–4

HOUSE 67 GAGO JANG 1965–7 1970–7

HOUSE 68 JUSU JANG 1965–8 1970–7

HOUSE 69 LER JANG 1965–4 1970–6

HOUSE 70 LER TANG 1965–2 1970–2

HOUSE 71 TEI JANG 1965–6 1970–7

NEW HOUSE 1 SANG TANG 1965– – 1970–6

NEW HOUSE 2 WANG WANG 1970–3

NEW HOUSE 3 SOPAOW KLEE

NEW HOUSE 4 YASANG TANG 1970–9

NEW HOUSE 5 SAFO TANG 1970–7

NEW HOUSE 6 BOWYING TANG 1970–7

NEW HOUSE 7 YATU TANG 1970–9

NEW HOUSE 8 PA JANG 1970–5

NEW HOUSE 9 TUNGSANG JANG 1970–10

NEW HOUSE 10 SERTO JANG 1970–14

NEW HOUSE 11 LENG JANG 1970–4

NEW HOUSE 12 YANGO JANG 1970–6

NEW HOUSE 13 SANG JANG 1970–7

NEW HOUSE 14 SAW TANG

△ = male
O = female
d = died before 1965 census
d = died after 1965 census

+ incoming person
– outgoing person
--- born since 1965 census
-*- separate household in 1966

TABLE 32

Changes in household composition of villages between 1965 and 1970

VILLAGE	No. of households in 1965	No. of households emigrated	No. of households created by sub-division	No. of households in 1970
A	21	—	5	26
B	5	3	—	2
C	6	6	—	—
D	12	8	—	4
E	13	4	1	10
F	4	4	—	—
BOREH	7	2	1	6
ISOLATED HOUSES	3	—	—	3
TOTALS	71	27	7	51
NEW HOUSES	—	—	—	14
GRAND TOTALS	71	27	7	65

was 8·0. For the 51 households of old stock in 1970 it was 8·5. The 14 new immigrant houses had an average of 6·6 giving an over-all average for the 65 households at Meto in 1970 of 8·2.

The lower figure for new arrivals cannot be regarded as suggesting an incipient change in Miao household structure. It is consistent with the fact that migrants are often new sub-divisions of older households. It is true that this tendency is not apparent in the cases of the households which departed from Meto but this is probably due to the fact that we have viewed the process from the emigration and not the immigration end. It is unlikely that all the emigrants re-formed in exactly the same households in their new locations.

The total population of the 71 households in 1965 was 570, and of the 65 households in 1970 it was 533. The sex composition of the 1970 population is shown in Table 33. Sex ratios continued to favour females, as shown by Table 34. A similar balance in favour of females was shown in births since 1965. The ratio of new births occurring in Village A was 1·14 and for births in the Meto settlement as a whole it was 1·25.

As marriage is strictly virilocal in Miao society, only women can be lost or gained by households through marriage and divorce. The over-all balance in this regard was against Meto in the five-year period, as shown in the Table 35 which takes account only of households

TABLE 33

1970 population by villages

VILLAGE	MALE	FEMALE	TOTAL
A	117	141	258
B	8	10	18
D	20	18	38
E	38	37	75
BOREH	11	19	30
ISOLATED HOUSES	5	10	15
TOTALS	199	235	434
NEW HOUSES	54	45	99
GRAND TOTALS	253	280	533

remaining for the total period. Two other mature women also joined the group from outside—a mother in House 65 and a niece in House 63.

Birth, death, and natural increase rates were assessed in the following manner:

1. We took as our starting-point for each village what we shall term a 'base population'. This figure was arrived at by eliminating from consideration any persons who had moved away from the village during the five-year period. For example, the second wife of the son of Faitei in House 10 and her four children were excluded. Also excluded were all women who had left to marry elsewhere. These persons were excluded because of uncertainty regarding their vital statistics for the

TABLE 34

Ratios of females to males, 1965 and 1970

Village A, 1965 (21 households)	1·3
Village A, 1970 (26 households)	1·21
Total complex, 1965 (71 households)	1·19
Households of old stock, 1970 (51 households)	1·12
All households, 1970 (65 households)	1·11

TABLE 35

*Gains and losses of women through
marriage and divorce 1965–1970*

VILLAGE	GAINS	LOSSES
A	12	12
B	2	1
D	—	1
E	1	3
BOREH	1	7
ISOLATED HOUSES	—	—
TOTAL	16	24

total period. Theoretically we should also have excluded incoming
wives and their children but we did not do so because we were not
certain of the arrival dates of all the wives.

2. We calculated a 'final population' by adding to the base population
the total of births and adoptions and subtracting the total of deaths.

3. We calculated a 'mean population' by adding the base and final
populations and halving the total.

4. Vital rates for the five-year period were calculated on the basis of
the mean population and divided by five to give average annual rates.

The results of the procedure are set forth in Tables 36 and 37.

TABLE 36

Births and deaths 1965–1970 by villages

VILLAGES	Base population	Births △	O	T	Deaths △	O	T	Final population	Mean population
A	196	36	41	77	6	9	15	258	227
B	13	2	3	5	—	—	—	18	15
D	24	7	4	11	—	1	1	38	31
E	59	9	10	19	1	2	3	75	67
BOREH	23	1	7	8	2	—	2	30	26
ISOLATED HOUSES	12	—	3	3	—	—	—	15	13
TOTALS	327	55	68	123	9	12	21	434	380

NOTE:
a. There were 4 adoptions in Village D and 1 in Boreh.
b. The total for mean population is calculated from the other totals.

TABLE 37

*Average annual birth, death, and natural increase rates
for period 1965–1970*

VILLAGES	Birth rate per 1,000	Death rate per 1,000	Increase rate per 1,000
A	67·84	13·22	54·63
B	66·67	—	66·67
D	70·97	6·45	64·52
E	56·72	8·96	47·76
BOREH	61·54	15·38	46·15
ISOLATED HOUSES	46·15	—	46·15
TOTALS	64·74	11·05	53·68

THE RISING MIAO POPULATION

At the time of the 1960 Census the birth-rate for the whole of Thailand was calculated on the basis of official registrations to be 34·7 per 1,000 and the death rate 8·4 per 1,000. Because many births may not have been registered, the true birth rate is probably considerably greater. It has generally been assumed to be around 45 per 1,000 and the natural increase rate to be between 3·1 and 3·4 per cent annually.[3]

In comparison the Meto Miao figures given above are very high. Before accepting them and drawing conclusions from them about the Miao future we must ask firstly whether they are accurate, and, secondly, whether they are typical.

It is possible that some births were recorded as falling within the five-year period when in fact they occurred before 1965 and were missed in the census taken in that year. It is unlikely, however, that this affected the result significantly because the earlier census was conducted with at least as much thoroughness as the later one. The degree of consistency amongst the returns from the different villages also suggests that the amount of error was not great. The lowest birth-rate figure for any of the five villages—56·72 per 1,000 for Village E— was still very much above the national average.

The death-rate figure is almost certainly accurate as the prolonged funeral ceremonies always make deaths in a village well known. A surprising feature of the statistics was the small number of deaths of

[3] H. V. Richter and C. T. Edwards, 'Recent economic developments in Thailand'. Paper given at the Seminar on Contemporary Thailand, The Australian National University, Canberra, 1971 (mimeograph), p. 2.

infants born in the five-year period. Still-born children or children surviving only a day or two after birth may possibly have been missed from the count but of the 123 recorded births only 10 died, an annual infant mortality rate of only 16·26 per 1,000.

The typicality of the figures is open to much more doubt than their accuracy. Several factors should be considered:

1. The sample was fairly small.

2. The period was short. A single short period could have circumstantial characteristics affecting its significance. For example, if it was a period of settled, relative prosperity—as this one was—marriage-rates would tend to be higher and death-rates lower. It may also happen to be a period relatively free from epidemic disease. Although such diseases do not commonly afflict Miao communities on a massive scale, the low number of infant deaths does suggest that 1965–70 was a healthy period.

3. Probably the most important factor in the high birth-rate at Meto was the polygynous unions of many of the men, which meant that they had more than one breeding wife coincidentally or a succession of breeding wives.

It has sometimes been argued that polygyny reduces birth-rates because the women have less frequent or less fertile intercourse owing to the preoccupation, lowered potency, or advanced age of their husbands. Even if this were true, it could apply only in circumstances in which some men were denied wives. When the sex ratio in a community strongly favours women, as at Meto, polygyny must increase production.

The unequal sex ratio at Meto probably does make it atypical of Miao communities in general. The estimates for the Miao population as a whole, quoted in Chapter Two, do not show a marked sex imbalance, although our own detailed studies leave us with some doubts on this score. In so far as Meto is atypical, it is probably so because of its relative wealth. As wealth derives from agricultural productivity, this in itself is significant because it indicates that the richer an area of land the faster the rise in population.

Even when allowance is made for all the above factors, it still seems probable that the Miao have a rate of population increase very much higher than the national average. Confined within narrow territorial limits they are already facing an economic crisis which, because of their greater population increase, is probably deepening for them more rapidly than for most communities in Thailand.

CHAPTER TWELVE
CONCLUSION

THIS book has both an ethnographic and a theoretical purpose. The first aim has been to describe, in the simple, abbreviated, and partial manner necessitated by a single volume, how the Miao live. The second aim has been to try to explain this way of life as a cultural system correlated with the ecology of the people. In particular we have been concerned to analyse the role of what we believe to be the main ecological factor in the Thailand setting—the cultivation of the opium poppy.

In Chapter Four we compared the Miao to birds which flock together in a good feeding place but scatter widely on new searches when the food is finished. Yaitong, the headman of Meto, went further and compared them to predatory birds. If this is how the Miao sometimes see themselves, it is certainly how they are almost invariably viewed by outside peoples with whom they come into contact. Like most popular conceptions of other people the image is grossly exaggerated but contains a core of truth.

The Miao attitude to land is exploitative in the sense that they aim to get the most out of it without apparent concern for conservation. This at least is generally the case in Thailand and accounts of them from other times and places indicate that it is a long-established characteristic, although apparently one more prominent on the frontiers of their population than amongst the people who have stayed behind in their Chinese homeland.

Their answer to exhaustion of resources has been to move onwards. Before that point has been reached better opportunity may have drawn them forwards. Thus their exploitative attitude to nature has been both a push and a pull taking them in all directions over the mountains of Indo-China but mainly southwards because that is the way the hills run. The attitude is not merely a quirk of psychology. How it arose may remain a mystery. It may have been forced upon them by defeat and harassment in the centuries of antiquity, or they may have been born an adventurous people. But whatever the case, it now accords well with other major aspects of their cultural behaviour.

For the Miao the food quest is not enough. It is not enough for any human beings, of course, but for them it is less so than for many peoples who live off the soil. At least as important as subsistence is the accumulation of wealth. A great part of their life interest is in working for display, in costumes, in silver jewellery, and in feasting with their spirits.

The accumulative motive is open-ended and therefore encourages exploitation. In the Miao case we can trace a further complexity in the pattern. Although they accumulate for display the main wealth item—silver—also has a utilitarian value of which they are equally well aware when they seek it. It can be converted into sustenance for movement into areas of renewed opportunity. Thus their cultural–economic system is conducive to a migratory way of life which facilitates exploitation and avoids its disadvantages.

The historical evidence suggests that the Miao were prone to migrate long before opium entered the picture. It cannot therefore be accorded the primary role in accounting for their movement. But there can be little doubt that it increased the rate of movement southwards from China and that in many cases once adopted by groups it left them with little choice but to keep on moving.

Poppy cultivation could serve their cultural incentives well. Given profitable outlets for the product it could easily become a major part of their economy creating an ecological dependence upon the particular environments suited to it. A feature of these environments is the narrow limits of possibilities they offer. The limiting factors in Thailand are not hard to see.

Firstly there is remoteness. If the Miao are to maintain a trading economy, necessary if they are to acquire wealth, in their mountain settings distant from market centres a crop is needed which is both easily transportable and profitable. No other crop yet known to them fulfils these criteria so well as opium. Its superiority over other possible crops varies, of course, in proportion to the remoteness of the community, and there are some groups of Miao who have been able to develop satisfactory alternatives. But for very many communities opium remains the only worth-while means of trade available. For all communities, too, it has at present other great advantages over any suggested alternatives: it has a certain market and a stable price, thus allowing calculation in economic life. Its price is so stable that it can function as a mode of currency in itself.

Secondly, the suitable environments are limited to certain altitudes where frequently the areas fit for cultivation are small. In the tropical region the opium poppy will grow well only above a height of 3,000 feet. Areas of suitable planting land, especially when the soil conditions necessary for opium are taken into account, at such heights in Thailand are rarely extensive. The area at Meto was one of the largest continuous areas we have seen. The situation is also made more difficult for the Miao by the fact that in their recent migrations they have usually been moving into hills which have already been settled by other tribes thus reducing the amount of land open to them even within the narrow range set by the opium poppy.

The effect of the small size of the areas may make anything other than dependence upon a cash-crop economy impossible, although, as we shall discuss in a moment, cultural factors leading to overcrowding more often cause this situation.

Thirdly, climatic factors in the environments chosen, because of their suitability for opium, encourage dependence on the crop as the main means of livelihood. Once a group is committed to opium growing as a major activity the utilization of much land for padi, the main subsistence crop in the area, becomes very difficult. The reason lies in the seasonal distribution of crops. Padi is harvested in November right at the end of the wet season. The opium harvest is usually not completed until February when half the dry season has gone. It is then too late to clear much new land, to allow the cut growth to dry in the sun, and then to burn it off. The opium harvesting takes all the group's energy. Therefore often only small amounts of bush land are cleared for padi even when it is available.

Padi could be planted on some of the land previously used for opium because the poppies, although harvested two months before padi planting, will have kept the soil relatively free of weeds. This does occur, but usually only in the declining years of a settlement when poor opium crops necessitate more production of food, because the group is reluctant to reduce its opium-producing area. The land also will not generally yield good harvests.

Climatic factors also dictate a priority for opium on land which it is envisaged might at some time be used for both crops. Although it is possible to follow opium with padi, it is very difficult to follow padi with opium. A new field being made in the jungle will be cleared by February and burnt off in early April. If it is to be used for padi it will be planted in late April. The crop will occupy the ground until early August. The period between the padi harvesting in November and the poppy planting the following July (with half a wet season intervening) would usually result in the ground's being so overgrown as to make clearing for poppy planting exceedingly difficult.

In many areas the seasonal factor encourages a further attachment to the cash economy through the necessity to have a crop which will keep the ground clear from the time it is cleared by burning at the end of the dry season until the poppy planting in August. The crop generally employed is maize, and most of the harvest is used for pig food thus creating a production complex: maize–opium–pigs.

As mentioned in Chapter Eight, at Pasamliem only a small amount of maize was grown because the altitude was too high. However, the high altitude also resulted in the grass growth on the fields between the time of the burning-off in April and the poppy planting in August being comparatively light and therefore easily weeded. Thus environment does affect the local pattern of crop use. But we may say that above an altitude of 3,000 feet the environment, in one way or another, favours the growing of opium.

Cultural as well as environmental factors also play a large part in committing the people to opium and limiting their periods of settlement. In some areas there would be sufficient land to enable a group large enough to have a satisfactory community life to maintain itself indefinitely. Indeed there are some groups which have been stable for forty years or more, but they are atypical.

Their comparative rarity is due to the willingness of the Miao to receive new comers into a territory. In Chapter Four we said that one of the reasons for this is that a large community allows the fullest blossoming of their cultural life. Another reason suggested was their desire to maintain the ideology of receptiveness and the widest network of friendly social relationships against the day when they themselves might have to join other communities. But a further reason not previously discussed is the existence of a general rule in the hills that unoccupied land is open to settlement by anyone. It is owing to the common acceptance of this rule by all tribes that inter-tribal fighting is unknown in the hills of Thailand.

The effect of the rule in encouraging the growth of settlements is twofold. Firstly it gives other Miao a claim to come into the area. Secondly it gives further impetus to the willingness of the residents to welcome them because their presence will help to secure the area against other tribes.

The rule is also yet another factor tending to increase the dependence upon opium. If a tribal group is practising swidden padi farming the areas to which it can claim occupancy are much larger than those actually under cultivation at any one time because they include fallow land. But even the rice swiddeners of other tribes have difficulty in maintaining right to land which they have not brought into use in recent years. A Miao group primarily devoted to opium cultivation has comparatively little land under padi and few fields obviously lying fallow. Therefore the areas surrounding the opium land are more likely to fall under alien occupation, thus leaving them a circumscribed territory from which they can gain a livelihood only by means of a cash crop.

Once the people have become primarily opium growers they tend to think in terms of that crop. Padi growers have only to glance one year ahead to see the necessity of more land for rotation. In the best areas opium may be grown for up to twenty years successively on the same ground. At Meto the average was about eight years. But at the time of first settlement eight years is a long time, especially if the grower thinks that he has enough land for at least one shift of fields. The prospect of land exhaustion is quite remote and even if contemplated not very frightening to a population conditioned for centuries to periodic migration.

An effect of the cultural–ecological system in which opium plays such a key part is that population densities frequently rise to degrees which either oblige or encourage the disintegration of settlements. In extreme cases movement is forced upon the people by absolute exhaustion of resources. In other cases it may begin as soon as productivity has begun to fall below the optimum, inducing the more enterprising people to look for better opportunities elsewhere.

Enterprise is fed by the success which opium allows. In Chapter Nine we pointed out that averaged over many years the income of the Miao would not be anything like as high as that at Meto during the period of the study or so much superior to that of other tribes as the figures then collected indicated. As we said earlier, for most people life is a slow rhythm of poverty and plenty, of moving, settling, and moving again. Nevertheless the relative prosperity which they may achieve in favourable conditions is an important factor attaching them to their way of life. More than with other peoples in the tribal region their aspiration level may run ahead of their current conditions.

The mode of life also supports, if it does not actually cause, other characteristics of the society of considerable economic and political significance. Firstly there is an absence of social stratification based upon wealth. Although the Miao have well-developed accumulative urges; although there are few social pressures preventing persons retaining for themselves what they have gained; and although some families do become rich and are capable of staying rich even for several generations; nevertheless generally fortunes ebb and flow with the tide of population movement which brings more people into the richer areas, thus constantly redistributing numbers according to resources.

Secondly, there tends to be an absence of enduring social or territorial links which can form a lasting basis for political organization. Not only clan sections but even families may separate to form different congregations elsewhere. Even when groups have been co-resident for a considerable period and a degree of political cohesion has developed, the fact that any of the constituent clan sections may depart from the alliance at any time means that secular leadership has no security beyond, at most, the clan.

Probably it is partly for this reason that the persons who often do become most important in large communities are the shamans, the basis of whose authority is not secular but religious, and therefore not confined to particular social groups. Their role in political affairs is certainly limited by the fact that this is not the sphere in which they directly operate. They are not judges in civil disputes, they do not preside at village meetings and they are not the intermediaries with outside authorities. But their indirect influence on decisions and on support given to secular leaders is often great, and in some circumstances it could possibly be critical.

Although conditions in contemporary Thailand are not comparable and events unlikely to take a similar course, it is worth noting, as evidence of the degree of influence shamans can have, the following passage in Savina's account of the attitude of the Miao at the time of the revolt in Tonkin and Laos from 1918 to 1921:

The people cannot conceive of being subordinate to another . . . The Miao are waiting for a liberator, a king, a *phoa thay* . . . But not everyone can be a *phoa thay*. He must be recognized and named by the shamans. It is from them that he receives, so to speak, his powers, and it is also by them that he is advised during the whole of the operations. For this reason one finds in all the wars undertaken by the Miao in the course of their history two insepara-ble elements: the political and the religious. This people turns its religion into a weapon to conquer its liberty and ensure its independence.[1]

The same factors which inhibit political organization within the society—the frequent movement and realignment of social groupings, and the absence of permanent bonds to particular territories—also contribute to the over-all ethnic identity of the Miao. Individual connections ramify widely. People travel freely and meet others who have travelled elsewhere. And so they come to know a common country beyond their separate settlements and all the different people who may lie in between. The opium economy, by promoting settlement in-stability and encouraging movement, must increase this effect.

Their ethnic identity, based upon their distinctiveness as a people, is also enhanced by another aspect of the opium economy in that objects of their trade, such as silver ornaments, silk thread to embroider tribal costumes, and oxen to sacrifice to the dead, have value only in the context of Miao society. The retention of their value therefore depends upon retention of the culture. This is not to say that the Miao are unaware of wider realities. They trade also to obtain food and material comforts; they are attracted by goods such as guns, radios,

[1] Savina, 1930, pp. 258–9.

and even wrist watches both because of their usefulness and because of the prestige they confer. It is possible that in time material incentives may displace the peculiarly cultural motives. But the process, if it occurs, is likely to be disturbing because it will mean the devaluing of important products of their toil.

That the Miao do have a strong sense of ethnic identity is obvious to all who know them well. It is also indicated by the fact that although they trade with other peoples and sometimes employ them they rarely intermix socially and they almost never intermarry, neither with the poorer tribes around them nor with the richer Chinese traders who frequently take women from other tribes.

It is true that some groups appear to have a stronger will to independence than others and that circumstances may develop a wish to belong to a wider society. At Pasamliem in 1958 I asked the people if they would like to have a school in the village and they were emphatically against it on the grounds that it would disrupt their society. In 1970 the question was put again to some of the same people at Meto. They said they would favour it provided that not all the children would have to attend. When asked whether the school should teach in Miao language or in Thai, Yaitong, the headman, replied: 'The language should be Thai, because we are only a small, poor people and when we go down to the town people laugh at us.'

The expressed attitude, however, is likely to disguise an inner conflict some of which may be very close to the surface. At Meto there was no prospect of establishing a school immediately, but children were offered by a trusted Thai official the chance of attending a boarding school for tribal children. From an initial batch of about 15 volunteers, only three appeared on the appointed day. One was Yaitong's own son but his father sacrificed a chicken, studied the omens, and refused to let him go.

Meto at the time was under growing stress as opium yields declined. As we said at the conclusion of Chapter Nine, when Miao visit the plains they may note the prosperity and ignore the poverty. If they are in a state where they are seeking alternatives to economic decline, they may see visions of themselves as rich wet-rice planters or even as workers in the towns. The difficulty may come when the gap is revealed between their hopes and the reality they can achieve.

Also at Meto there were additional reasons for despondency. Some attempts at migration had failed. They had been told by certain officials that their crop was evil and their methods of farming harmful and inefficient. Their Karen neighbours were becoming restive at what they claimed was damage to their territory. Rumours of Miao villages involved in fighting with the Government were penetrating to them.

Their changed attitude, therefore, was an attempt realistically to appraise their situation. Nor is it to be discounted as evidence of an adaptability which may provide the basis for new relationships with the wider society. But their very sensitivity to suggestions of inferiority indicated their awareness of their cultural distinctiveness. In other circumstances their reaction could be to reassert their independence.

The record of the Miao in other countries shows the strength of their will to determine their own destiny. Savina writes: 'In their history . . . we see uprisings of a multiple, successive and almost regular character. . . . They have never had a proper country, but they have never, on the other hand, known bondage and slavery.'[2] It is indeed freedom from bondage that the Miao seek to maintain. Complete independence they do not expect except perhaps when the false promise of it is deliberately held out to them by propagandists who know that it can never really be their lot for long.

All the Miao whom we have ever met have a strong desire to live in harmony with the people who rule the land. They know that they are not a nation. They know too that their trade and their inter-communication with relatives in other parts of the country depend upon peace and order. If they are caught up in war they may, as Savina says, show 'a bravery and courage . . . superior to other peoples'[3] but for most of them it is a catastrophe which they would gladly avoid.

In Meto and the other communities we have studied peace and good relations have prevailed, recently increased, we hear, in the case of Meto by personal visits by the King of Thailand. But in some other parts of the country disastrous fighting has broken out between the Miao and Government forces. Some of the accounts reaching the outside world present this as a Miao tragedy only, but the truth is that it is a tragedy for both Miao and Thai, made worse by the fact that in many cases the conflict has been brought to a head by the action of outside forces acting for interests other than those of either party.

It is a dual tragedy because each party suffers and yet each has right on its side. It is not a question of crime and punishment, nor of a power struggle, but partly of misunderstanding and partly of genuine confluct of legitimate interests. It is tragic because circumstances much more often than bad intent set the scene and decide the course of events. This can be made clear by a consideration of the main issues in the conflict—opium and land use.

The Thai view on both issues was expressed in an official statement

[2] Savina, 1930, p. 236.   [3] Ibid., p. 233.

by General Prapas Charusathira, Minister of the Interior, in August 1966:

Nearly all the tribal peoples have come into the region because it has offered them either new opportunity or refuge from foreign domination. They are friendly to the Thai people. If there has seemed to be little concern with the 'tribal problem' until the last few years this is because we could afford to leave them to make their own adaptation to the country of their adoption without disturbance to their social organisation and tribal integrity. The past policy of the Thai Government towards the tribes has been extremely tolerant. Most of them are recent immigrants. The Miao tribe for instance began to move into Thailand only one hundred years ago and the majority of them have probably entered the country within the last fifty years. They have been allowed to cross the border freely and to occupy land to which they have no legal right. Within the hill area of Thailand they have been permitted to move from place to place as they exhausted the fertility of one piece of land after another. They have been given the protection of the law but have not been required to fulfill any of the obligations of Thai citizens such as the payment of taxes or military service.

This policy was in tune with the wishes of the tribes. They were independent people who wanted to be left alone . . . But the policy of non-interference could not indefinitely continue . . . Because of their inefficient methods of cultivation the tribes have been steadily despoiling the land of the region. Parts of it have been permanently ruined for agriculture. The removal of forest cover has not only depleted timber resources but has interfered with the watersheds of the rivers which irrigate the great rice plains on which the economy of the nation depends. Also, in the case of several of the largest tribes, their income has been derived from the cultivation of the opium poppy and the Government is determined to suppress opium growing for the sake of the welfare of its own people and others in the world . . .

The tribe of most immediate political importance is probably the Miao. They occupy the most remote and mountainous parts of the border region. They are the most migratory of all the groups. They have been the most involved in opium growing and therefore must be most subject to economic redirection with the opportunities it will provide for malicious misrepresentation . . .

Our policy aims to improve tribal welfare while respecting tribal integrity. It is not the intention of the Government to force the tribal peoples to give up their traditional ways of life and become exactly like the Thai people. They may continue to practice their own religious and distinctive customs as long as they wish. By doing so, they make a contribution to the rich cultural variety of the Thai nation as a whole. There is no attempt to break up their social groupings or to disturb their residence in the hills. The sole political requirement placed upon them is that they have loyalty to the King and abide by the laws of the country. In return, the Government will make every effort to promote their economic and social development. Our policy is one of integration rather than assimilation, although no obstacles will be placed in the way of tribal peoples who do wish to identify themselves with the Thai.[4]

Question has often been raised as to the sincerity of the Government's intention to suppress opium production. Because it makes the best story, it has become almost customary for foreign journalists to claim that officials in high places and low gain profit from the trade, but in their next sentences the writers will often criticize the Government for interfering with the way of life of the tribes. At least these contradictory sentiments reveal the dilemma of the Government, which is a more important reason than corruption for lack of will in efforts at prevention.

One would be foolish indeed to deny that corruption exists and that it is a serious problem. We have referred to it in Chapter Ten. But the amount of it and the extent to which it influences official action can easily be exaggerated. Only a very small minority of officials are in positions where they could gain from the trade and most of these do not do so. There are other more enlightening angles than that of corruption from which the policy of opium suppression may be examined in order to understand the manner in which it is applied and the problems which it is likely to encounter.

The statement quoted above gave two reasons for the policy—the welfare of the Thai people and that of other peoples in the world. It is the second which has so far provided the greater impetus. The United Nations, particularly at the urging of the United States Government, has put pressure on the Thai Government to which it has responded because of concern for its international reputation. This is one of the foreign forces to which we alluded earlier as helping to precipitate the Thai–Miao tragedy.

Lately, however, the first reason has become increasingly important. In earlier times opiate addiction in Thailand was mainly a Chinese problem, but following the total ban on opium-smoking imposed in 1957 the use of heroin spread rapidly amongst the Thai until today there are probably at least a quarter of a million who habitually use the drug. The social cost to the nation provides a strong motivation for wishing to stop opium supplies. The high number of habitual users should also dispose of any suggestion that Thailand gains much economically from opium production, because the amount it consumes is probably greater than the amount it produces.

The cessation of production could mean a serious economic drain because the addicts, who are unlikely to disappear overnight, would then turn to outside sources for their supply. Therefore, until neigh-

[4] Prapas Charusathira, *Thailand's Hill Tribes*, Department of Public Welfare, Bangkok, 1966, pp. 2–8 (English version).

bouring countries make equal efforts to suppress production, the Government is making an economic sacrifice in its own efforts to do so—a sacrifice which earns it no good will amongst the Miao.

From the Miao point of view opium is their main means of livelihood. Considering that opium addiction among them is kept within tolerable limits and that they are almost entirely free from the abuse of other drugs such as alcohol, the social cost does not outbalance the economic gain. For them there can be little conviction in the argument that they should abandon production to suit the welfare of other peoples, who obviously want opium. Therefore the actions of the Government in interfering with their trade seem like unwarranted interference. The reasons for it are hard for them to understand. Into this situation add a small dash of official corruption and the belief soon spreads that they are being harassed in order to be better exploited. Add also active anti-Government propaganda by foreign radio and trained agents, then the mixture becomes explosive.

A paradoxical element in the situation—one of the probably ineradicable misunderstandings which contribute to the current tragedy —is that the very interference which brings the Government such hostility is the chief support of Miao prosperity. If opium were made legal everywhere in Thailand tomorrow the Miao economy would collapse. Not only would the legal price be very much lower than the present price, but their comparatively small farms and simple techniques could not compete with modern methods of mass production elsewhere.

The Thai Government rarely interferes with actual production in the tribal areas. The United Nations has recommended only a gradual elimination as alternative cash crops are introduced. On the other hand there is a growing awareness amongst the Miao of the disadvantages of opium and a willingness to seek alternatives, which will probably increase as population growth demands more continuous use of the land. Given time and patience the situation may be relieved by a convergence of the interests of both parties in a programme of crop replacement.

But can time and patience prevail? At present the two sides are impelled by contradictory motives—the one to get rid of opium-growing and the other to retain it. Each side is urged on towards collision by outside pressure—the Miao by propagandists who tell them their way of life is threatened and the Government by the force of world opinion. Sympathy is surely deserved by both parties. If a collision occurs the Miao, as the smaller people, are bound to be by far the heavier sufferers. But whether it occurs or not the Thai are in a sad moral predicament—they will be criticized either for action or inaction.

On the second major issue—land use—the case for the Government, as stated in the passage quoted above, is that Miao methods of farming have three bad results:

1. They destroy land for further agriculture.

2. They deplete timber resources.

3. By interfering with watersheds they endanger the agriculture of the river plains on which the economy of the nation depends.

The Miao case is that the land they use is the only land available to them and that the methods they practise are the only ones they know which can give the standard of living they want.

There appears, therefore, to be a real conflict of interest. How serious it is depends upon how true are the criticisms made of Miao methods. Again and again the Miao have received extreme criticism from writers for their forest destruction. Savina says 'They are the ones who cut down the majority of old forests of Asia', although, with the sympathy for the Miao typical of him, he says that they cut down trees out of necessity 'since they do not have an inch of land on the plain.'[5] In his book on the peoples of Thailand Seidenfaden writes:

The Maeos, like other hill tribes, are great forest destroyers . . . This whole-sale destruction of the forest of the northern hills is a very harmful business resulting in the denudation of them whereafter heavy rainfalls wash the soil down in the valleys thereby preventing the growing up of new trees. No wonder the Thai government is now trying to tie down the Maeos to certain restricted areas.[6]

The Report of the socio-economic survey conducted by the Department of Public Welfare in 1962 gave a much more moderate view:

Signs of erosion in the hills are minimal indeed and the secondary forest cover regenerates usually very quick, if an adequate period of fallow is allowed to the abandoned clearings. The land under cultivation is only a small proportion of the total forest area in the hills of Northern Thailand. The cut-ting of trees in itself would not constitute too great a problem, since the hill forests have not been economically exploited.[7]

The Report of the United Nations Survey Team in 1967 was more cautious. It stated that the estimate of $5\frac{1}{2}$ million acres of forest land affected by shifting cultivation was probably not an exaggeration and that 'from the angle of the forester concerned with the conservation and management of forests for the purposes of timber and other

[5] Savina, 1930, p. 179.
[6] E. Seidenfaden, *The Thai Peoples*, Siam Society, Bangkok, 1958, p. 131.
[7] *Report on the Socio-Economic Survey of Hill Tribes of Northern Thailand*, 1966, p. 30 (English version).

production and the preservation of soil and water resources, such a state of affairs is justifiably serious',[8] but it concluded with the statement:

It may be summarized that within the biotic, climatic, soil and human setting of the ecosystem in the Hill Tribe areas, no very serious or lasting deterioration is at present noticeable. We have cautioned, already, against being complacent about this, in the light of a prospective expansion of human and related livestock pressure upon the secondary vegetation stages within that ecosystem. We need scarcely record that the forests occur where they do because of the climate and related ecological conditions, and that they do not themselves 'add to' the rainfall, as so often thought by the layman![9]

This seems to us a balanced judgement regarding the position in the Hill Tribe areas. Forest cover will remain over the greater part of the northern hill region because the topography and soil types make it unsuitable for agriculture by any known methods. In so far as serious damage to water retention is caused by forest removal it is more likely to be done by lowland farmers clearing the lower slopes of the hills than by Miao clearing the mountain tops where the forest in any case is usually thin. The same holds true for the destruction of timber resources. Teak, the most valuable Thai timber, cannot grow at the Miao altitude, and the timbers which are found there are not suitable, either because of their type or their sparse distribution, for commercial exploitation.

Thus two of the reasons commonly given for condemning Miao methods—the endangering of agriculture on the plains and the depletion of timber resources—have no great general validity, although adverse effects may be produced in limited areas justifying protective action. The worst that can happen in most areas is that once tree-shrouded hill-tops will become clothed in grass, a process which has occurred in many countries of the world where a flourishing agricultural economy continues to survive at the lower levels.

We come, then, to the third reason—that Miao methods result in the destruction of the land for further agriculture. If in fact wooded areas were to change to grassland, then there would be much truth in this charge. The commonest type of grass which invades swiddening areas—*Imperata cylindrica*—is difficult to clear, inhibiting to secondary forest growth, and unsuitable for pasturage. But the chief sufferer would be the Hill Tribe cultivator himself. Therefore the strongest grounds for criticizing Miao methods lie in the context of Miao welfare—a fact sometimes not clearly enough recognized. If there is no great concern for their welfare then there need be no great worry,

---

[8] Phillips *et al.*, 1967, p. 22.   [9] Ibid., p. 31.

even if the most fateful prognostications are fulfilled. The hill tribesmen must fade away as the long green grass invades their settlements,
and then in time the slowly regenerating forest will cover their graves.

There are many persons in Thailand—both within Government
departments and outside them, especially those associated with the
King's Programme of Assistance to the Hill Tribes—who do see the
situation in the context of tribal welfare and are concerned to ensure
that measures taken to deal with it will be such as will protect and if
possible promote favourable prospects for the tribal peoples. How great
is the need for such measures? The answer will depend upon how
serious the threat of declining resources is judged to be.

If the population were to remain at present levels, it is probably
not highly serious. The evidence, admittedly based on impression
rather than scientific study, suggests that opium land cultivated to
exhaustion over an average period of ten years will generally revert to
forest within fifty years. This seems a very long period compared to
the maximum of ten years usually required for the regeneration of padi
land which has been cultivated for only a year. But on the other hand
the opium land will have given five times as much use. Therefore it is
not obvious that the Miao system of continuous cultivation is less
productive or more harmful to resources than the rotational method,
especially if greater damage to watersheds during the longer period
the fields are without forest cover can be largely discounted.

The viability of the Miao system, however, depends upon frequent
migration to new areas while the old are left alone to recover. This is
becoming increasingly difficult as population pressure, not only
amongst the Miao but also amongst neighbouring peoples, reduces the
scope for it. The study of Meto contained in this book shows how
serious the situation is becoming.

It is this situation which lies at the root of Miao unrest. It is
exacerbated by the Government's committal to reduce opium production and it may have been exacerbated by other events, but no
true appreciation of the situation can be gained if attention is paid only
to these factors because they are the mere irritants to an economic
sickness which was rapidly spreading in any case—the sickness of land
shortage.

Yet it is not absolute land shortage which is currently troubling the
Miao but restriction of their freedom to move. Therefore the belief of
some of their well-wishers that their discontent would be entirely
removed by the granting to them of definite land titles is an over-
simplification. Savina intuitively recognized the extended nature of
their claims when he wrote 'The Miao people are without property,

without their own country. The day the Miao can say "This field is mine; this country is mine." they will stop revolting.' [10] What they seek is the right to till wherever they can find the chance. They would welcome legal ownership of one field provided it did not stop their moving on to another, because only by so doing can they cope with the demands of their present economy and its associated cultural values.

We have suggested that the foreclosing of opportunities for migration owing to general land pressure will force stability upon them. Then surely great economic changes will be required. It is difficult to foresee exactly the form they will take but they will probably include a reduction in the importance of opium, irrespective of political or social pressures to the same end.

A condition for successful stability must indeed be the granting to them of some form of secured land tenure. As Savina wrote, 'This people has travelled far enough in the world to merit a little rest, and has toiled long enough on the mountains to deserve its place in the sun.' [11]

Savina also wrote: 'It is very difficult to say today what will become of the Chinese and Indochinese Miao in 500–1,000 years from now, since we cannot even tell what will then comprise China and Indochina. But these races will not disappear for all that and it is probable that, for many centuries yet, the Miao will keep their old customs and will continue to speak the age-old language of their ancestors. They will be to the future Asia what the Basques and the Bretons are to Europe.' [12]

If, 500 or 1,000 years from now, when our present and several future licences have run their courses, the spirits should decree a period of hard labour for the many sins by then accumulated, it should not surprise us, nor displease us, to find ourselves once more among the Miao in the beautiful bush-clad mountains, we hope, of northern Thailand.

[10] Savina, 1930, p. 236.   [11] Ibid., p. 239.
[12] Savina, 1930, pp. 285–6.

REFERENCES

ANONYMOUS WRITER, 1831. 'Observations on the Meaou-Tsze Mountaineers', *Canton Miscellanie*, Vol. 3.

DE BEAUCLAIR, I., 1956. 'Culture Traits of Nine Chinese Tribes in Kweichow Province, South-West China', *Sinologica*, Vol. 5, Zurich.

——, 1961. '"Miao" on Hainan Island', *Current Anthropology*, Vol. 2.

BEH, Y. T., STEPHEN, C. H., YANG, and W. R. MORSE, 1938. 'Blood Groups of the Aboriginal Ch'wan Miao of Szechwan Province, West China', *Man*, No. 66.

BERNATZIK, H. A., 1947. *Akha und Meau*, Wagner, Innsbruk.

BIGOT, A., 1938. 'Ethnologie sommaire de l'Indochine française', *L'Indochihe française*, Hanoi, Nov.

BROUMTON, 1881. 'A Visit to the Miao-Tsze Tribes of South China', *Proceedings of the Royal Geographical Society*, No. 3.

BRUK, S. I., 1960. *Peoples of China, Mongolian Peoples Republic and Korea (Nasaleniye Kitaya, M.N.R. i Kori)*, Moscow, Academy of Sciences, U.S.S.R., Institute of Ethnography imeni N. N. Miklukho-Maklay, 1959. (Translated by U.S. Joint Publications Research Service, No. 3710, Washington, D.C., 1960.)

CHAPMAN, E. C., 1967. *An Appraisal of Recent Agricultural Changes in the Northern Villages in Thailand*, paper presented to the Sixth Academic Conference of the Agricultural Economics Society of Thailand, Bangkok, 1967 (mimeograph).

CHARUSATHIRA, PRAPAS, 1966. *Thailand's Hill Tribes*, Dept. of Public Welfare, Bangkok (English version).

CHINESE PEOPLES' REPUBLIC, 1965. *Jen-min Shouts'e (Peoples' Handbook)*, Pekin.

CLARK, C., and N. R. KASWELL, 1964. *The Economics of Subsistence Agriculture*, London.

CLARKE, S. R., 1911. *Among the Tribes in South-West China*, London.

DAVIES, MAJOR H. R., 1909. *Yun-nan: The Link between India and the Yangtze*, Cambridge.

FREEMAN, J. D., 1955. *Iban Agriculture*, H.M.S.O., London.

GEDDES, W. R., 1954. *The Land Dayaks of Sarawak*, H.M.S.O., London.

——, 1956. 'The Chinese Institute for National Minorities', *Journal of the Polynesian Society*, Vol. 65, No. 1.

——, 1967. 'The Tribal Research Centre', in *Southeast Asian Tribes and Minorities and Nations*, ed. P. Kunstadter, Princeton, N.J., Vol. 1.

GEIL, W., 1911. *Eighteen Capitals of China*, Constable, London.

GILMAN, F. P., 1891. 'The Miaotze in Hainan', *China Review*, Vol. 19, No. 1.

GRAHAM, D. C., 1926–9. 'More Notes about the Chwan Miao', *Journal of the West China Border Research Society*, Vol. 3.

——, 1937. 'The Customs of the Ch'uan Miao', *Journal of the West China Border Research Society*, Vol. 9.

——, 1939. 'Note on the Ch'wan Miao of West China', *Man*, Nos. 171–2.

——, 1954. *Songs and Stories of the Ch'uan Miao*, Smithsonian Institute, Washington.

GRAVES, R. H., 1869. 'The Miao-Tsze', *Chinese Recorder*, Vol. 2.

HALPERN, J. M., 1960. 'The Natural Economy of Laos (typescript), University of California, Los Angeles.

HAUDRICOURT, A. G., 1947–50. 'Introduction à la phonologie historique des langues Miao-Yao', *Bulletin de l'École française d'extrême-orient*, Vol. 44.

HINTON, P., 1969. *The Pwo Karen of North Thailand—A Preliminary Report to the Department of Public Welfare.*

——, 1969. *Tribesmen and Peasants in North Thailand*, Tribal Research Centre, Chiengmai.

HUDSPETH, W., 1922. The Cult of the Door Amongst the Miao in South-West China, *Folk Lore*, Vol. 33.

——, 1937. *Stone-Gateway and the Flowery Miao*, Cargate Press, London.

INTERNATIONAL BANK FOR RECONSTRUCTION AND DEVELOPMENT (I.B.R.D.), 1966. *The Current Economic Position and Prospects of Thailand*, Washington (mimeograph).

IZIKOWITZ, K. G., 1951. *Lamet: Hill Peasants in French Indochina*, Etnografiska Museet, Gothenburg.

JAMIESON, C. E., 1923. 'The Aborigines of West China,' *China Journal of Science and Arts*, Vol. 1.

JANSE, O. 1944. *The Peoples of French Indochina*, Smithsonian Institute, War Background Studies, Washington.

KEEN, F. G. B., 1963. *Land Development and Settlement of Hill Tribes in the Uplands of Tak Province*, Dept. of Public Welfare, Bangkok.

KEMP, E. G., 1921. 'The Highways and Byways of Kweichow', *Journal of the Royal Asiatic Society, North China Branch*, Vol. 52.

KOPPERS, W., 1930. 'Tungusen and Miao', *Mitteilungen der Anthropologischen Gesellschaft in Wien*, 60.

LACOUPERIE, ALBERT TERRIEN DE, 1887. *The Languages of China Before the Chinese: Researches on the Languages Spoken by the Pre-Chinese Races of China Proper Previously to the Chinese Occupation*, London.

LEACH, E. R., 1954. *Political Systems of Highland Burma*, G. Bell & Sons, London.

LE BAR, F. M., G. C. HICKEY, and J. K. MUSGRAVE, 1964. *Ethnolinguistic Groups of Mainland Southeast Asia* (map), Human Relations Area File Inc., New Haven, Conn.

LIN YUEH-HWA, 1940. 'The Miao-Man Peoples of Kweichow', *Harvard Journal of Asiatic Studies*, Vol. 5.

LOCKHART, W., 1861. 'On the Miautsze or Aborigines of China', *Transactions of the Ethnological Society*, London, No. 1.

LYMAN, T. A., 1968. 'Green Miao (Meo) Spirit-Ceremonies', *Ethnologica*, Neue Folge, Band 4, Brill, Cologne.

McCARTHY, J., 1900. *Surveying and Exploring in Siam*, John Murray, London.

MARLOWE, D. H., 1969. Upland–Lowland Relationships: the Case of the S'kaw Karen of Central Upland Western Chieng Mai, in *Tribes and Peasants in North Thailand*, ed. P. Hinton, Tribal Research Centre, Chiengmai.

MICKEY, P. M., 1947. *The Cowrie Shell Miao of Kweichow*, Peabody Museum, Harvard.

MILES, D. J., 1968. *Report to the Tribal Research Centre*, Chiengmai (mimeograph).

MONINGER, M. M., 1932. 'The Hainanese Miao and their Food Supply', *Lingnan Science Journal*, Vol. 11.

MOSELEY, G. (ed.), 1966. *The Party and the National Question in China*, M.I.T. Press, Cambridge, Mass.

MOULY, R. D., 1946. 'Hainan, l'île aux cent visages', *Bulletin de l'Asie Française*.

NATIONAL STATISTICAL OFFICE, 1963. *Household Expenditure Survey*, B.E. 2506, Bangkok.

NEW YORK TIMES, 1971. Report 21 November.

PENDLETON, R. L., 1962. 'Thailand, Aspects of Landscape and Life', *American Geographical Society Handbook*, New York.

PHILLIPS, J. F. O., W. R. GEDDES, and R. J. MERRILL, 1967. *Report of the United Nations Survey Team on the Economic and Social Needs of the Opium-producing Areas in Thailand*, Bangkok. [The authors' names do not in fact appear on the title-page of the report.]

PLAYFAIR, G. M. H., 1876–7. 'The Miaotzu of Kweichow and Yunnan from Chinese Descriptions', *China Review*, Vol. 5.

RICHTER, H. V., and C. T. EDWARDS, 1971. 'Recent Economic Developments in Thailand', Paper given at the Seminar on Contemporary Thailand, the Australian National University, Canberra (mimeograph).

ROJANASOONTHON, SANTHAD, and F. R. MOORMAN, 1966. *Soil Survey Report No. 8*, Land Development Dept., Bangkok.

RUEY YIH-FU, 1960. 'The Magpie Miao of Southern Szechuan', in *Social Structure in South-East Asia*, ed. G. P. Murdock, Chicago.

SAIHOO, PATYA, 1946. 'The Hill Tribes of Northern Thailand' (typescript), SEATO, Bangkok.

SAINSON, CAMILLE, 1904. *Nan-tchao ye-che, Histoire particulière de Nan-tchao*, Paris.

SAVINA, F. M., 1930. *Histoire des Miao*, Société des Missions Étrangères de Paris, 2nd ed., Hong Kong.

SCHOTTER, A., 1908. 'Notes Ethnographiques sur les Tribus de Kouy-tschou (Chine)', *Anthropos*, Vol. 3.

——, 1911. 'Notes Ethnographiques sur les Tribus de Kouy-tschou (Chine)', *Anthropos*, Vol. 6.

SEIDENFADEN, E., 1958. *The Thai Peoples*, Siam Society, Bangkok.

SHRYOCK, J. K., 1934. 'Ch'en Ting's Account of the Marriage Customs of the Chiefs of Yunnan and Kweichow', *American Anthropologist*, Vol. 36.

SWINHOE, R., 1871–2. 'The Aborigines of Hainan', *Journal of the Royal Asiatic Society, North China Branch*, No. 7.

STAVENHAGEN, RODOLFO, 1971. 'Decolonialising Applied Social Sciences', *Human Organisation*, Vol. 30, No. 4.

THE THAILAND GOVERNMENT, 1965. *The Thailand Government Survey of 1965*, Bangkok (in Thai and English).

——, 1965. *Thailand Facts and Figures, 1965*, Ministry of National Development, Bangkok.

——, 1966. *Report on the Socio-Economic Survey of Hill Tribes in Northern Thailand*, Department of Public Welfare, Bangkok. [First published as a mimeograph in [1962.]

THWING, E. W., 1896. 'A Legend of the Ius', *China Review*, Hong Kong, Vol. 22.

TING, V. K., 1921. 'On the Native Tribes of Yunnan', *China Medical Journal*, Vol. 35.

TOURS, B. G., 1923. 'Notes on an Overland Journey from Chungking to Haiphong', *Geographical Journal*, Vol. 62, No. 2.

UNITED NATIONS, 1963. Commission on Narcotic Drugs, Report of the Eighteenth Session, Economic and Social Council Official Records: Thirty-sixth Session, Supplement No. 9, New York (E/3775; E/C.N. 7/455) paragraph 90.

——, see also under Phillips.

VANNICELLI, LUIGI, 1956. 'Il culto religioso presso i Miao', *Festschrift anlasslich des 25-jahrigen Bestandes des Institutes fur Volkerkunde der Universitat Wien*, 1929–1954, Verlag Ferdinand Berger, Wienna, sect. 3.

WESTERMEYER, J., 1971. 'Use of Alcohol and Opium by the Meo of Laos', *American Journal of Psychiatry*, 127:8, February.

WILLIAMS, E. W., 1845. 'Notices of the Miao-tze or Aboriginal Tribes Inhabiting Various Highlands in the Southern and Western Provinces of China Proper', *Chinese Repository*, Vol. 14, No. 3.

WINNINGTON, A., 1959. *The Slaves of the Cool Mountains*, Lawrence and Wishart, London.

WIRTZ, H. A. M., 1958. *Report interimaire au Gouvernement Royal du Laos sur L'economie Agricole du Laos, et le Developpement des Services Agricoles*, F.A.O., Rome.

WU LIEN-TEH, 1959. *Plague Fighter, The Autobiography of a Modern Chinese Physician*, Heffer, Cambridge.

YOUNG, GORDON, 1962. *The Hill Tribes of Northern Thailand*, Siam Society, Bangkok.

INDEX

PLATE 1

a. Miao sashes

b & *c*. Miao heads

PLATE 2

b. When eating with the spirits of the dead use a long spoon

c. Festival ball game

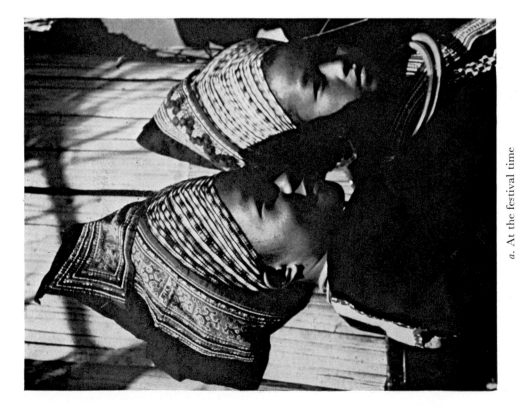

a. At the festival time

PLATE 3

b. Lowtong, the headman of Meto, and his brother Ger

a. Festival ball game

PLATE 4

a. Meto territory from 10,000 feet

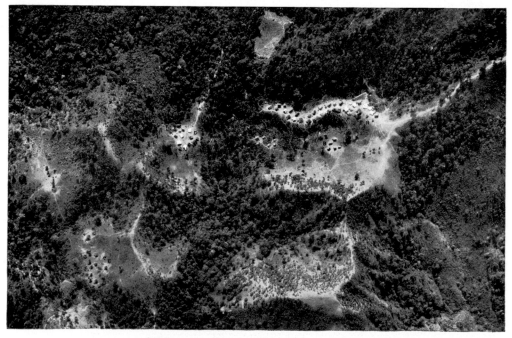

b. The main Meto settlement from the air

PLATE 5

a. Mother and children at Pasamliem

b. Area of Meto countryside including fields 125 to 129 and 153 (bottom) and 152, photographed in 1966. Bwotong's farm-house is in centre of field area

PLATE 6

a. Fields Nos. 172 to 188. Areas which have been used for padi are visible at left, right and centre

b. Pasamliem 1958

PLATE 7

a. Old fields to be replanted

b. Field newly cleared from secondary forest growth

PLATE 8

a. Landscape in the poppy season

b. Padi field at time of harvest

PLATE 9

a. Harvest time in field
No. 195

b. Poppy planted among
unharvested maize

PLATE 10

c. Indian hemp for cloth-making growing in a maize field at Pasamliem

b. Karen hired workers helping with harvest

a. Fields just after the first weeding

PLATE 11

c. Embroidering bands for kilts

a. A sugar cane juice extractor at Pasamliem

b. Weaving at Meto

PLATE 12

c. Carrying home the maize from the field

d. Grinding it for pig food

a. Marking the batik design

b. Stitching the kilt

PLATE 13

b. Scraping off the opium

a. Tapping the poppies

PLATE 14

a. Girls in Pasamliem

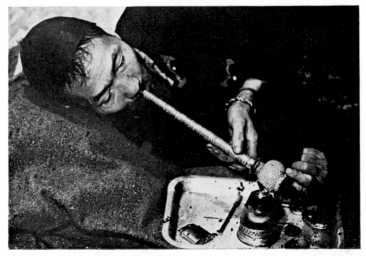

b. Kalaow smoking opium

PLATE 15

a. Boys playing pan pipes on way to fields

b. Leju, the daughter of Bwotong

PLATE 16

a. New voices from outside

b. Dawn in the Hmong hills